THE
PACIFIC
CROSSING GUIDE

THE
PACIFIC
CROSSING GUIDE

Second Edition

Royal Cruising Club Pilotage Foundation
in association with the
Ocean Cruising Club

Originally edited by Michael Pocock
Revised by Ros Hogbin

ADLARD COLES NAUTICAL
London

Published by Adlard Coles Nautical
an imprint of A & C Black (Publishers) Ltd
37 Soho Square, London W1D 3QZ
www.adlardcoles.com

First edition 1997
Second edition 2003

ISBN 0-6182-8

A CIP catalogue record for this book is available from the
British Library.

A & C Black uses paper produced with elemental chlorine-
free pulp, harvested from managed sustainable forests.

Typeset in Sabon 9½/12 pt
Printed and bound in Singapore
by Tien Wah Press Limited

CAUTION

Whilst every care has been taken to ensure that the information contained in this book is accurate, the RCC
Pilotage Foundation, the authors and the publishers hereby formally disclaim any and all liability for any
personal injury, loss and/or damage howsoever caused, whether by reason of any error, inaccuracy, omission or
ambiguity in relation to the contents and/or information contained within this book. The book contains
selected information and thus is not definitive. It does not contain all known information on the subject in hand
and should not be relied on alone for navigation use: it should be used in conjunction with official hydrographic data. This is particularly relevant to the plans which should not be used for navigation.

The RCC Pilotage Foundation, the authors and publishers believe that their selection is a useful aid to
prudent navigation, but the safety of a vessel depends ultimately on the judgment of the navigator, who should
assess all information, published or unpublished.

Plans and diagrams have been based with permission on British Admiralty Charts and Publications and where
foreign information was used, permission was sought from the Hydrographic offices of Australia, Canada, Ecuador,
Fiji, France and the United Kingdom (Licence No HO 363/960/624/01), Japan, Mexico, New Zealand, Solomon
Islands, US Defense Mapping Agency and USA National Ocean Service.

Plan 28 on page 109 is for illustrative purposes only – it does not meet the Canadian Charts and Nautical
Publication Regulations of the Canadian Shipping Act.

Plans nos 45, 46, 53, 54, 55 and 56 were based on parts of charts NZ 955, NZ 9558, NZ 5122, NZ 5123, NZ
532 and NZ 5322 with the permission of the Hydrographers RNZN.

Plans nos 26, 29, 32, 47, 63, 65, 67, 69 and 70 contain nautical information reproduced from NOAA's National
Ocean Service charts, with permission.

CONTENTS

Contents

PART III • PORT INFORMATION

EDITOR'S PREFACE

The excitement I felt as the final lock gates of the Panama Canal opened, revealing the Pacific Ocean to me for the first time, was palpable. I crossed the Pacific with my husband as part of a circumnavigation. We travelled along the classic South Pacific route and reached Tonga and New Zealand in our first season; returning to Fiji and Vanuatu on the way to Australia in our second.

The route we took provided an unforgettable journey through many of the world's best cruising grounds. In terms of what the Pacific has to offer, however, it represented just one ploughed furrow taken from a field of possibilities. There is so much more to explore both north and south of our track. We will go back!

In the meantime, the opportunity to share our findings with others who are contemplating a Pacific crossing has been a valuable one. And that value has been enhanced immeasurably by receiving quantities of feedback from a whole range of Pacific cruisers. I hope I have managed to include most of them in the acknowledgements section. Without this help, and short of travelling personally to all the island groups scattered over millions of miles of ocean, the task would have been impossible.

Even so, by its very nature, some of the information supplied is subject to change at relatively short notice – as soon as you have finished painting one end of a suspension bridge, the other is already in need of attention! I would therefore like to reinforce the message that up-to-date information from people currently out in the Pacific is always welcome and can be sent at any time to the RCC Pilotage Foundation or the publishers.

It has been my privilege to take the helm from Michael Pocock for the second edition of *The Pacific Crossing Guide*. The fruit of his labours in the first edition provided me with an excellent starting point from which to develop the book. In addition, the use of colour throughout this book has made a huge difference to the visual impact of the guide. You can almost smell the ocean in its shades of iridescent blue.

The distinction between the terms 'crossing' and 'cruising' guide is worth spelling out, because this still remains open to confusion. There are many excellent cruising guides giving detailed information about one or more specific island groups within the Pacific – some are listed in Appendix A. They discuss the minutiae of nooks and crannies off the beaten track and extend the scope of anchorage-by-anchorage cruising for the Pacific liveaboard fraternity.

However, this 'crossing' guide, contained in one volume, concentrates on the ocean as a whole. It is concerned with the different options available for getting from one side of the Pacific to the other. It gives more than an overview, in that it aims to provide enough detail to answer the questions where?, when? and how?, but it does not attempt to provide exhaustive information about every port of call along the way. The ports selected represent major stops across the Pacific, but in some of the larger countries or smaller island groups, there will be other ports of entry not detailed in this book.

The Pacific Crossing Guide aims to appeal to a broad readership, spanning those whose first ocean crossing begins in the Pacific, as well as seasoned ocean wanderers looking for new ideas for their next cruise. I hope it manages to broaden the horizons of the first, whilst holding the attention of the second. My main aim is that it will spur ocean cruisers on into the Pacific, so that they may experience the wonders of this marvellous ocean at first hand for themselves.

Ros Hogbin
2003

FOREWORD

Crossing the Pacific in your own yacht is a challenge that most of us don't tackle; writing a book to help others make that journey is also a challenge. Ros Hogbin has now done both and the Pilotage Foundation is indebted to her for editing this second edition.

This new edition has built on substantial foundations laid down by Michael Pocock; it has expanded coverage of the options for routes across and around the ocean, given a more detailed treatment of Pacific weather and a full analysis of the communications available to ocean voyagers. Port information has been updated and new ports added. We have also introduced full colour throughout the book which we hope will make it more attractive to use.

Given the scope of this book, it is not possible for one person to have first hand up-to-date knowledge of all the ports covered. The joint venture with the Ocean Cruising Club has continued with this edition and we have been fortunate to receive help from so many members of both clubs, who have been cruising in the Pacific. Some are mentioned later by name but we are most grateful to everyone who has responded to the editor's requests for information.

As always we will be pleased to receive comments and feedback on this new edition which can be sent either to our website: www.rccpf.org.uk or via the publishers.

Francis Walker
Director, RCC Pilotage Foundation

THE RCC PILOTAGE FOUNDATION

In 1976, an American member of the Royal Cruising Club, Dr Fred Ellis, indicated that he wished to make a gift to the Club in memory of his father, the late Robert E Ellis, of his friends Peter Pye and John Ives and as a mark of esteem for Roger Pinckney. An independent charity known as the RCC Pilotage Foundation was formed and Dr Ellis added his house to his already generous gift of money to form the Foundation's permanent endowment. The Foundation's charitable objective is 'to advance the education of the public in the science and practice of navigation' which is at present achieved through the writing and updating of pilot books covering many different parts of the world.

The Foundation is extremely grateful and privileged to have been given the copyrights to books written by a number of distinguished authors and yachtsmen including the late Adlard Coles, Robin Brandon and Malcolm Robson. In return the Foundation has willingly accepted the task of keeping the original books up to date and many yachtsmen and women have helped (and are helping) the Foundation fulfil this commitment. In addition to the titles donated to the Foundation, several new books have been created and developed under the auspices of the Foundation. The Foundation works in close collaboration with three publishers – Imray, Laurie, Norie & Wilson, Adlard Coles Nautical and On Board Publications – and in addition publishes in its own name short-run guides and pilot books for areas where limited demand does not justify large print runs. Several of the Foundation's books have been translated into French, German and Italian. The Foundation runs its own website at www.rccpf.org.uk which not only lists all the publications but also contains free downloadable pilotage information.

The overall management of the Foundation is entrusted to Trustees appointed by the Royal Cruising Club, with day-to-day operations being controlled by the Director. All these appointments are unpaid. In line with its charitable status, the Foundation distributes no profits, which are used to finance new books and developments and to subsidise those covering areas of low demand.

THE OCEAN CRUISING CLUB

Many of us belong to both the Royal Cruising Club and the Ocean Cruising Club whose joint memberships have contributed to the information to be found in these pages. A shared project, such as *The Pacific Crossing Guide*, is a bond between the clubs. This bond has now been extended to other publications sponsored by the RCC Pilotage Foundation and this gives us great satisfaction.

From small beginnings in 1954, the Ocean Cruising Club has grown to a membership of over 1600 in over 40 countries, with a worldwide network of nearly 100 Port Officers. An ever increasing number of our members are passing through the Panama Canal and heading west. I am delighted that they have subscribed to the information that Ros Hogbin (a member of both clubs) has compiled for this edition.

In conclusion, let me wish all those who use this book great enjoyment during their crossing of the Pacific, an ocean that is huge in area and so very rich in delightful cruising opportunities.

Mike Pocock
Commodore 1997–2002
Ocean Cruising Club

Covering almost half the earth's surface, the Pacific Ocean offers a wide range of sailing conditions, landfalls and experiences.

Like every ocean crossing, careful planning is required when undertaking passages through the Pacific. The variation in climate over the latitudes, the isolation and great distances travelled make self-sufficiency an essential requirement – right down to a complete inventory of on-board spares.

The rewards are the sights, the scenery and the people encountered from island to island. There is so much to discover, from the lush green forests and dramatic peaks of the Marquesas with their shy accepting peoples, to the friendliness of the New Zealanders with their islands' tremendous variety of landscapes and wildlife.

Memories last for ever after a Pacific crossing. Memories of the journey itself, with warm nights and a myriad of stars; boisterous passages in the reinforced tradewinds and spectacular landfalls with their colour, noise and newness. Impressions remain of dark tropical nights safely at anchor, with the village church choir at practice and surf booming in the background on the outer reef. But the abiding recollection, which stretches beyond the cruising, the island friends and personal achievements, is simply the vastness of this great ocean.

The small village of cruisers that work their way through the Pacific each year, support and pass on their knowledge to each other, and *The Pacific Crossing Guide* is a compendium of that knowledge.

The Pacific is an ocean to be visited and enjoyed. Prepare carefully and the rewards will be all the sweeter.

Terry Stamper
Rear Commodore, West Coast North America
Ocean Cruising Club

ACKNOWLEDGEMENTS

I have drawn on a large number of Pacific crossers, past and present, for help in compiling this second edition. Many are members of the Royal Cruising Club and/or the Ocean Cruising Club and all have been most generous in taking the time to ensure that the information we publish is as accurate as possible.

Dr Nicholas Davies and Hugh Marriott have very kindly updated their separate chapters on health and radio communications, and Andrew Edsor has provided much needed information on e-mail and satellite technology.

Many who have recently crossed the South Pacific or live at one end or the other have helped to update all aspects of this classic route. In alphabetical order they are: Neil and Suzanne Ablitt (*Maude*), John Cornelius, Don Coulam (*Impetuous*), John Davies, Valerie and David Dobson (*Kanaloa*), Jerry Dzugan (Sitka), John and Helen Fleming (*Flame of Gosport*), Ian and Susan Grant (*Rebel X*), Michael Henderson (Guam Port Authority), Tom and Vicky Jackson (*Sunstone*), Kerrie and Danny Kennedy (Dive Gizo), Nina Kiff (*Wetherley*), Don Laing, Tim Le Couteur (*Hesperine*), John Maddox, Ken and Prue McAlpine (*Mischief*), Misty McIntosh (*Tamoure*), Richard Markie (Paradise Village Marina), David Mitchell (*Ondarina*), Capt Silila F Patane (Port Administration, Pago Pago, American Samoa), Hank Pennington (Kodiak), David and Annette Ridout (*Nordlys*), Lew Sabin (Whangarei Town Basin Marina), Peter Seymour (Blue Water Rallies), Rex Sherman (American Association of Port Authorities), G K Soucoup (*Maritime Express*), Philip Stewart (*Tsolo*), Geoff Taylor (Copra Shed Marina).

There have been many others who have crossed further afield and given me much assistance in cruising areas that I have yet to explore: Neil and Ginger Blum (*Jennie*) (Marshalls, Gilberts and NZ), William Bourne (*Iseult*) (Japan), Jerry Dzugan (Sitka), Lyn and Jim Foley (*Sanctuary*) (Alaska and Japan), Michael Henderson (Apra, Guam), Noël Marshall (*Sadko*) (Micronesia and Japan), Hank Pennington (Kodiak), Kitty van Hagen (*Duet*) (Alaska and Western Seaboard), Janet and Michael Young (*Don Henry*) (Australs).

Finally, I would like to thank my husband Andrew, for his helpful suggestions in response to my chapter drafts, and Francis Walker, who managed to keep sight of the overall picture, while I soldiered on with the fine detail.

Plans, diagrams and images

I am very grateful to the cartographer, Alan Whitaker for the meticulous way in which he converted all the existing plans into full colour for this edition, as well as providing new artwork for Parts I and III. His use of colour and attention to detail has greatly enriched the visual element of the *Guide*.

The following people have supplied images for the book: Annabel Finding, Joanne Gambi, Andrew Hogbin, Noël Marshall, David Mitchell, Bill Perkes, Marcia Pirie, Michael Pocock, Lisa Shamer, Kitty van Hagen, Simon van Hagen and Sepha Wood. Their colourful contributions (which are individually credited) have captured the essence of the Pacific – the journey across it, its peoples and islands.

Language and spelling

It is worth pointing out that the spelling of place names throughout the Pacific is subject to some variation, according to the source of your information. Some differences are minor – such as the Strait of Juan de Fuca or the Juan de Fuca Strait; the Tuamotu Archipelago and the Tuamotus. Others, however, particularly among the Pacific Island groups, are markedly different according to which chart or book you are reading. Fijian names are notable in this respect: Mbengga and Beqa are one and the same place – the first being the phonetic spelling of the second. Although the early navigators used the local names for islands, they only learned them by word of mouth and therefore spelt them phonetically. This is often how they appear on charts. Other examples are the international airport at Fiji, spelt Nadi, but pronounced 'Nandi'; in the Northern Cook Islands, Suwarrow is known as 'Suvarov' and frequently spelt that way; general usage refers to the Marquesas, although French charts call them the Îles Marquises.

Closer to home, British and American readers will find a degree of variation in their own terminology, when they encounter one another on their Pacific crossings. The glossary in Appendix G may therefore be useful to help the reader on both sides of the Atlantic. I am grateful to Anne Hammick, who originally compiled this list for *The Atlantic Crossing Guide*.

PART I

PREPARATIONS

1 Crossing the Pacific

The Pacific Ocean

The Pacific Ocean is by far the largest ocean on the planet. It is more than twice the size of the Atlantic and covers almost a third of the earth's surface. At 165 million sq km (64 million sq miles), its area is greater than that of all the earth's land masses combined. Dropping down more than 11km (6 miles) from the surface, the Challenger Deep in the Mariana Trench is the deepest place on earth – extending almost 3km (1.6 miles) further than Everest is high.

The Pacific is bordered by substantial continents: the Americas to the east and Australasia and Asia to the west. However, the ocean itself, for the most part, is a huge expanse of water, empty of all but the smallest spots of land. There are spatterings of tiny island groups and numerous minute coral atolls in the central and western Pacific, as well as the Galapagos Islands in the east and the Hawaiian Islands further north. Even so, the sum total of these republics, kingdoms and protectorates make up an exceedingly small part of the vast ocean that surrounds them.

An idyllic anchorage in the lagoon of Toau, one of the Tuamotus. Photo Andrew Hogbin.

Why cross the Pacific?

Just as there are boats of many sizes and shapes out on the ocean, people are drawn towards crossing the Pacific for numerous different reasons: because of its hugeness, for a sense of achievement, to discover its islands and peoples, to enjoy its remoteness and beauty, to live life at a slower pace, in a simpler way. They may wish to tackle it in a season, as part of a circumnavigation, or stay within its boundaries for years of exploration. Whatever the reason, crossing the Pacific is a unique experience. It is an ocean rich with possibilities. Whether journeying through the South Pacific from the Galapagos to Fiji, or venturing north to Japan and Alaska, there is an incredible amount to see and do.

The Pacific is *not* an ocean to be crossed in one giant leap. Apart from being an eccentric idea in mileage terms, it defeats the purpose of the crossing. The Pacific is an ocean that needs time – typically six to eight months for a South Pacific crossing from Panama to New Zealand. To cross the Pacific is still a great adventure. It is true that some of the hallmarks of the pioneering age have disappeared. Cruising yachts now tend to be larger and more comfortable, and they are well equipped with everything from communications systems to watermakers. The number of people crossing along the most popular trails has also definitely increased. However, the Pacific Ocean is enormous and a crossing is still a major undertaking, demanding commitment and self-sufficiency and offering great rewards in return.

What does a Pacific crossing involve?

The commitment required to leave the shores of the developed world behind for an extended period is still considerable. The majority of sailors planning a Pacific crossing fall into two categories. The first are those whose home ports are in Europe. They will have crossed the Atlantic already and so will have experienced an ocean crossing, as well as the more relaxed cruising lifestyle shaped by time spent in the Caribbean. For them, the major commitment is to pass through the Panama Canal. They will then no longer be able to return home via a relatively short and direct Atlantic circuit. In practical terms they are thus committed either to a circumnavigation, or to an extended period in the Pacific.

The second set of sailors are those originally based on the west coast of America. They do not necessarily need to commit to a circumnavigation. It is possible to cross via the South Pacific and return to the west coast via Japan and Alaska, for example. The greater step in this case will be the transition from coastal cruising to ocean passage-making. Ready access to the facilities of the developed world will diminish as the ocean miles increase. They will find themselves among palm-clad atolls, drawing on their own resourcefulness, while the local community relies on subsistence fishing and small-scale copra production for its livelihood.

A third category of sailors, for whom neither of the above points will require much adjustment, are those originally from Australia or New Zealand. For them, crossing the Pacific signals their long-awaited homecoming!

Whether your Pacific crossing is a new departure, or the next stage in a continuing journey, it is likely to take more than six months. During this time, particularly if travelling in the tropics, you will find that your pace of life slows right down, in rhythm with the island people you meet. It is wise to allow this to happen. Priorities change. The complexities of life in the fast lane recede and become irrelevant. You may find a simpler way to live and gain new freedom.

Which way across?

There is arguably no better place to start a Pacific crossing than on the west coast of America, and then to follow the standard route across the South Pacific from east to west. This route may be the most popular, but don't let that put you off. It is a classic route, not to be missed:

- It remains in the tropics for most of its length.
- It makes full use of the tradewinds.
- It calls in at some of the most beautiful islands and atolls on earth.
- There are enough people crossing to form sociable communities, as well as plenty of space off the beaten track for those who prefer solitude.

Most people cross the Pacific along the classic route. It offers the longest cruising season (from February to October), and maximises the time spent in fabulous locations. It follows the wind and consists of a series of reasonably spaced hops from island to island, after the first couple of ocean passages have been made.

However, it is not the only route across the Pacific. Crossings from west to east are possible, but not as straightforward. It is not advisable to contemplate such a crossing directly back through the South Pacific to Panama, since this would involve a tough uphill battle against the tradewinds for most of the way. Crossings from the western Pacific to the Americas may be accomplished by travelling north out of the tradewinds and skirting round the North Pacific rim via Japan to Alaska. This type of crossing is far from tropical, and is more likely to involve challenging weather conditions and time constraints. For these reasons, fewer sailors take this option, although Japan and Alaska are fascinating cruising destinations in their own right. If you have already cruised the South Pacific, however, and are considering a Pacific circuit, or if your starting point is

Hannabella *sailing in the tradewinds. Photo Andrew Hogbin.*

New Zealand or Australia and you do not wish to head into the Indian Ocean, this route is worth considering.

Many people remain in the Pacific for a number of seasons, enjoying different island groups each year and crossing part of the ocean, but returning to their home port at the end of the season. Australians and New Zealanders will typically cruise to Tonga, Fiji and the Solomons between May and October, and Americans will head for Hawaii, and then on to Alaska for the summer, before making their way back home.

The geography of the Pacific

For most people, the geographical relationship of all the islands and archipelagos in the Pacific remains a mystery, until something such as a Pacific crossing is planned. Even an initial glance at a map of the Pacific does not necessarily clarify matters, but presents a mass of tiny dots, with unfamiliar names, in acres of blue.

There are approximately 20 000 islands in the Pacific Ocean, most of which are concentrated in the south and west. Some of the larger islands, such as the Japanese islands and the islands of north-west North America, originate from the adjacent continents. Others, such as the Hawaiian Islands, are high volcanic islands, which have risen from the ocean floor. A third type of island is the low coral island, such as the islands of French Polynesia.

The Pacific can be divided up in two main ways, politically and ethnically. From the point of view of those planning a crossing, political divisions are the most helpful way of identifying the different island groups and their locations.

Principal island groups in the South Pacific

The Galapagos Islands, belonging to Ecuador, lie just south of the equator, approximately 900 miles out from Panama. They are often the first port of call before heading further south-west into French Polynesia, but they have relatively little in common with the rest of the Pacific islands. The most prominent political bloc that stands across a wide tract of the South Pacific is French Polynesia, which includes the Marquesas, the Tuamotus, Tahiti and the Society Islands and the Australs to the south.

After the Galapagos, the Marquesas are the closest to Panama. They are a group of high islands with no fringing reefs. The island of Nuku Hiva, which is probably the best-known name in the group, houses the centre of administration. To the south-west of the Marquesas lies the Tuamotuan Archipelago which, being made up of coral atolls, has no high land at all. The lagoons contained within the reefs are surprisingly large, measuring on average about 32km x 14km (20 miles x 9 miles). Mururoa Atoll, where the French have conducted their nuclear testing programme, is in the south-eastern corner of the Tuamotus, a long way off the commonly used route. Two unique islands stand on their own to the east of the southernmost Tuamotus: Pitcairn Island (the ultimate home of the Bounty mutineers) is only just outside the boundaries of the Tuamotus, while Easter Island lies 20° further east in the most isolated position in the whole Pacific.

Beyond the Tuamotus lie the Society Islands, named by Captain Cook in honour of the Royal Geographical Society, under whose patronage he was sailing when he first called at Tahiti. The administrative capital of the whole of French Polynesia is Papeete on the island of

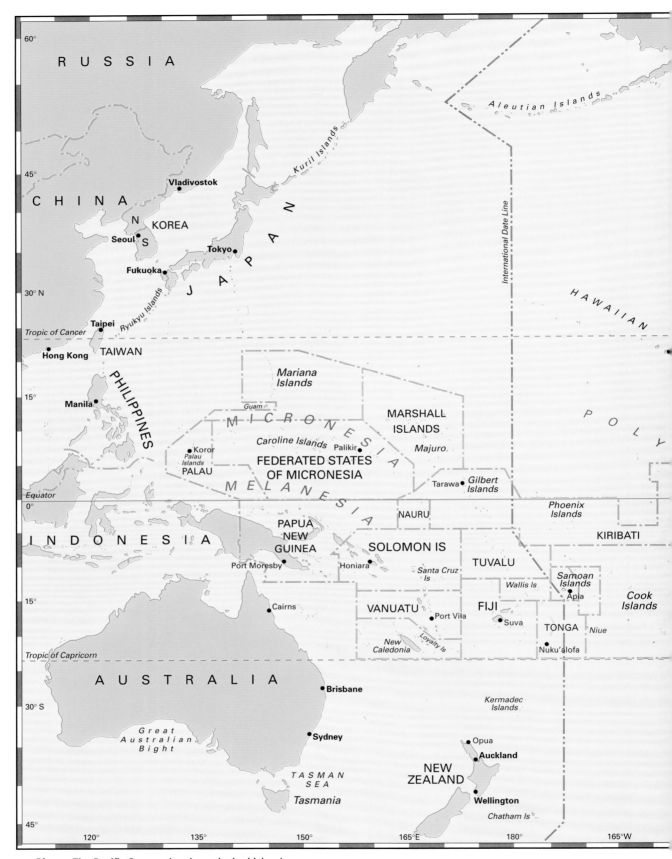

Plan 1 *The Pacific Ocean, showing principal island groups.*

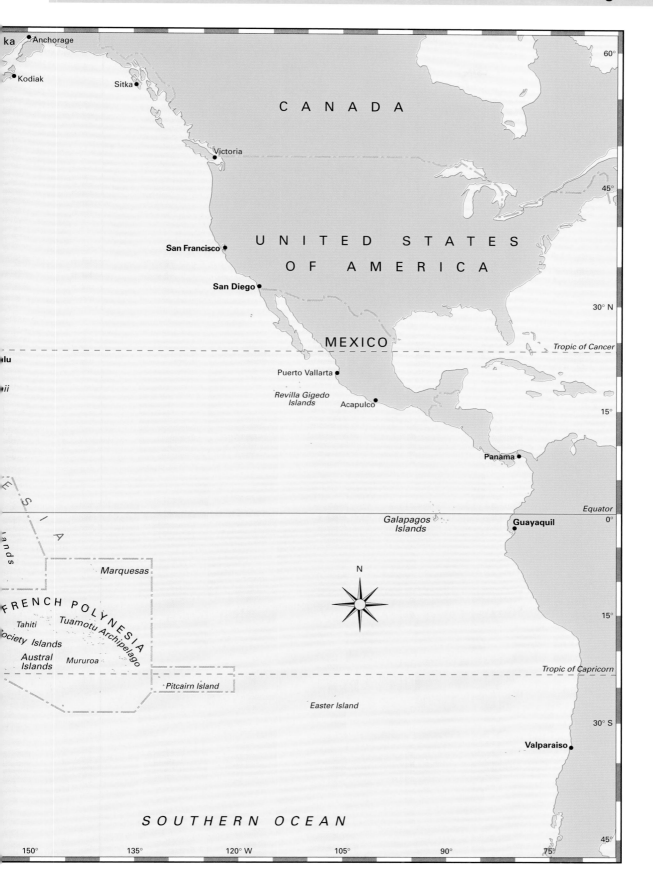

ka •Anchorage

• Kodiak   Sitka •

60°

C A N A D A

Victoria

45°

U N I T E D   S T A T E S

San Francisco •

O F   A M E R I C A

San Diego •

30° N

MEXICO

Tropic of Cancer

Puerto Vallarta •

lu

ii

Revilla Gigedo
Islands   Acapulco •

15°

Panama •

Equator

Galapagos
Islands   Guayaquil •

0°

E

S

I

A

N

ands

Marquesas

F R E N C H   P O L Y N E S I A

Tahiti   Tuamotu Archipelago

15°

ociety Islands

Austral   Mururoa
Islands

Tropic of Capricorn

Pitcairn Island

Easter Island

30° S

Valparaiso •

S O U T H E R N   O C E A N

45°

150°   135°   120° W   105°   90°   75°

Tahiti, which is the largest island in the Societies and lies at the windward end of the chain. The famous resort island of Bora Bora lies at the opposite, leeward, end.

The Australs lie south of the Societies, rather off the beaten track for westbound sailors. The significant features of the Societies and the Australs are that they are nearly all high islands with fringing reefs. Their principal attraction is that they contain delightful, sheltered lagoons inside their reefs which are accessed relatively easily. Between French Polynesia and New Zealand lie the Cook Islands, the Kingdom of Tonga and Fiji. All these island groups are independently governed, but have strong ties with New Zealand and previously with Great Britain.

The Cook Islands are spread over nearly 900 miles in a north–south direction, immediately west of the Societies. The Southern Cooks are more closely grouped than the rest and include the island of Rarotonga, the administrative centre of the group. Only three islands in this group – Rarotonga, Mangaia and Atiu – are high islands, and only the first two and Aitutaki have fringing reefs, with limited passes. The Northern Cooks are a very widely scattered collection of small atolls of which only Penrhyn and Palmerston have villages, and only Penrhyn and Suwarrow have lagoons with adequate passes to permit entry.

Beyond the Cooks, the Kingdom of Tonga forms the southern limit of the South Pacific islands. Tonga is a long chain of islands, divided into three distinct groups. The Vava'u group is at the northern, windward end with Neiafu as its administrative centre. The relatively lonely Ha'apai group is halfway down the chain, and the leeward south-western end is taken up by the Lulunga, Nomuka and Otu Tolu groups. These, although technically three separate groups, are seldom referred to as such and are more generally thought of as the islands surrounding Tongatapu, the largest island in the kingdom, containing the seat of power in the capital Nuku'alofa. Nearly 200 miles to the north of the Vava'u group lies a remote outpost of Tonga called Niuatoputapu Island (known by passing sailors as 'new potatoes'). Continuing from Tonga to the south-west, there are one or two isolated hazards, but otherwise only 900-odd miles of open sea to the northern tip of New Zealand.

To the west of the northern Cooks and north of Tonga are American and Western Samoa. American Samoa is US territory and a useful distant outpost. Its capital is Pago Pago (pronounced Pango Pango). Western Samoa, close by, is self-governing, with strong ties to New Zealand and an equally shared fervour for rugby football. The two territories form a small group of islands; most of them are reasonably high with little or no fringing reefs. The Samoan Islands provide a helpful stepping stone for yachts that have passed through the Northern Cooks en route from French Polynesia to Fiji.

The Fijian Archipelago spreads across the dateline and covers a very large area. There are two large islands, Vanua Levu and Viti Levu, separated by a wide but reef-strewn channel and surrounded on three sides by reefs and islands. The greatest spread is to the southeast, where the Lau group form the most significant part. Between Fiji and Australia are Vanuatu, previously the New Hebrides, and New Caledonia, another highly valued French possession. Vanuatu is now independent, but has a unique Anglo-French background.

South of the Tropic of Capricorn, the Southern Ocean is almost completely empty all the way from the coast of Chile to New Zealand.

Islands in the North Pacific

In the western Pacific, north of the equator, there is a vast area of ocean filled with island groups extending all the way up towards Japan. These are the less frequented groups in Pacific crossing terms, and so their relative positions are generally unfamiliar. The Solomons and Papua New Guinea are situated in the far west, to the north of Australia but south of the equator. From there, heading north into the northern tropics are the Palau Islands, Caroline Islands and the Marianas. Heading east from the Carolines are the rest of the Federated States of Micronesia, the Marshalls, and the republic of Kiribati, which extends east to include the Phoenix Islands and the Line Islands.

Much further to the north of the Line Islands are the Hawaiian Islands, which stand alone on the limit of the tropics, just south of the Tropic of Cancer. North of the Hawaiian Islands there is a wide expanse of almost empty ocean, which stretches up to the islands of the North Pacific rim. These islands consist of Japan to the north-west, then heading north-east, the Kuril Islands and the Kamchatka Peninsula, belonging to Russia. The Aleutian Island chain, belonging to the USA, stretches around the north of the rim and joins Alaska and the western seaboard heading south-east.

Ethnic groupings – Polynesians, Melanesians and Micronesians

Different areas in the Pacific can also be defined by three major ethnic groupings. Although these groupings do not fit with political boundaries, and therefore for route planning purposes are of limited geographical use, they are of particular interest from a cultural and historical point of view. These groups occupy distinct areas of the ocean. Polynesians are found in the central and South Pacific, including the islands of Hawaii, Samoa, Tonga and New Zealand. Melanesians inhabit the south-west Pacific, north-east of Australia and south of the equator, including the Solomon Islands, Vanuatu, New Caledonia and Fiji. Micronesians live in the western Pacific, north of the equator, on islands such as the Carolines, the Marshalls, Kiribati and the Marianas.

2

Pacific Winds and Currents – A Seasonal Approach

To cross the Pacific is first to dream. In fact, the Pacific, more than any other ocean, entices the dreamer with promises of endless tradewind sailing in clear blue skies. But what of the reality? A cruise through tropical waters in the South Pacific will certainly have moments of near-perfection, where reality far outstrips the best imagined ocean passage. However, the Pacific as a whole is vast, and subject to tremendous variations in wind and weather, according to season and location.

Once the nitty-gritty of the planning process begins in earnest, two major considerations focus the mind:

• Most Pacific cruising is seasonal, and highly dependent on the incidence of hurricanes, cyclones or typhoons in three main areas at specific times of the year.
• The Pacific Ocean stretches up and down the latitudes in both hemispheres. It cuts across a range of different wind systems and weather conditions even in a typical season (and many would argue that such 'textbook' seasons rarely occur). In an *un*-typical season, for instance during a strong El Niño year, the pattern of prevailing winds and currents will alter significantly, which may have a knock-on effect for crossings that year.

In general, the direction of a Pacific crossing is determined by prevailing winds and currents within the relevant span of latitudes. Therefore, crossings in the tropics and sub-tropics take place from east to west, and higher latitudes facilitate passages from west to east.

The origin of Pacific wind systems

The wind systems of the world exist because the sun heats the earth's surface and atmosphere to a greater extent at the equator than at the poles. This hot air rises and moves out towards the poles in both hemispheres, creating a band of low pressure at the equator. The air then cools and falls, creating two areas of sub-tropical high pressure at about 30°N and 30°S, and finally it flows back towards the equator, setting up a vertical circular motion. The earth's rotation deflects this motion, so that in the northern hemisphere, circular flow is clockwise around the high, with tropical easterly tradewinds to the south and westerlies to the north. The southern hemisphere mirrors this: anticlockwise

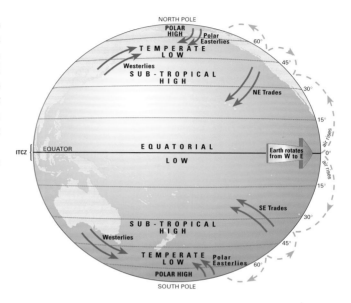

Fig 1 *Simplified wind circulation around the Earth.*

rotation around the high, easterly trades to the north, and westerlies to the south. In addition, there are two areas of high pressure at the poles, and where the polar easterlies meet the temperate westerlies (at about 60°N and 60°S), bands of low pressure form.

These distinct areas of high and low pressure are fairly well defined in the Pacific as a whole, since the bulk of the ocean is relatively free of large land masses, which tend to modify such systems. The pressure systems shift seasonally with the movement of the sun across the latitudes: northwards during the northern hemisphere summer, and southwards during the southern hemisphere summer.

Wind systems across the Pacific

The wind systems described below are given as a guide only, and not a guarantee. Even the most typical of seasons is controlled by the incidence of tropical revolving storms and the need to steer clear of them to safety when the season has ended. Anomalies such as the El Niño phenomenon give rise to even greater irregularities. (These anomalies, as well as tropical revolving storms, are considered in subsequent sections.) Plans 2 and 3 show the different wind patterns spanning the Pacific Ocean in January and July.

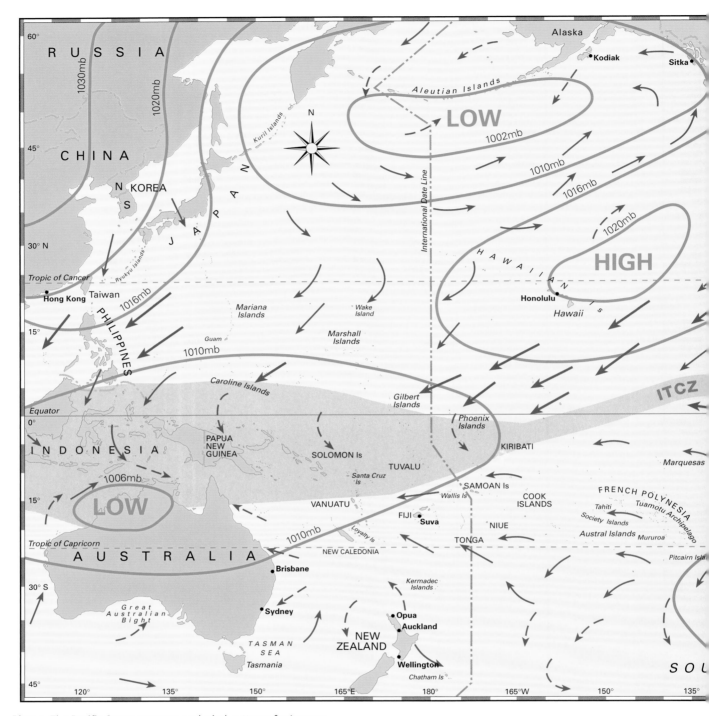

Plan 2 *The Pacific Ocean pressure and wind patterns for January.*

South Pacific wind zones

The standard route westwards across the South Pacific, from Panama to New Zealand, cuts across several wind and weather systems:

- The Inter Tropical Convergence Zone (ITCZ), or Doldrums
- Tradewinds
- Variables
- The South Pacific Convergence Zone (SPCZ) and
- Westerlies

It is therefore a useful route to consider first, since these systems may also appear along other Pacific routes.

Inter Tropical Convergence Zone (ITCZ) – the Doldrums

The journey from Panama at 9°N to the Galapagos at the equator is likely to be affected by the Inter Tropical Convergence Zone (ITCZ), known historically as the Doldrums. The ITCZ is a region of high temperature and low pressure along the equator. Its width can range from 50 miles to 300 miles. East of longitude 160°W, it

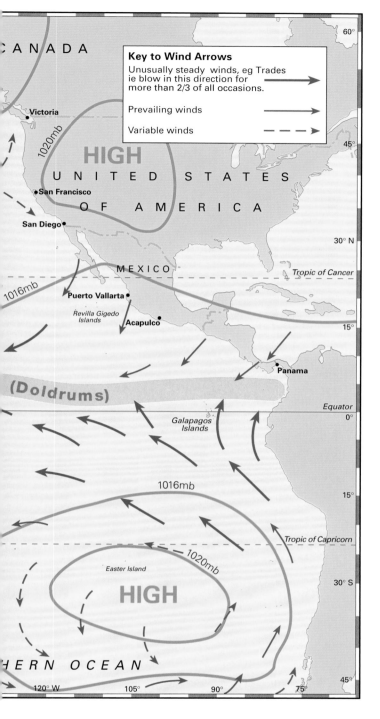

and condenses, resulting in heavy rain squalls and violent thunderstorms.

In the northern hemisphere spring, when most people depart from Panama, the ITCZ may stretch for a large part of the passage down to the Galapagos. One option is to wait in the Las Perlas Islands (known for their wildlife) until the ITCZ has moved north, which may then allow favourable winds to establish for the passage westwards.

Tradewinds and the south-east Pacific high

Once clear of the Galapagos and heading into the southern hemisphere, the tradewinds begin to establish themselves, and may hold throughout the passage of more than 3000 nautical miles to the Marquesas. In which case, the sailing conditions really do live up to the original dream and can be superb, in steady south-easterly winds and clear blue skies dotted with the odd patch or two of cumulus. If the south-east Pacific high (see Plan 3), an almost stationary system located at approximately 30°S, records a particularly high pressure, the tradewinds will be correspondingly stronger and vice versa.

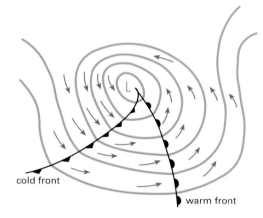

Fig 2a *Northern hemisphere low with trailing warm and cold fronts.*

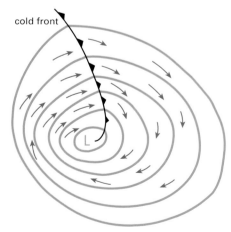

Fig 2b *Southern hemisphere low with trailing cold front (a mirror image of the northern hemisphere, when rotated around its horizontal axis).*

lies in the northern hemisphere all the year round, shifting between the equator (March–April) to 12°N (August–September). It is much more variable in position in the western Pacific, moving south of the equator from November or December until April or May. Conditions of very light winds and calms persist along its length and the weather is hot and sultry. It is also an area of vigorous convection activity. The tradewinds to the south collect a great deal of moisture on their way back to the equator. This hot, moisture-laden air rises

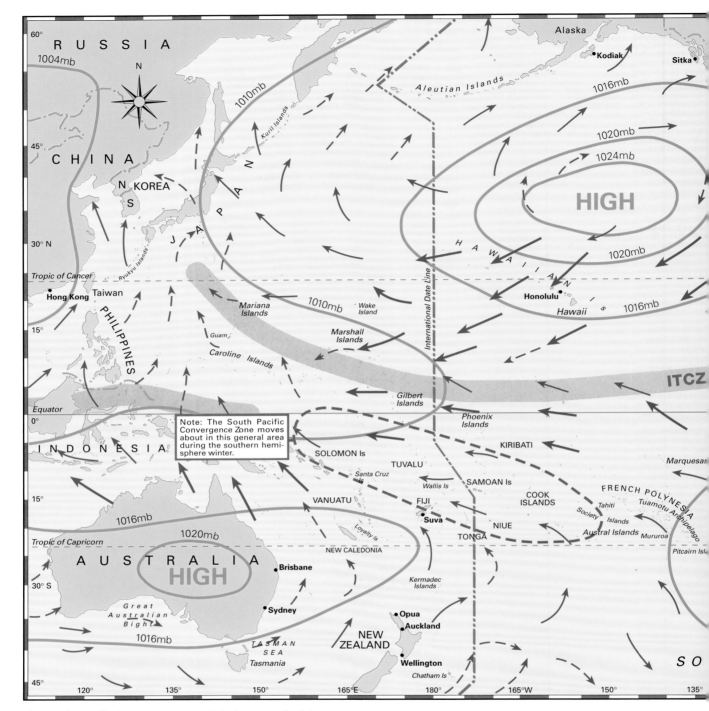

Note: The South Pacific Convergence Zone moves about in this general area during the southern hemisphere winter.

Plan 3 *The Pacific Ocean pressure and wind patterns for July.*

Variables, and the passage of lows and highs moving eastwards

At the other end of French Polynesia, proceeding south of 15°S, the tradewinds may begin to give way to a band of high pressure, with associated light and variable winds in the area sandwiched between the tradewind belt and the prevailing westerlies in the higher latitudes below. Continuing west, quite often the wind will go into the E and NE and lighten. It may go all the way into the N and perhaps die altogether. The accompanying weather is hot and dry.

These light, variable conditions are influenced by the passage of highs and lows (with associated frontal systems) in the higher latitudes moving eastwards across the Pacific from the Southern Ocean, Australia, the Tasman Sea and New Zealand. If a cold front passes further to the south, it is quite likely that a complete anticlockwise backing from SE right round to N will occur. Note that the wind backs, rather than veers – a mirror image of the clockwise wind shifts found in the northern hemisphere (see Fig 2a and b showing a comparison of northern and southern hemisphere lows).

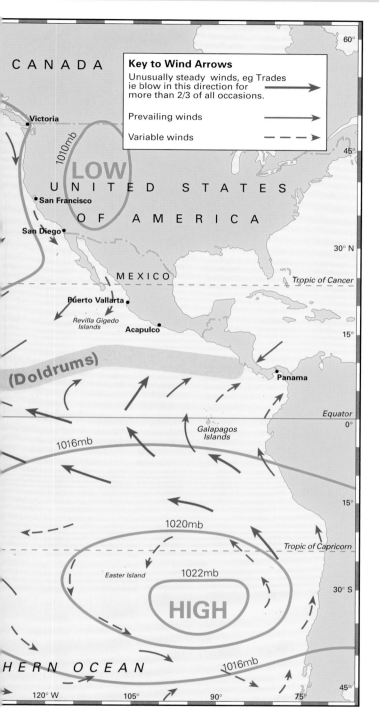

The South Pacific Convergence Zone (SPCZ)

The South Pacific Convergence Zone (SPCZ) is a region of enhanced convection (frontal) in the western Pacific, which slopes ESE approximately from the Solomons (5°S 150°E) to Tahiti (20°S 150°W). In the southern hemisphere winter (July), the SPCZ is poorly developed, while the ITCZ is strong across the Pacific. In the following months, during the transition to the southern hemisphere summer (January), a region of intense convection over northern India moves SE, the SPCZ develops, and the ITCZ over the western Pacific becomes weak. From April onwards, intense convection moves back northwards, the ITCZ strengthens, and the SPCZ weakens as it moves westwards towards the equator.

The SPCZ is a phenomenon that is mentioned in weather synopses from French Polynesia westwards (but not usually beforehand), and is marked as a dashed line on many of the weather charts. It is in constant motion and very often interacts with the front or trough of a low sweeping eastwards across the South Pacific. Depending on the strength of the front and/or trough and the amount of energy in the convergence, the meeting can be anything from fairly benign to quite dramatic. A ridge of strong high pressure can also interact with the SPCZ.

Conditions in the area of the convergence can become quite violent. In early 1991 four yachts leaving Bora Bora westbound ran into 70 knots for several hours. One boat was rolled 135°, sustaining considerable damage. The boats back in Bora Bora experienced 60 knots of wind, and five ended up on the reefs or beaches (deep anchorages and doubtful holding). In September of the same year, north of Vava'u, Tonga, four boats were sailing southbound at night in a pleasant 12 knot breeze from the NE, when they ran into 70 knots from the SW in a dramatic wind shift. In each case the position of the SPCZ, as nearly as can be determined, was directly across their track.

This is not to say that destructive winds are always going to be experienced at the SPCZ, or that these winds will not be experienced elsewhere, but the SPCZ is a relatively easy thing to keep track of and is well worth monitoring.

Variables and westerlies

The start of the southern hemisphere summer heralds the arrival of the cyclone season, and with it the necessity to leave the cyclone belt. A popular option for those that have reached Tonga or Fiji (in latitudes 18–21°S) is to head for New Zealand at 35°S. New Zealand is in the variables, with a regular incidence of strong winds, often from the west. It is standard practice on this passage to make as much westing as possible in the first part of the 1000 nautical mile journey, before the likelihood of westerlies increases.

The wind may then die, before shifting gradually to the NW.

If the front is not too far south, quite strong NW pre-frontal winds can be experienced. There are often rain squalls prior to the passage of the front, when the wind goes into the SW, and it may blow very hard as the new high fills in from the west.

If a particularly strong high develops, often after the passage of a front, then the tradewinds above it will become reinforced or augmented (possibly reaching 35 knots, with correspondingly close isobar spacing). These will persist until the high moves off or weakens.

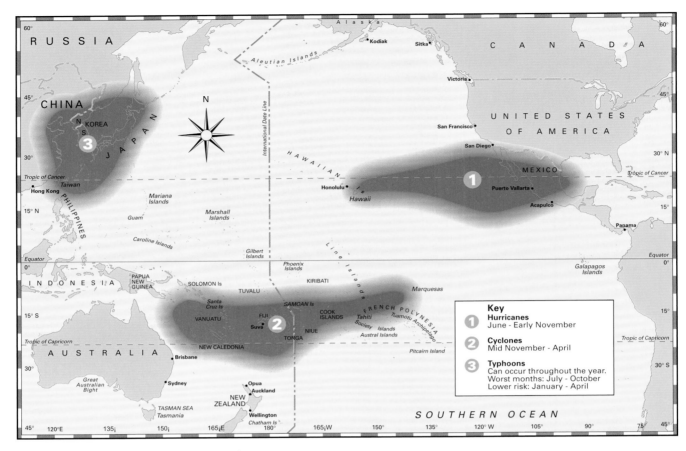

Plan 4 *Tropical revolving storms – areas and occurrence.*

North Pacific wind zones

The ITCZ

The wind zones described for the standard South Pacific route also appear in the relevant latitudes in the North Pacific. The ITCZ remains north of the equator in the eastern Pacific. In the west it moves south during the northern winter. In the far west it disappears in summer and winter, and only develops in spring and autumn. The eastern portion of the ITCZ displays typical Doldrum weather. However, travelling west, the incidence of easterly prevailing winds increases.

Tradewinds and the North Pacific high

In the northern summer, the winds rotate clockwise around a huge area of high pressure in the North Pacific (see Plan 3 for July). On the southerly side of the high (situated at approximately 30°N), NE trades that span the Pacific blow consistently in a curved band. They have a large northerly component near the American coast, and at the far western end of the Pacific they are replaced by the SW monsoon.

Monsoon activity

Monsoon activity in the extreme western Pacific affects some routes north and equatorially in this region. A strong winter high over Asia produces NE winds in the China Sea and causes the NE monsoon to develop between 5°N and 30°N in the far western part of the North Pacific. In December and January particularly, these winds contribute to strong NE trades, which span the Pacific in a consistent belt. The waters off the Philippines, Taiwan and Japan are particularly affected by stormy conditions in mid-winter. During the periods of changeover between NE and SW monsoons (in spring and late summer), calms and variables prevail. A summer low over Asia affects the SE trades of the far western Pacific, deflecting them to the SW. The SW monsoon is accompanied by squalls and gale force winds.

Between the equator and the ITCZ west of 180°, a NW monsoon season appears between December and March. This affects the Solomons, Papua New Guinea and Northern Australia. The wind gains a greater westerly component moving southwards, ie it is mainly N or NE near the equator and becomes NW further south. Conditions are generally fairly moderate, but squalls do occur with increased wind.

Variables and westerlies

On the polar side of the high is a narrow band of variable wind which shifts from approximately 35°N in the summer to 25°N in the winter. This band is influenced by the tradewinds in the east and the SW monsoon in the western Pacific. In the higher latitudes, westerlies prevail, blowing strongly in the winter and more gently in the summer months.

Tropical revolving storms

Pacific cruising is seasonal because of the incidence of tropical revolving storms (see Plan 4). These go by different names according to area – hurricanes, cyclones and typhoons.

Hurricanes

Hurricanes in the East Pacific are a risk mainly off the coast of North America between 10° and 30°N and are associated with the hurricane season in the Caribbean. June to October is the season of greatest activity, but the beginning of November is probably still a risk. It is generally thought that these hurricanes are only active for some 1000 miles or so off the shoreline. In reality, this is a dangerous assumption as they are capable of travelling well out into the Pacific and, on average, two a year will reach Hawaii. They are small intense hurricanes generated in the Gulf of Mexico and travelling on a north-westerly route, particularly in mid-summer. Unlike a true Caribbean hurricane – which can be 600 miles across – these are only about 120 miles in diameter.

Cyclones

The cyclone season south of the equator is from mid-November until April. The cyclone area extends from the coastline of Australia, north of Brisbane in the west, to Tahiti, and very occasionally the Marquesas in the east. The northern limit is generally believed to be about 5°S, and 30°S is about as far south as they are likely to reach.

Typhoons

Typhoons are to be found in the West Pacific. They occur west and north of the Carolines and the Marianas, including the northern part of the Philippines, and onwards to the coastlines of China and Taiwan. July to October are the worst months, but in practice they can happen in any month. There is reckoned to be a lower risk from January until late April.

The period from June through to October is considered to be free of tropical storms in the South Pacific. May is not entirely safe, as witnessed in 1994. Every few years yachts are caught in tropical storms, some of which reach cyclone strength. There are very few really good cyclone holes in the tropical South Pacific. To be safe it is better to go either to the northern hemisphere, or south to New Zealand or Australia. New Zealand is generally free of cyclones, but not completely, so one must monitor reports. The Queensland coast is subject

to cyclones, but there are many safe havens there. When approaching the Australian coast, be conscious of the often strong south-setting East Australian Current. Many boats have been lost when caught there in a 'Southerly Buster'. If a 'Southerly Change' is forecast (that's an Aussie description of the passage of a cold front), be extremely careful about approaching the coast. If a strong wind warning is added to it, you must definitely avoid closing the coast unless you can get inside the current before the 'Buster' hits, the west wall of which is usually 3 to 7 miles offshore.

Pacific Ocean currents

Broadly speaking, the surface currents that flow in the Pacific echo the wind direction in each region. The tradewinds are responsible for the North Equatorial Current (at approximately 15°N) and South Equatorial Current (which follows the equator), both flowing westwards. Between them, the Equatorial Counter-current flows eastwards. In higher latitudes, the currents generally flow eastwards, with smaller circular currents and areas of variable current in the mid-latitudes (see Plan 5).

The most detailed information will be found in routeing or pilot charts which are published in two sets for the North and the South Pacific. Each set has a separate chart for each month of the year and the information covers wind, currents, fog and the incidence of tropical storms. If you have access to a set, it will of course be useful. However, a full set is bulky and relatively expensive to buy and is only able to give information relating to an 'average' year.

North and South Equatorial Currents and associated currents

The North Equatorial Current approaches the Philippines in the western Pacific and curves north and eastwards to form the warm water Kuro shio (or Japan Current) to the east of Japan. A branch of this current flows into the Sea of Japan and through the Tsushima Strait, forming the Tsushima Current. The Kuro shio then heads east and divides into several branches: the North Pacific Current moves eastwards and eventually south; some current flows south before the Hawaiian Islands; some passes north of the islands and then turns south much nearer to the coast of California. Some branches of the Kuro shio head north from Japan and meet the Okhotsk Current, a southward flow of the Kamchatka Current. Upon nearing North America, part of this current heads into the Gulf of Alaska and part forms the California Current.

The South Equatorial Current flows to the Solomon Islands in the west and heads south to form the East Australian Current, then circles eastwards towards

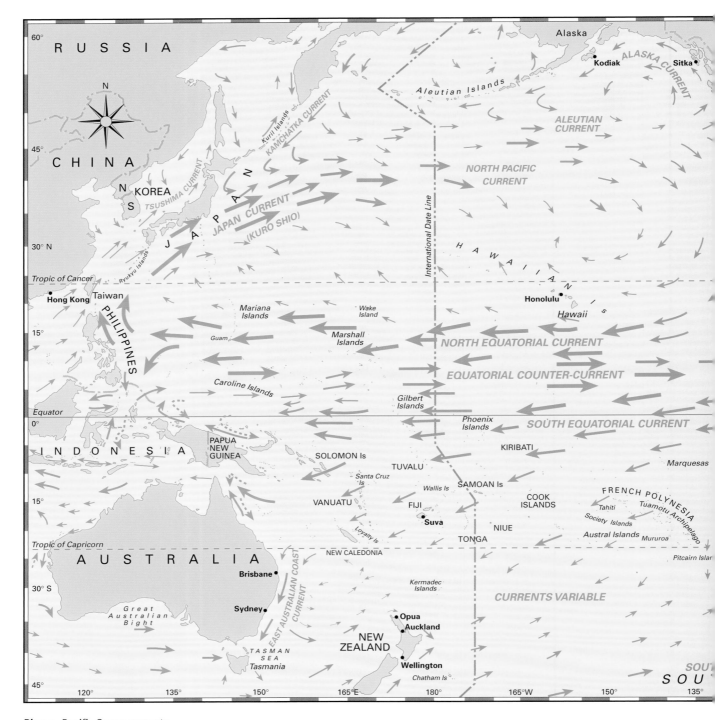

Plan 5 *Pacific Ocean currents.*

South America. It reaches the coast at 45°S. One branch continues in high latitudes eastwards between Antarctica and South America and the other flows north as the Humboldt (or Peru) Current.

These currents are also distinguished by temperature differences. Westerly-flowing equatorial currents are warm and remain warm as they flow outwards from the equator towards the poles on the west side of the Pacific. Easterly-flowing currents are cold and remain cold as they flow back towards the equator on the east side of the Pacific.

Pacific currents and passage-making

The well-worn track through French Polynesia, the Cooks, Tonga or Fiji and on down to New Zealand is blessed with a fair stream almost all of the way, except perhaps the last leg. Equally, those heading across the North Pacific by way of Hawaii to Asia will enjoy a fair stream, once they have escaped the grip of the Equatorial Countercurrent, and until they meet the effects of the north-easterly Japan Current in the closing stages.

Accurate information is more important when making

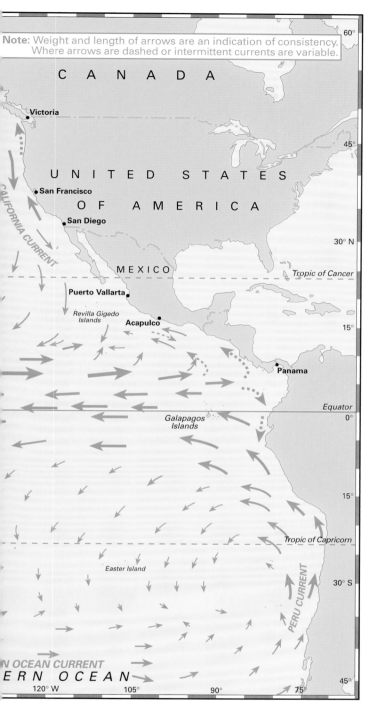

Note: Weight and length of arrows are an indication of consistency. Where arrows are dashed or intermittent currents are variable.

course to the Australs will gain some benefit, they would gain even more if they hung south all the way and then rode the Peru Current up the coast of South America.

Those who work their way to the north-east through the Solomons and on to the Marshalls will have a very changeable time, and if they can find the countercurrent they might well use it to good advantage.

Only those who go well north, returning to the USA or Canada from Japan in the westerlies, will have a fair stream in that part of the ocean.

From El Niño to La Niña: the Southern Oscillation

The Southern Oscillation (SO)

The Southern Oscillation (SO) is a term used to describe pressure differences across the tropical part of the Pacific Ocean. It is constantly present as a large-scale pressure oscillation, which 'see-saws' across the great width of the Pacific year by year. The SO was first mentioned in scientific literature in the 1920s by C T Walker, using data collected from measuring stations in Tahiti and Darwin. By the 1960s, a connection had been made between pressure differences and changes in sea surface temperature (SST). SSTs were then used to describe the different states of the SO.

In any particular year, the SO exhibits the characteristics of one of three main phases: the warm phase (El Niño), the cold phase (La Niña), or the 'normal' phase (in between the two). In fact, no phase is particularly 'abnormal', they are merely different – in the same way that summer and winter are different. The most well-recognised of these states is the El Niño phase (or El Niño phase of the Southern Oscillation – ENSO). El Niño has received progressively greater media coverage in recent years, mainly because of its severe impact on climate and weather in the Pacific and far beyond.

El Niño

El Niño is a Spanish name, meaning 'Christ Child'. It has been used by fishermen for centuries to identify the warm currents that appear off the coast of Peru around Christmas time. Today, the term 'El Niño' is used to describe the whole phenomenon, complete with the anomalous currents, winds and weather patterns that stretch far beyond the Pacific.

Every year in December, whatever the state of the SO, the warm El Niño *current* appears for a short while. If the year is a 'normal' one, this warm water dissipates soon afterwards and cold waters return to the eastern tropical Pacific. The larger-scale El Niño phenomenon occurs approximately every 3–7 years, when the warm El Niño current continues to build and persists for several months into the following year.

a passage into the North Pacific from the equator, such as from the Galapagos to Hawaii. Inevitably one finds a foul stream in a latitude in which it should be fair. Nobody complains when the opposite occurs! GPS information, combined with accurate log readings, help to identify the existence of a set. If the countercurrent has shifted southwards and hits you sooner than expected, then the only answer would seem to be to turn north abruptly and try to cross it in the least time.

West-to-east crossings are not so well favoured. The yachts that leave New Zealand and hold a southerly

In a 'normal' year, the easterly tradewinds blow across the tropical Pacific and a mass of warm water piles up in the western Pacific – the sea surface at Indonesia is about 0.5m higher than that at Ecuador and its temperature is 8°C higher. In addition, a southerly wind blows up the Peruvian coast and acts in conjunction with the tradewinds to push water away from that coast. This water is replaced by an upwelling of cold, nutrient-rich water from deeper levels.

The onset of an El Niño event always takes place at the same time of year, although its strength may vary. It is characterised by the following features:

- Unusually high pressure in the western Pacific and lower pressure in the eastern tropical Pacific.
- The tradewinds reduce in strength in the central and eastern tropical Pacific.
- Stronger westerly winds blow in the western Pacific, so warm waters from the west flow back eastwards, forming a band of warm water along the equator.
- The ITCZ is displaced southwards, and anomalous northerly winds may increase.
- The flow of water away from the Peruvian coast stops and a static layer of warm water builds up. This prevents nutrient-rich cold waters below from surfacing, which in turn decimates local fish populations – they struggle in the elevated temperatures and their food supply is cut off.
- Weather is affected dramatically. Torrential rainfall moves eastwards with the warm water, causing flooding in Peru and drought in Indonesia and Australia.
- El Niño conditions may peak in July of the affected year, or may persist until the end of the year and into the early months of the following year.

In 1982–3 a very severe SO occurred, and five cyclones moved as far east as French Polynesia. The 1997–8 event was the strongest on record and developed more quickly than any El Niño for the past 40 years. Both rapidly made an impact on weather, marine ecosystems and fisheries in the eastern Pacific. The South American fish industry was devastated and coral reefs across the Pacific died. Drought conditions extended to India and Sri Lanka and even as far as southern Africa, precipitating disease and malnutrition.

From a yachtsman's point of view, an El Niño event may affect planning in the following ways:

- Weak, even fluky, tradewinds caused by a weaker than normal high pressure area between South America and the central Pacific will equate to a slow passage west.
- Warmer than normal surface water extending into the central and eastern tropical Pacific can cause tropical cyclones to move much further east than is usually the case. This would certainly be a good reason to delay arriving in Polynesia until late May or June if a moderate El Niño was in progress.

Should a major El Niño be in progress, it might be prudent to enjoy a season in Central America and leave a Pacific crossing until the following season. It is uncommon for a second El Niño year to follow hot on the heels of the first.

Much observation and study has been done on the subject by the scientific community. Meteorologists and climatologists are clear that the SO in its various phases contributes in a major way to global weather dynamics. The El Niño phenomenon is now well known, and prediction is made much easier and far more accurate by satellite and SST measurements. Most meteorological offices, certainly the major ones, will be a good source of information on its status. Websites such as www.pmel.noaa.gov – the Pacific Marine Environmental Laboratory of NOAA (the USA-based National Oceanic and Atmospheric Administration) – provide good background reading on the subject.

La Niña

La Niña is the opposite phase of the SO to El Niño. It is characterised by unusually low pressures in the west and high pressures in the east. The tradewinds are strong and there is less likelihood of tropical storms moving east. The SSTs are anomalously cold in the eastern and central equatorial Pacific – as much as 3°C cooler than usual. Rainfall is less in this area. Cold La Niña events sometimes (but not always) follow El Niño events. The onset of La Niña might prompt an early start to a Pacific crossing, with the aim of getting to Polynesia in March or April.

Weather Information

When travelling across the South Pacific via the standard route, it is most important to keep a good eye on what is going on around and above your position. As with anywhere else, it is necessary to separate land breeze, sea breeze and local phenomenon effects, which generally occur near high islands, from the general shifting of wind due to the approach of a frontal system.

The steady state of the South Pacific trades is SE. When the wind shifts to the E and NE, particularly with diminishing velocity, then you should be looking for a frontal system to be moving towards you from the SW or W.

When the velocity *decreases* as it moves to the N and NW, there may not be much strength in the front, but if the wind velocity *increases* considerably as the wind moves into the N and NW, the chances are pretty good that the frontal passage is going to bring fresh wind with it when the wind shifts to the SW. When the wind is blowing out of the northern quarter, it is worth thinking ahead about shelter from the SW and S.

Weatherfax

Many yachts are equipped to receive weatherfax charts, either through a dedicated receiver or via a laptop computer and SSB radio. A selection of broadcasting stations covering a large area of the Pacific are listed below. All frequencies are upper sideband. For those using a modem hooked up to a computer, the frequency will have to be adjusted by about 1.9 kHz. All times are in UTC, and all schedules are daily. Schedules are up to date as of 2002. See http://weather.gov/om/marine/radiofax.htm for a comprehensive list of worldwide marine radiofacsimile broadast schedules; or the *Admiralty List of Radio Signals, Vol 3 (2001–2)* NP283/2.

Point Reyes, California (call sign – NMC) 4346/8682/12730/ 17151.2/ 22527 kHz transmits schedules at 1104/2324 (part 1) and 1115/2335 (part 2). Their tropical analysis is broadcast at 0755, 1608 and 2212 and covers from 30°N to 20°S and east of 145°W. It shows the ITCZ, which is a help for sailing out of the Gulf of Panama. It also gives information for the NE and NW Pacific.

Honolulu, Hawaii (KVM70) 9982.5/11090/16135/ 23331.5 kHz transmits a schedule at 0533, 1150, 1733 and 2350. Their tropical surface analysis is transmitted at 0148, 0800, 1350 and 1956. These charts cover 40°N to 40°S and from 105°W to 120°E. This tropical chart covers from about 1000 miles west of the Galapagos to over the top of Australia, but it does not show fronts.

Wellington, New Zealand (ZKLF) 5807/ 9459/13550.5/16340.1 kHz transmits a schedule at 1100 and 2300. They transmit a surface analysis at 1000 and 2200 for the south-west Pacific; this is excellent as it shows the fronts, and usually the South Pacific Convergence Zone, as a line of long dashes. Quite often the SPCZ will appear as an extension of a cold front associated with a low centre quite far to the south. They also have a surface analysis for the Tasman Sea at 0900/2100. This chart is very useful when sailing between New Caledonia, Fiji, New Zealand, Australia and Tasmania.

Charleville, Australia (VMC) 5100/11030/13920/20469 kHz took over from Canberra and Darwin on 1 July 2002, broadcasting on the same frequencies and now run from the Bureau of Meteorology. Their surface analysis at 0245, 0845, 1430 and 2015 gives a good picture of what is moving across the Australian continent and out into the Coral and Tasman Seas. They transmit a schedule at 0015 and 1215 in two parts, and a gradient level wind analysis at 0600 and 1800. This goes out to 180°, so it covers the tropical areas west of Fiji. They transmit other charts that may be of interest if you are heading further west.

Other stations that may be useful for routes in the North Pacific are:

Tokyo, Japan (JMH) 7305/9970/13597/18220, 23522.9 kHz, which transmits a schedule at 0340.

Kodiak, Alaska (NOJ) 4298/8459/12412.5 kHz, which transmits a schedule at 1838.

English language weather reports

To supplement the weatherfax charts, it can often be helpful to get someone else's opinion and analysis of what is going on. Yachts that do not have weatherfax often rely on one or more of the following broadcasts. All that is needed is a good short-wave receiver or transceiver, with a BFO switch.

Tony's Net (ZLIATE) 14315 kHz (20 metre ham band) at 2100. There are always plenty of relays available. Hams can call in and give their positions and request weather. At about 2130 or so, John (VK9JA) from Norfolk Island (Tasman Sea) will come up, take positions of those boats wishing for weather information, and then will go off to another clear frequency, often 14302.5 kHz, and give a synopsis of weather for the south-west Pacific, including the SPCZ, and then give a forecast for the various positions where yachts are located, as well as island groups. While it is useful to be a radio ham, and be able to talk to these folk, it is not essential. Often a yacht that may be in the general area will be getting information that is equally applicable to others.

Panama Connection Cruisers Net 8107 kHz at 1330, gives weather from Panama to the Galapagos.

Coconut Breakfast Cruisers Net 12365 at 1330, gives weather for the Marquesas, Tuamotus and Society Islands. It can also be used to obtain an overview of the weather for the last part of the passage to the Marquesas.

Russell Radio (SSB) 6515 kHz at 1900 with Ritchie Blomfield, and 13137 kHz at 2000–2100 and 0400–0445 with Des Renner. Des also gives an excellent weather forecast on 4445 kHz from 1930–2000 and 0700–0800 (New Zealand Standard Time). A small charge may apply to this service.

Bob McDavitt also operates out of New Zealand, and his book *Mariners Met Pack South West Pacific* is an excellent reference work for this area. He gives a free weekly e-mail overview of the SW Pacific weather, which can be obtained by e-mailing mcdavitt@met.co.nz. He also offers a routeing service at a charge of NZ$50 per report, which could be useful for the tricky passage down to New Zealand.

Pacific Maritime Mobile Net 14313 kHz (20 metre ham band) at 0400 is run by Fred (KH6UY) from Honolulu, Hawaii (sometimes 14300 kHz if 14313 kHz is busy). The warm-up session is from 0400 to 0430, which is followed by the roll call for yachts on passages spread out all over the Pacific. They give a position and a weather report and, by participating, one more bit of weather information becomes available to others. Besides, a good picture of the weather can be learnt simply by listening.

For yachts heading to Australian waters:

Townsville Radio (VIT) 2201/4426/6507/8176/12365 kHz transmit weather forecasts for the Coral Sea area from Vanuatu to the Queensland coast at 0003 and 1203, and the coastal waters of Queensland down to Fraser Island at 0603 and 2003.

Sydney Radio (VIS), same frequencies as Townsville, transmits a Hi Seas forecast for the south-east area off the Australian coast, including the Tasman Sea and the waters surrounding Tasmania at 0703 and 1903.

Penta Marine Radio Communication (Penta Comstat – VZX) is a private HF radio communications service for yachts and pleasure craft. They re-transmit weather forecasts for the Queensland and New South Wales coasts (see their comprehensive website at www.pentacomstat.com.au for details).

They also offer a service (for a membership fee) that may be useful, particularly if you wish to be able to be contacted by 'people back home'. They can receive faxes, phone calls, radio messages, etc, and will advise, via their traffic list, if there is a message for any particular yacht. You can call them on the radio or, on arrival, call them on a land line and they will be able to forward the message.

Penta Comstat can be paid by credit card authorisation, which is very convenient. Their postal address is 170 Mobbs Lane, Firefly, NSW 2429, Australia. Tel: +61 2 6559 1888 or Fax: +61 2 6559 1885.

There are many other sources of weather, such as local weather usually given on commercial or state stations in the various island groups. Fiji seems to have a good weather service and they broadcast in English.

3

Preparing to Go

The boat and its equipment

There are many different approaches to ocean voyaging and almost as many boats to match. The boat you choose will depend on a number of factors – not least, the depth of your pocket. Your choice will also be affected by the type of ocean traveller you turn out to be. The more you are able to discern this in advance, the easier it will be to find the boat that fits. After all, the boat you buy or build is likely to be your home for several years. Are you aiming to visit only the major ports of call, or do you enjoy exploring remote anchorages? Does onboard comfort rate more highly than overall boat speed and performance? Do you prefer the quiet and simple life, with as little recourse to engine use as possible? Or is navigation and communications gadgetry, coupled with heavy-duty power consumption, nearer to your style of cruising?

The boat

The right choice

It is most likely that a great many readers will already own their chosen yacht and be beyond the point of no return on this subject. For their peace of mind, these pages are not intended to be dogmatic. There are enough writers already who will advocate one particular boat type and construction and assert that no other is suitable. This attitude is fallacious. Just take a look at the yachts in the Bay of Islands in New Zealand as the fleet comes in towards the end of the year. An incredible variety of yachts complete successful Pacific crossings each season – from wooden monohulls to GRP multihulls, and all shapes and sizes in between.

Choosing the boat is an inevitable compromise between comfort and performance. Comfort compromises performance, and vice versa. Lifelong sailors, particularly those who have taken part in serious racing, will find that the sacrifices in performance that often have to be made in search of large internal volume and sophisticated home comforts are not always acceptable. They will opt for a more spartan regime and retain the speed and responsiveness that means so much to them. For others, for whom the sailing is not as important as the arriving in new places and the joy of living on board, to compromise comfort afloat would be a mistake.

It is important to assess, as best you can, your own cruising philosophy. You will then be less likely to buy into a lifestyle that, for example, extols the virtues of small handy boats with limited headroom and perhaps no engine, only to find that when you reach the Pacific, the larger, more comfortable boat with the lusty diesel engine anchored close by causes covetousness and discontent.

Construction

Out in the wilds of the Pacific there is very little help available for those in trouble. With this in mind, it makes sense to choose a reasonably rugged construction. This is not to say that the only choice is steel. Granted, it is the most rugged material and the most likely to survive a stranding, but prospective purchasers should be aware that steel boats of less than 15m (50ft) are inevitably heavy. They need large sail plans to achieve a decent performance and, particularly with regard to the deck, maintenance is a constant concern. If these features can be accepted, then steel is not expensive, the welding techniques for home building are not difficult to acquire, and certainly there is a large proportion of steel yachts at large in the Pacific.

In all other forms of construction, there are lightly built and heavily built examples. Too light is risking vulnerability in a bruising situation; too heavy is merely a negative factor in optimising performance.

Ease of handling

In order to be a good ocean traveller, the most vital quality that a yacht needs is an ability to track well and be easy for the automatic steering systems to manage. Unfortunately, this is the most difficult characteristic for the amateur to judge. Many of the pundits will say that a long keel is an absolute essential. This is very much open to debate. Plenty of lateral area is very valuable, and spreading it fore-and-aft is no bad thing, but the modern configuration with the rudder on a separate skeg is generally far superior when properly conceived.

Much the most critical characteristic is the balance of the hull lines. In simple terms, the relationship between the form of the bows and the stern must ensure that, as the vessel rolls, the flotation values are not varying and creating a strong tendency to yaw. Broadly speaking, a full stern should be balanced by a full bow and the worst possible concept is the double wedge that is broad and flat across the stern and pencil sharp at the bow. This type is a development of the racing classes that are sailed by large crews, who work hard to regulate the sail area so that the yacht always sails at an optimum angle of heel. For a small crew, it is important that the yacht is heel tolerant, for otherwise they will be worn out by constantly shortening sail.

The sail plan

Eric Hiscock, in his classic book *Voyaging Under Sail* (1959), advocated a maximum area of 400sq ft (36sq m) for any single sail that had to be handled by a crew of only two. This is probably just as valid today with regard to the mainsail. The advances in roller headsails and improved sheet winches suggest that headsails of 45sq m (500sq ft) are not unreasonable. If there is a willingness to accept the added complications and expense of fitting powered winches, then the sky is the limit if you have a bottomless purse. A modern design with a single mast will have a mainsail of about 36sq m (400sq ft) when the overall length is of the order of 13m (44ft) and the waterline about 11m (36ft).

Size has more virtue when on long passages than it does when on short day passages. On day passages, if the mainsail is too big and heavy it becomes less worthwhile to hoist, and so the day is spent under headsail only or under power.

Engine power

Those sailors who have been cruising since the early days, when engines were of doubtful reliability, grew to believe that a good sailor only used his engine as a last resort. This attitude, quite naturally, generated a feeling that a successful cruise is measured in inverse proportion to the number of engine hours used. Younger sailors, not influenced by such beliefs and used to the reliability of modern diesels, may have no time for any such prejudice. To them, there is no virtue in struggling on in frustrating conditions when a turn of the key will solve it all. The point that is being made is that it is up to each of us to identify our own attitudes and do things the way we want to, without fear of censure from others. If it is accepted that the engine will be fired up when progress gets slow, then buy a boat with a decent amount of power, fit a large enough fuel tank, and have a full-size propeller.

Speed under power is only critical in that the Panama Canal authorities insist on a capability of a minimum of 5 knots (but bear in mind that extra charges may be levied for yachts unable to complete their transit in one day, and thus a minimum speed of 6 knots would be desirable). The other significant need for speed arises if you plan to call at places such as Mopelia, at the western end of the Society Islands, where the outflow in the pass is frequently in excess of 6 knots.

Performance

The speed of a boat only gives a partial picture of its performance. Speed on passage is related to the waterline length of the yacht – or, to be more precise, to the square root of the waterline length. Where there is adequate wind in a favourable direction, a well-set-up yacht can expect to make average daily runs of around 20 to 25 times the root of the waterline. A 9m (30ft)

waterline yacht should be able to average between 110 and 135 miles a day under sail. Performance is a very broad term and should not be confined to an equation only related to the length of the daily run. It is a well-tried and repeated argument that says that faced with a passage of, say, 20 days, one day more or less is of little consequence when comparing it to the quality of life aboard during those 20 days.

There are many aspects of performance that should be considered, not least of which is the weatherliness of the design. A yacht whose design promotes comfort at the expense of windward performance will reveal this compromise in adverse conditions. If such a boat is not able to turn effectively to windward, the crew will at times struggle with a lack of confidence in their craft. To make an analogy with choosing a car, only a few of us are concerned with ultimate speed. If we choose a powerful car it is in order to have a reserve of power for difficult situations. The more powerful version flattens out the hills and is less demanding on the driver; and the same can be said of the more powerful yacht. Heavy weather is much less wearing for those with the ability to keep going with confidence. Ultimately, the difficult decision lies in identifying an acceptable middle way, which best solves the problem.

Rig considerations

The rig is a subject that calls for a great deal of serious thinking before departure. It is something that can be modified if funds will allow, and proper preparation is the key to an easier and safer life at sea. With the development of modern sail handling techniques, there has been a drift away from the division of the rig into two-masted arrangements. The majority seem to favour a single mast for the greatest efficiency at sea. Admittedly, the ketch or yawl has some merit when reaching and when the mainsail is lowered in heavy weather situations. On the other hand, the mizzen is no great asset in upwind or downwind sailing. For a great many owners there is a conflict of interest between the increased paraphernalia that is mounted on the stern, solar panels, windmills etc, and the overhang of the mizzen boom.

The almost universal use of roller headsails has generated a great deal of discussion on the layout of the foretriangle. It is generally accepted that the principal roller headsail must have a back-up provision of some sort. This will vary from a second roller system on a permanent inner stay, to an emergency inner forestay that can be set up when needed to take a heavy weather sail fitted with piston hanks. This second type can also support a twin headsail rig. The simplest version is the traditional cutter rig with the inner forestay at two-thirds the height of the mast. There are variations on this theme, with a fixed inner stay much closer to the main forestay, and these presuppose the concept of sailing on an either/or basis, rather than double headed as on a pure cutter.

Poled-out genoa on a downwind run. Photo Andrew Hogbin.

Below decks

The choice of layout below deck will depend very much on the size of the crew or the frequency of visitors. Where there is going to be more than one couple on board for a longish period, then separate cabins, giving a reasonable degree of privacy, will ward off the onset of strife. The feature that is so often forgotten is the need for good practical sea-berths in a comfortable, well-ventilated part of the yacht. There must be a sufficient number of sea-berths for all bar one of the crew. On long ocean passages it should seldom be necessary to have more than one person on watch at a time.

The galley is the centre of life at sea in that mealtimes are the high points of the daily routine and, unlike short local passages, the crew are not going to survive on sandwiches and snacks. Once over the first 48 hours, most crews develop healthy appetites and will thrive on a diet of good meals. The galley should be close to the hatchway for good ventilation, and handy for the cockpit where so much of life is lived.

There is a tendency in new yachts to provide much smaller chart tables, even in quite large boats, on the basis that modern electronic navigation systems place much less demand on chartwork. This is unfortunate, because in a well-laid-out yacht the chart area serves many purposes in harbour as well as at sea. It is the ship's office, it is a writing desk, and even a drawing board. A great deal of clutter can accumulate on the chart table that would otherwise be spread over the saloon table.

Draught

Finally, there will always be endless discussions on the ideal draught for cruising the Pacific. There is a school of thought that strongly advocates the use of a lifting keel to be able to reduce draught to an absolute minimum – this in order to have greater freedom to explore the lagoons and anchor closer to the beach. Were there no sacrifices to be made to achieve this end, then what cruising sailor could argue against it? Extreme shoal draught is, however, bought at a price. There is an inevitable loss of stability to be accepted. To make the most of a lifting keel it is necessary to have a lifting rudder; this is a difficult piece of engineering, and very likely the trunking for the lifting keel will inhibit the internal layout.

The ultimate shoal draught ocean cruiser is the modern multihull, of which there are an increasing number. They are a breed apart, and their advocates are always very enthusiastic. Their large plan area makes them very comfortable platforms for living, particularly in harbour. Perhaps their greatest weakness is that they are not by nature good load carriers, nor are they self-righting from a knockdown. When crossing the Pacific, the benefits of being able to take on stores in quantity where they are well priced, and to avoid buying in the more expensive islands, are undeniable. It is a recognised fact of life that all ocean cruising yachts end up, at some stage or other, much more heavily laden than ever allowed for by their designers.

The equipment

The mast, rigging and sails

Probably the most important aspect of the rig, with regard to an intended Pacific crossing, is to ensure that the running gear is well prepared. The time spent running on one or other gybe will be greater than on any other point of sail, and the ability to bring a pole into use quickly and easily is vitally important. The transformation to a more comfortable motion, when a properly balanced and well-set-up goose-winged (wing and wing) rig is achieved, is the most satisfying feeling. Probably the most ideal arrangement is to have twin poles, on twin tracks, stowed vertically on the forward face of the mast with the heels uppermost. The hoist can remain attached at all times and a foreguy and aftguy should be readily available. If the end fitting of the pole is well designed, the jib sheet can be led through it and chafe should not be a serious factor.

The twin headsail rig is another good option, depending on the right conditions (which may be less prevalent in the Pacific than in the Indian or Atlantic oceans). Once again, the key for shorthanded sailing is to be able to deploy both poles easily, thus facilitating any necessary change in sail plan. It is highly desirable for one person on watch to be able to raise and lower the poles effectively. They should also be able to drop or furl the sails independently of the poles.

The control of the main boom should be well considered. For crew safety, the boom should be guyed forward at all times. Either a kicking strap or a vang to the rail, keeping the boom pulled down, helps to flatten the sail and stabilise the spar. Vertical movement of the boom allows varying twist in the sail, giving a tendency for the yacht to roll, and increases chafe as the cloth moves constantly against the leeward rigging.

Rigging failures occur most frequently around aft lower shrouds, which are very often undersized in standard specifications. A lower shroud is a relatively short wire with a limited degree of elasticity. Violent motion in a seaway both in strong winds and very light ones creates a nodding action at the crosstrees which is resisted by the lower rigging. The limit of movement is finite, creating a strong shock loading which results in fatigue, and possibly even failure in under-sized rigging. The upper terminals should be regularly inspected, particularly the inside plates of tee-bar sockets.

Mast steps are strongly recommended. In Chapter 4 the importance of eyeball navigation is mentioned, and a means of quickly reaching the lower crosstrees is very worthwhile. With a small crew, hoisting someone to the masthead at sea is a major exercise in a bosun's chair. With steps, the person in the chair can do so much more to help. It is a good idea to run a line from the upper steps to the cap shroud, to prevent a backing jib from snagging on a step.

The good news is that at the end of the voyage, if heading towards New Zealand, there are first-class riggers and sailmakers ready to help, at prices that any European or American sailor will find very reasonable.

The engine

The most significant thing to be said about the mechanical parts of the yacht is that the crew need to be sufficiently familiar with the needs of the equipment, to be independent of local assistance for the entire crossing. Pacific islands do not have a great number of competent diesel mechanics with experience of small yacht installations. It is well worth acquiring the necessary skills to complete all the routine maintenance, and to develop a certain amount of diagnostic ability before departure. An adequate supply of filter elements, pump impellers, alternator belts and sufficient lubricating oil are absolutely essential. Spare injector pipes and nozzles are worth considering.

There is a much repeated and very valid doctrine that says that the secret of a reliable diesel is to feed it only the cleanest fuel. As far as the installation is concerned, this translates into first-class filtration, with an easily inspected bowl on the coarse water separating filter and the means of extracting sludge from the lowest parts of the tanks. This is an ideal point at which to mention the dreaded bacteria that can grow in a diesel tank, and subsequently block filters and bring the machinery to a grinding halt. By all means use an approved additive, but what is far more important is to avoid any accumulation of water in the tank. The bugs cannot breed without water, and pure fuel is not at risk. It is good practice to keep the tanks well-filled whenever possible. Therefore transfer fuel from cans as soon as there is room in the tank, which will reduce the formation of condensation in the airspace. A gravity tank can have a drain cock on a small sump at the bottom, below the lead-off for the supply line, but a keel tank should have a permanently installed hand pump taking fuel from the lowest point, which must again be well below the end of the suction line to the filter.

There is, when space permits, a very good case for having at least a small day tank that operates on gravity. This resolves the problems of a failed lift pump and eases the difficulty that may be experienced in bleeding the system. The opportunities to take on fuel directly from a pump are limited across the Pacific, and the probability that fuel will have to be carried in cans is strong. This is no bad thing because it provides another filter in the line and, if a syphon device is used for transfer, then there is always the chance that some sludge may not get any further than the bottom of the can. Some very efficient filter funnels are available, particularly in the USA; these are sometimes known as Baja filters on account of the poor quality of Mexican diesel.

Ground tackle

This is a difficult subject and opinions vary. The fact is that there is almost always going to be a risk of fouling a coral patch and, to put it mildly, rope and coral do not go together very well. There is no substitute for heavy chain and lots of it. Most anchorages are less than 20m (66ft) deep. The ability to anchor on chain in deep water is limited by the crew's capacity to recover its weight. Using 10mm chain, a 15kg (33lb) anchor and an efficient hand-operated windlass, recovery in 17–20m (56–66ft) is inevitably going to be a major grind. A powerful electric windlass will cope with a bit more, but it will still be a slow operation. In view of all this, it is doubtful whether there is any advantage in carrying more than 75–90m (246–295ft) of chain on the main rode (and, for the most part, you will generally be using less than 50m (164ft)). For really deep water situations it is necessary to use your heaviest anchor and a length of heavier chain combined with rope. In order to reduce the risk of the rope snagging the coral, use 15–20m (49–66ft) of chain, and make sure you are still able to recover this heavy gear effectively.

Electronics

Navigation equipment and autopilots have all but moved out of the 'luxury' category in modern ocean voyaging. Failure of the GPS should not be considered a total disaster, providing you carry one or two hand-held sets as back-up. There is also much to be said for carrying a good sextant and knowing how to use it (see Appendix A 'When All Else Has Failed'). Certainly GPS has become so well established that no other position fixing system can compete. It cannot be emphasised too often, however, that accuracy is only useful alongside an awareness of the limitations of the chart that is being used. Many Pacific charts are compiled from data provided by surveys carried out many years ago and may be in error by as much as 2 miles. A large number of yachts are equipped with radar, which can be reassuring at night for establishing distance off, although in most cases, landfalls in the dark are best avoided. As a generalisation, it is fair to say that fog is not a hazard on a South Pacific crossing, but may well be encountered in northern waters.

A reliable echo sounder is extremely useful, if only to reassure oneself that there is adequate water when its clarity is poor. Modern autopilots are fiendishly clever and, for what they do, remarkably power efficient. With regard to the mechanical elements, one may be able to improvise or fit a back-up, but a failure of the inner electronic workings will be beyond the ability of most owners. To this end, there is a very strong case for a purely mechanical self-steering system using a wind vane, such as the Monitor or Aries, which is independent of electrical power and much more easily maintained or repaired.

Another good option, which is less power-hungry, is a small tiller pilot driving a mechanical self-steering system. This provides the convenience of electronic controls for setting the course to steer, as well as consuming little power. A back-up system is also easily affordable.

Auxiliary generating systems

As a general rule, the simpler the systems, the less it will cost in time, money and effort to maintain them. It is very easy to add gadgetry, but it is more difficult to match this with the increase in charging required. For the larger, more sophisticated, yachts, equipped with microwaves, watermakers, freezers and so on, a properly installed AC generating set is a viable option. For even quite modest yachts there is nowadays a significant tendency towards a daily power consumption that calls for a worthwhile means of charging, other than the alternator on the main engine. The evenings in the tropics are long and dark, and a good standard of lighting is a joy. The typical Pacific cruising yacht has an arch across the stern with a fair area of solar cells, and often a wind generator as well. Solar cells, although far from cheap, are now much more cost efficient than they were several years ago and, provided they are well sited (above the awnings), make a useful contribution. The tropical sun is certainly powerful, but sadly the days are short.

The merit of wind power is that if there is a constant breeze, the input is also constant, day or night. However, there is the danger of injury that results all too often from careless contact of scalp or fingers with those merciless blade tips. The unit should be mounted

The typical kit on a blue water cruising yacht: solar panels, bimini with water-catching spout, wind-vane steering gear and wind generator. Photo Andrew Hogbin.

so that the disc of the blades is well above head height. It is also worth noting that their efficiency is reduced when sailing downwind, and so a combination wind/ towgen is worth considering. The towed generator provides a useful but modest charge in consistent sailing conditions. However, its drag may have a slight impact on boat speed, and care must be taken to prevent it interfering with the streaming of a fishing line.

Cookers, fridges and watermakers

The choice of cooker must rest with the owner and be dictated by the available space and the cost. The installation is all important. Life at sea without a cooker that swings freely to at least 45° each way is not going to be very pleasant. If the kettle will not stay in place in all conditions, then something is in need of improvement. The hangings must be secured so that the unit cannot become unshipped in the event of a serious knockdown. The propane supply should be remote in a draining locker, and a total capacity of 18–20kg (40–44lb) in two containers should be sufficient. The main supply line should be made of copper with a shut-off valve where the flexible connection to the cooker is connected. Safety devices that sniff in the bilge are an asset, but there is no substitute for good discipline and turning off the supply after use.

Fridges and freezers are much more reliable nowadays and very commonplace on board. The worth of a genuine freezer must depend on the individual's desire to carry stocks of frozen provisions for long periods, considered alongside the extra charging requirements that go with freezers. In all cases, check the insulation surrounding your appliances for thickness and efficiency. A small fridge can be operated entirely by the 12V DC supply, and although it is a significant drain, it is not so serious that it cannot run continuously, relying on input from solar or wind energy with intermittent use of the main alternator. All refrigerating equipment has to have a cooling facility for the returning coolant, and for the simplest and smallest installations an air-cooled radiator is sufficient. Beyond this, a sea-water cooling circuit is required or a so-called keel cooler – which is not necessarily sited on the keel. A serious freezer will often rely on an engine-driven compressor, clutched in for an hour or so, night and morning. Apart from the inconvenience of having such a strict charging regime, there comes a time when the yacht is lying in a marina and the neighbours may, very reasonably, object to long hours of engine fumes and noise.

A watermaker pump that is belt driven off the main engine is less of an embarrassment as it is never likely to be in use in harbour. There are some very good DC-powered small-capacity watermakers, but for larger output the pump has to be more powerful and must either be driven off the main engine or by an AC motor with a generator running. Those with the ability to make their own water are lucky indeed. They are free from the risk of infection from doubtful local supplies and they can shower at sea with an easy conscience. It is well worth having a sizeable reserve tank capacity, so that you are not forced to go to sea to make water sooner than you wanted to leave. It goes without saying that good maintenance is vitally important. It is also necessary to purge the system if it is going to be unused for more than a few days.

Dinghies and outboards

Your dinghy is equivalent to your car when shore-based: it will be well used. The wear and tear on dinghies is a major factor, and is the principal reason why so many sailors want a hard dinghy. To most people this conjures up a picture of constantly having to land directly on sharp coral and haul the dinghy across it. This is not really the case. Most landings are beach landings, albeit very often on crushed, fairly abrasive, coral sand. The emphasis on beach landings highlights the need for a craft that is easy to leap out of forwards and quickly, and light enough to lift clear of the surf rapidly. If the parent yacht is large enough to carry two dinghies, then that is surely the ideal arrangement. The prospect of one dinghy going adrift without a reserve to go and salvage it is not a happy one in some remote atoll with no other yachts to help. A second dinghy can also provide some valued independence, when crew members have different tasks to fulfil on opposite sides of the anchorage.

An outboard motor is more or less essential, depending on your dinghy usage. For some, whose requirements are for short journeys in fair conditions, it is considered a valuable luxury. In such cases, the outboard will not usually be larger than 2–3hp and will be easy to pass up on board and stow. For those who scuba dive, for instance, at sites typically a couple of miles away from an anchorage, an outboard that allows the dinghy to plane is considered vital. In this case, larger engines, ranging from 8hp to 25hp, may be regularly used. The drawbacks are increased petrol consumption and the additional weight of the outboard, which will need a hoisting system (eg a halyard shackled to a rope cradle) to bring it on board.

Spares

The difficulty and the cost of obtaining spares in remote parts of the Pacific is far more serious than anywhere in the Caribbean. However, overdoing the buying of spares is a definite possibility that will damage the trim of the yacht and also the budget. The line has to be drawn somewhere. The priority items must be for those systems that will be badly missed if they are rendered useless for the lack of a part – the heads, for instance, or the main engine. There is bound to be a quantity of spares that are never used and that might be considered an expensive waste. At the end of the voyage it is worth assessing what spares have been used. At the same time

The dinghy, seen here going ashore in Moorea, must be a sturdy workhorse. Photo Andrew Hogbin.

it is worth adding up what those same spares would have cost if air freighted from home, always supposing that the right thing arrives first time! The unused spares will begin to look cheap compared to the cost of one awkward item sent by air. Sometimes you may even be able to sell some of your surplus items to a fellow sailor at your final destination.

Self-sufficiency is the key to economic survival in remote places, and successful self-sufficiency depends on adequate spares and tools. Keeping the show on the road is a major challenge that has to be addressed.

Spares can be divided into two categories: those that are necessary for routine maintenance, and those that are required to repair some unexpected failure. Take the heads as an example once again. There are service kits available, depending on make, that provide all the necessary seals and washers that should be routinely replaced when servicing. With repeated daily use, the need for a service is going to come round a lot more frequently than in an ordinary sailing season. So how many kits are needed? In addition to all the servicing parts, what items can fail the test of time and break miles from anywhere? The toilet is a horrible thing to work on, but it is much better to grasp the nettle long before leaving so that one is familiar with its innermost workings and ready to fix it when there is nobody else to turn to.

This argument applies to all the essential items of equipment, particularly the engine. A spare alternator is well worth carrying. Any sign of a charging failure, and it is not difficult to change the unit. The average owner is not likely to stand much chance of repairing the faulty alternator itself. When the yacht reaches New Zealand, then the expertise is available. In the meantime, the spare will have been as useful as the spare tyre in your car. It is very important to carry an up-to-date wiring diagram of the electrical circuits. It is much easier to diagnose the problems with a clearly drawn circuit diagram to study. Batteries have a habit of failing at the most inconvenient times, and it is important to be able to monitor their condition independently and to know how to rearrange them to eliminate one that has gone down.

One member of the crew should have a good grounding in elementary sail repairs and an adequate supply of thread, needles and sticky-back cloth. Regular close inspection of the seams and some timely stitching will often save much more than the proverbial nine. A sewing machine is a very useful thing to carry, but very few of them will cope with more than 6oz cloth and heavier material will have to be sewn by hand.

Good tools, and plenty of them, are bound to be needed sooner rather than later. A comprehensive set of spanners together with a good socket set will repay their cost in no time. Sets of taps for threads of different sizes, coupled with a supply of set screws and machine screws to match, are invaluable. When it comes to improvising a repair, where perhaps a thread has stripped, it may prove possible to drill and tap to a larger size. A small electric drill, either cordless with a charging unit or with leads and crocodile clips on to the battery, is very useful. In a boat there are so many occasions when it is difficult to drill with two hands, and the hand-drill is too long anyway.

It is worth giving some thought to the provision of a small folding workbench that can be set up in the cockpit and clamped in position complete with a vice. The facility to work in the fresh air and the wind while under the awning can make even quite unpleasant jobs almost bearable.

In the event that it is necessary to order replacement parts by fax or on the internet (where it may be possible to source a more local agent, rather than relying on parts from home), exploded diagrams showing spare part numbers and names for all equipment are essential. International couriers operate in most major centres, and parts can arrive within a matter of days. Make sure that 'replacement parts for yacht X in transit' is clearly shown above the address to avoid import tax.

Fishing gear

To many Pacific sailors there is nothing more satisfying than hauling in fresh fish on passage. If the advice in Chapter 6 is followed on preserving fish, then the larger the catch the better – within reason. Because there is no control on which fish will take the lure, the gear must be strong. Towing a 9kg (20lb) tuna at 7 knots inevitably creates some impressive strains. The accepted technique for fishing on passage is to tow an unweighted lure based on a double hook 5–8cm (2–3in) long wrapped in bright material; shredded plastic bags in sharp colours, as well as silver wine bags, are effective. Smaller hooks can be used, to avoid losing gear to big fish. The trace should be wire of around 45kg (100lb) breaking strain, not less than 2.4m (8ft) long. There needs to be a first-class swivel to match, and the line to the reel or spool needs to be equally strong and at least 61m (200ft) in length. Whether the line is stored on a reel with a brake mounted on the aft rail, or merely wound round a piece of plywood, is a matter of choice. The fact is that the catch will almost inevitably have to be hauled in hand over hand, so 4mm multiplait and a good pair of leather gloves is a useful outfit for the job. The difficult bit is the final effort of bringing the trophy in over the guard rails and not kinking the trace as it is done. A gaff hook is very useful for this task. Plenty of spares are essential and these will double as welcome gifts among the islanders. Stainless hooks are well worth the extra cost.

Charts and books

A Pacific crossing requires a great deal of information in book and chart form (for some suggestions of recommended reading, see Appendix B). It is possible to get by with fewer than the ideal number of charts, but the more

A great trevally, caught on a long line with a homemade lure on a double hook. Photo Michael Pocock.

you skimp, the greater the danger of a premature termination of the crossing. There are many yachts that have to pick their route according to their chart inventory. In the worst case, this results in so much wasted opportunity as some of the most desirable venues become inaccessible. On the other hand, to call up the chart agent and order a complete portfolio is beyond the reach of many people's budgets. To spend so much on charts that will only be used once in one's lifetime is, to many, a gross extravagance. Restrictions on photocopying charts are much less stringent in the USA and, if there is a good-quality linear copier available, some very good copies can be made – always supposing that one can gain access to the originals. Borrowing is the ideal answer, or buying second- or third-hand from someone who has just completed their cruise and has come ashore.

The approved doctrine says that an uncorrected out-of-date chart should never be used for navigation. In the Pacific there seems to be some justification for ignoring that doctrine; much better an old chart than none at all. Just remember Captain Cook, who had to make his own after he had arrived! Whatever chart you are using, new or old, to believe that it is 100 per cent correct would in many cases be dangerously naïve; the surveys are old and seldom perfect in respect of longitude. The use of radar and eyeball navigation is important in these cases. If any night landfalls are going to be attempted, then an up-to-date List of Lights is extremely useful, bearing in mind that the upkeep of lights and other navigational markers in the South Pacific islands is not necessarily as stringent as that in the USA or Europe.

Tidal information is not a number one priority. In a large area of the central part of the Pacific Ocean the range is small and the time of high water is close to noon every day. Local almanacs will be valuable around the rim. The possibility of having to resort to astro navigation makes a proper nautical almanac a necessity. However, if it is only being used as a back-up to GPS it need not be updated every year. Instructions are included for use in the year following, and in extremis it would not be beyond the realms of possibility to use it a third year by applying the corrections twice. This only applies to the sun and the stars. For the moon and the planets, a current almanac is essential.

There are a number of helpful pilotage guides for island hopping, such as *Charlie's Charts of French Polynesia* and Warwick Clay's *South Pacific Anchorages*. (See Appendix B for further suggestions.) All charts and books need to be acquired before departure; they are not sold along the way, which of course results in a great deal of illicit photocopying of borrowed material!

Adaptations for tropical living

There are a number of ways in which it is possible to prepare for the different priorities for living aboard in the tropics. Good ventilation below deck is an absolute necessity. If the boat has not been built with a generous

Ventilation is a major priority. Note the security bar across the hatch opening, which allows it to be left open when the crew are ashore. Photo Michael Pocock.

supply of hatches and vents, then some action must be taken to add them. Good sensibly designed dorade-style vents are a bonus at sea, as are skylights and hatches that still have enough shelter to be left open a crack in moderate conditions. Fitted canvaswork covers that allow a leeward skylight to be held open without the spray finding its way below are easily made and very useful. In harbour, a good windscoop for the forehatch makes a big difference to air movement right through the yacht. Security bars across the openings allow the skylights to remain open while the yacht is locked up and cuts down on the oven-like interior that would otherwise result.

It is worth making loose cotton covers for the bunk cushions. They are much cooler to sit on and they can be regularly laundered and refreshed. In the hottest areas only an undersheet is necessary at night, and other bedding can be cleaned and put away deep in a locker. On passage it is possible to keep cool by wearing the minimum or no clothing, subject to reasonable respect for the burning power of the sun. In harbour, however, it is necessary to remain cool and be respectably dressed. Ashore, in some islands, this means long trousers for men and skirts for women. In order to

Moongazer's fine sun awnings are very extensive and give her superb protection in the heat of the day. Photo Marcia Pirie.

avoid the risk of hookworm ashore or stepping on stonefish in the water, shoes should be worn at all times in the tropics. Excellent plastic sandals can be bought cheaply and easily in all the French islands.

Where there is a threat of mosquitoes, there is a need for very thorough protection for the whole yacht. It should be possible to fit a screen or net across every opening until the whole yacht is impregnable. This does of course drastically cut down the airflow, and thankfully it is not necessary that often, mainly in the early evening. Burning mosquito coils is quite frequently sufficient. The technique is to place the coil where the air is leaving the yacht, not where it enters – the principle of this being that the coil cancels out the tempting smells of humanity that would otherwise lure the mosquito upwind. By siting the coil in this way there is less risk of the fumes upsetting sleeping crew members.

Awnings

Last but by no means least is the equipment necessary to provide shade on deck. Harbour awnings do not need much deliberation. They are vitally important, because so much of life is spent in the cockpit. There are many well-established ways of setting them up. What is more difficult to achieve is shade in the cockpit at sea while still being able to work the gear. Some sort of folding, bimini-type awning is essential, and if, as is so often the case, the mainsheet is sited forward of the hatch, then a roll-up blind that can join the bimini to the companionway dodger (or spray hood) is an added bonus. Everything in this respect must be robust and not capable of being destroyed at the first hint of bad weather. Naturally the awning would be furled in strong wind conditions, but it must be furled in a neat, secure manner so that it will survive.

Under the cockpit awnings all but the smallest yachts will want a respectable cockpit table, either fixed or removable, but sufficiently stable for entertaining guests. So much social life occurs in the cockpit that it is important to give serious thought to these factors. If barbecues are going to be a frequent occurrence, then the opportunities will be endless! The best equipment can be obtained from US sources.

4 Cutting the Ties and Setting Sail

The boat, brim full with ocean-going equipment, is ready. The route has been decided (see Part II) and you've pored over numerous Pacific charts. The departure date is fast approaching. However, before you can finally cast off into the Pacific, there are issues of people and paperwork to consider.

The crew

Couples and families

The great majority of small yachts crossing the Pacific are crewed by couples in stable relationships. This is a dynamic that works well on such a long crossing, particularly since the opportunities for jumping ship are not that frequent! Compatibility is key, and teamwork of the essence, when weeks are spent at sea, living at close quarters. Fewer partnerships disintegrate at the end of a crossing (although it does happen occasionally) than blossom into wedlock.

Some families with children ranging in age from infants to teenagers can also be found, particularly on the South Pacific route. Younger children tend to thrive on such a crossing. They make friends easily and meet up with them in different anchorages. They tend to be adaptable and receptive to their new environment. Home schooling via correspondence course is well established in the UK and the USA, and the combination of school in the morning and snorkelling in the afternoon can be a winning formula.

Teenagers (particularly only children) may begin to tire of the slow pace of the Pacific cruising lifestyle, making reference to 'yet another set of palm trees'. In this case, the faster pace of a formal rally may help. Very few 20-year-olds undertake such a crossing with their families; they are busy doing other things.

Larger crews are chiefly found among the organised rallies. This is perhaps a good thing because where there is a sharp differential in age between sections of the crew, each age group will find compatible friends from other yachts, and will tend to spend time with them in port.

There should be no difficulty maintaining crew morale when crossing the Pacific, unless of course the skipper is going to follow the example of an early pioneer, one Captain Bligh! Sailing from east to west should never need to be a test of endurance, whereas the reverse direction crossings will require a greater degree of fortitude.

Singlehanded cruising

Singlehanders always form a small percentage of the fleet and many people would applaud them for taking on the oceans alone. HF radio has improved their lot marvellously as they are no longer so completely out of touch. The Pacific is far from being dense with commercial traffic, so the risk of being run down is less than in some other parts of the world.

Friendships are soon made with other singlehanders and there is, it would seem, a tendency to congregate at the major stopovers rather than explore the lagoons in solitude. Nuku Hiva, Papeete, Neiafu and Suva are popular gathering places – the latter, in particular, on account of the very pleasant facilities at the yacht club where the bar and lawns provide a uniquely affordable meeting ground.

The relationship between singlehanders and the rest of the fleet is interesting. It is noticeable that some singlehanders are much more popular and made to feel welcome than others. The characteristics that are most likely to cause couples to fight shy are an occasional tendency for the lone sailor to believe that he has found a willing audience for a blow-by-blow account of his last epic passage, or a tendency to turn up at mealtimes without much thought as to how he might reciprocate – if only to bring an occasional bottle. Sympathy is not a good basis for a long-term friendship. This is not a generalisation about singlehanders, for the majority are good contributors to the sailing community. It is just a few who can become very clingy, slightly sad people, who spoil the image for the others.

Changing crew

Taking on extra crew at short notice is a risky business. The skipper is always responsible for the welfare of the crew members listed on arrival, so that unless crew leaving the yacht have purchased their flights out of the country, the authorities will not grant outward clearance with a reduced crew list.

Crew changes are always easier at the bigger islands with international airports – if only because the arriving crew members (who will presumably be coming in on a single ticket) will have an easier time with Immigration if the skipper is there to meet them with the ship's documents. In any case, it is a wise precaution to write to the new arrivals before they travel, on official-looking paper with the yacht's rubber stamp, confirming the arrangement for them to be signed on. Papeete–Tahiti or Honolulu/Nadi–Fiji offer the best connections for transcontinental routes.

Pets

Finally, spare a thought for the prospects for any four-footed or feathered members of the crew. The great majority of crossings end in New Zealand or Australia, and those countries' regulations concerning imported animals are not only very strict, but they are also extremely expensive to observe. Cats and dogs may not be landed, and twice-weekly inspections will be made at the owner's expense. A substantial bond has to be deposited; this is forfeit if the animals are ever found to be missing from on board.

Managing the paperwork

Finance

One of the challenges for those who are setting off on a great new adventure – one that will involve a significant time away from home – is to so order their affairs that financial and domestic horrors do not have to be resolved at long range. Admittedly, modern communications systems are such that a greater number of sailors can now manage things from on board by e-mail or fax. For the rest, distance will still be an issue for some time to come, and a home base through which paperwork can be sifted is essential.

The first issue is the simple matter of having ready cash on board; this has the trying habit of constantly needing replenishing. The most commonly held view is that unless quite large sums are involved, the cheapest and most economical method of transferring funds is by way of an ordinary credit card such as Visa. The handling charges are relatively small when dealing with sums of less than £1000 and, of course, the service is immediate. There are still some places where credit card transactions are not possible, and the answer to this is to carry a small reserve of US dollar or sterling traveller's cheques. It is also useful to keep some US dollars in cash, well hidden for use in very remote areas.

However, credit card transactions are only economical if the account is settled within the credit-free period. To this end, a system of prompt payment by someone with authority to transfer funds is essential. It is possible to employ your bank to conduct these sorts of affairs, but make sure that you are happy with the sort of service they offer before making a commitment to this course of action. If you persuade a member of the family or a friend to take on the job, it must be appreciated that this is no small task and the person you choose must be completely trustworthy. If their own domestic problems take an unfortunate turn for the worse, then you do not want to be left in the lurch or have your funds used to solve their problems!

There are a number of businesses based in the UK and the USA, run by people with a close connection to the ocean cruising scene, who provide services specifically for long-term cruising people. They will collect and forward mail, search for and obtain spares and charts, and take on the settling of accounts if required.

Mailings

Just as the fax machine once provided near-instant access to friends and family worldwide, e-mails have now superseded this mode of communication; internet cafés can be found in the unlikeliest of places (for further details on keeping in touch by e-mail, see Chapter 5). However, when you have been away from home for months or even years, there is still something wonderful about receiving personal post – greetings cards or a hand-written letter for instance – by 'snailmail'.

There are two main approaches to the issue of where to receive mail. Some crews prefer to allow their mail to accumulate at a forwarding address that never changes, and then call for a dispatch when they reach a location. They will wait until they know for certain where they will be for a period and then phone or fax to ask for their mail to be forwarded. The alternative approach calls for a degree of forward planning that is not always easy: giving correspondents a schedule of mail drops for a period ahead. The difficulty of this is forecasting the correct latest dates for mail to arrive, and then sticking to the schedule. Post office practices vary from country to country, but in many cases mail is only held for a specific time and then is returned to the sender. Mail addressed Poste Restante in French Polynesia, for instance, will only be held for 14 days. With uncertain delivery times and uncertain passage times, this sort of margin is just not big enough. It is strongly recommended that whenever a mail drop is arranged, you should write ahead from the yacht explaining how you will be travelling and asking that mail should be held for arrival.

Passports and visas

There are a number of passport and visa issues that need to be considered before departure. For instance, if the voyage is going to be a long one, it is important to look ahead to your passport renewal date and where you will be when it needs renewing. It is a problem to consider renewal in Australia because at some stage an entry visa will be required and this will not be issued unless the applicant's passport is valid for the whole period covered by the visa. Different nationalities will encounter different problems; but for UK passport holders, the USA and Australia are thought to be the only countries in the Pacific where it is important to have a valid visa before arrival. You may wish to consider additional pages in your passport, to accommodate the number of different stamps you will collect as you travel from country to country.

Ship's papers

Proper documentation for the yacht is essential. Full registration is much the best, but SSR is generally accepted. It is well worth carrying a supply of photocopies to avoid losing possession of original papers.

One last tip on the subject of preparing the paperwork is to suggest that a supply of colour photos of the yacht is sometimes very useful. Friendly relations with officials can often be encouraged by the presentation of a picture. Sometimes these are pasted on the office wall, and some officials keep a scrapbook and are pleased with a new contribution. It all goes with the handshake that is often much appreciated, and creates a more human relationship that can pay enormous dividends yet costs so little.

Formalities

The general principles regarding clearance procedures are really no different in the Pacific to anywhere else in the world. It is always best to play safe and to fly the Q flag on arrival in any new country. The ship's papers and the crew's passports must be in order and, with a few exceptions, you must arrive with a proper clearance certificate from the country that you have just left.

It can fairly safely be said that throughout the Pacific there are no instances of obstructionism for the sake of it by Customs officers. If you turn up in an official's office dressed for the beach, it is more than likely that the procedures will be difficult. The fact is that you will have insulted this man, who, in his own country, is an important official, and he will have no respect for your conduct.

The most important approach is to establish a human relationship as soon as possible. A civilised greeting and a handshake, if the opportunity arises, is the proper way to start on the right foot. A perpetual smile and a lot of patience are the tickets to success. It must be understood that someone else invented the system, and all that the officials are doing is seeing that the system is adhered to. Trying to suggest ways of increasing efficiency is not a way to make friends. If you succeed in creating the right atmosphere of mutual respect, then clearance is likely to be a light-hearted affair with plenty of smiles and laughs all round. But it may take a little while. Nobody understands a person in a hurry!

Within the Port Guides in Part III a section for each harbour has been included that describes as far as is known the procedures that will be followed. Certain countries have special requirements of their own, notably French Polynesia, where, for non-EU citizens, a bond has to be deposited with a local bank; this is only returnable when outward clearance is completed. The very strict New Zealand clearance procedures for overseas-registered yachts caused much public outcry and they have now changed back to the old system. This involves standard visits from Customs, Ministry of Agriculture & Fisheries (MAF), and Immigration. New Zealand and Australia are particularly strict about the import of certain foodstuffs, and will confiscate all fresh and frozen foods, some grains, honey and nearly all tinned meats. But this is no great hardship if you can manage to arrive with low stocks, because you are arriving to find better shopping facilities and lower prices than in the countries that you have just left.

When all is said and done, no guide to the Pacific can be up to date in respect of formalities for very long. Procedures are constantly changing, and the only way to avoid unpleasant surprises is to keep comparing notes with fellow sailors, particularly those who have radio contacts further on down the line.

Pacific cruising techniques

At last, after months or perhaps years of initial preparations, the time comes to make the break and set sail across the Pacific. More than half of those heading off will have crossed at least one ocean already; therefore this guide does not aim to be a textbook on ocean cruising in the wider sense of the word. This section relates particularly to the Pacific, and to some of the techniques that can be used when cruising through its waters.

What, you may ask, is so special about cruising in the Pacific? First and foremost, as has already been said, it is not a puddle to be leapt in one bound. A fair-sized leap is to be expected at the outset, when following the classic route across the South Pacific. Thereafter, until the final stage, it is a matter of smallish hops from one stepping stone to another: delightful, extraordinary stepping stones that repay those who linger among them.

The passage out from the Galapagos to the Marquesas is at least 100 miles or so longer than the Atlantic crossing leg from the Canaries to Barbados. If you skip the Galapagos and head directly to the Marquesas from Panama, the distance will be very nearly 4000 miles, which is a significantly long passage by anyone's standards. It is likely to be a passage that will start slowly and end quite fast. It will mean a number of weeks at sea with all the issues that this presents:

Drinking water

Water capacity, if no watermaker is carried, is a serious consideration. Rainwater collection cannot be relied on, so an adequate tank capacity and strict discipline is essential. If there is the least doubt about water supplies being sufficient, then the pressure pump, if fitted, should be turned off and the manual pump should be used throughout. Salt water should be used whenever possible. Never add dry salt to fresh water when cooking vegetables; use a suitable proportion of sea water. On the other hand, beware of dehydration as a result of insufficient drinking.

Fuel reserves

Depending on the capacity of the yacht's fuel tanks, a sensible strategy for consumption must be agreed at the outset. Conditions can be very light between Panama and the Galapagos, and if you are not one to wait endlessly for the wind, you will probably need to carry extra reserves for this leg – and more so if you are heading directly for the Marquesas. There is now a fuel storage tank in Nuku Hiva, making re-fuelling in the Marquesas a viable option.

Sailing strategies

Light-weather sails can be worth their weight in the first two weeks and perseverance is the watchword. Close study of the routeing charts to understand the flow and counterflow of the ocean currents is well worthwhile. They are only a guide, however, and – particularly if it is an El Niño year – all predictions can well be adrift (see Chapter 2 for further information on winds and currents).

There is a high proportion of running and reaching in an east–west crossing, but opinions will vary as to whether there is likely to be sufficient consistency to warrant converting to twin running sails. What is certain is that the running gear will be used in earnest, and that as the wind varies its use will come and go. Properly braced by forward and aft guys and a topping lift, the pole can be rigged in such a way that, as the wind draws ahead, the headsail can be let draw to the leeward side and the pole remain set to windward. When the wind goes aft once more, the headsail can be re-set to its outer end by the sheet that had never been unrigged. For those moving up from small boats, it should be explained that it is usual to rig the pole with the sheet free-running through the end fitting. It should of course be braced so that there is no movement to and fro in the fitting to cause chafe.

Chafe is a major concern both on the sails and on the running rigging, and not just for the initial passage. If at all possible, the aim must be to remain independent of professional sailmakers until New Zealand or Australia. Baggywrinkles are one solution, but anti-chafe patches on the sails are more reliable. Cut out from a roll of sticky-back cloth, these should be applied to that part of the mainsail in line with each pair of crosstrees on both sides of the sail. What is more, a second set, to correspond with the crosstree positions when reefed, should also be applied. Any overlapping headsails should have patches on the leeches to combat the wear of the crosstree end fittings, which should be well wrapped in tape or, even better, hide. Sheets and guys must not be allowed to lead across the guard rails for long periods.

Ultraviolet is another enemy against which you must make a strong defence. The tropical sun may only shine for a 12-hour day, but it does so with a relentless power that rots sailcloth much too fast. If twin running sails are set and the mainsail is lowered, then there should be

no hesitation in digging out the sailcover and putting it on. At any stopover where the yacht is going to sit at anchor more than literally just overnight, put the sailcover on and prolong the life of the sail.

Watchkeeping

There is less commercial traffic in the open areas of the Pacific per square mile than in the North Atlantic. This raises the vexed problem of whether or not it is necessary to keep watch at night. Both schools of thought exist, and the non-watchkeepers evidently sleep well and most survive. This is not an attitude that a responsible publication can support, and the decision for everyone to turn in and trust in faith is a purely personal decision – and one that should not be taken lightly. Very few sailors will claim that there is always a watchkeeper permanently on deck for every minute of the day and night. There should, however, always be one of the crew up and about and alert for danger. A scan of the horizon every ten minutes or so should be sufficient. Just as important as keeping a good lookout against collision is the importance of being ready to cope with any change in conditions, or change in the state of the gear. Far more damage to the gear will occur if the noise of a flapping sail, or whatever, must first wake someone from their slumbers and then continue till they rouse themselves to investigate.

Watchkeeping regimes are very much a matter of personal choice and will depend on the numbers on board. In most cases, this will be two, when the most popular timetable seems to be based on three-hour spells at night, with some longer division of the day and fairly flexible arrangements around mealtimes. Some crews prefer to do the same watches every day but others prefer to alternate, so the programme must be adapted to suit. Some two-handers lengthen the night watches to allow the off-watch crew a good chunk of sleep. Some watch systems only operate formally at night. What is important is to agree which deck operations will need two persons and which ones can be carried out by either one. The approach to this varies from those men who sail 'singlehanded with my wife', to those for whom each partner is capable of all simple operations without disturbing the other. This must surely be the ideal.

Reefing

Reefing is invariably easier with two people on deck, but in a yacht of 12m (40ft) or less the gear should, in this day and age, be devised so that the job can be reasonably easily done without calling all hands. Lazy jacks are a great help in this regard. There is a school of thought, more usually among less experienced sailors, that says that all reefing gear should be led aft to the cockpit for safety. A reluctance to leave the cockpit is a contentious issue. Sooner or later (sooner if regular inspections are not routine), an emergency will occur that requires prompt action on the foredeck; and this is when the sailor who is reluctant to leave the cockpit will find himself in a strange situation with which he might have so easily been more familiar. By all means take some gear aft if reefing is to be handled by two of the crew. If not, store it all together, by the mast, and keep it simple.

Adequate winch power is a great asset. The days when the yacht had to be turned into the wind and the boom lowered into the gallows before a reefing operation could begin are, one hopes, a thing of the past. If the reefing is to be done by only one person, then clearly the controls of luff and leech must be handy to each other. A mast-mounted halyard winch is no problem, but too many yachts have the reef pendants led to a small winch mounted on the main boom. In this position it is horribly difficult to apply any real power and the sail will have to flog for far too long as the slack is drawn in. One of the most difficult operations, particularly with the advent of full-length battens, is to pull down a reef on a dead run. The battens will wrap themselves around the athwartships rigging, sometimes with expensive results. The proper procedure is to harden the mainsheet slightly and ease the vang before commencing, and then ease only small amounts of halyard at a time. Each time the sail is lowered, the reef pendant must be hardened up so as to maintain leech tension. In this way the sail is shortened by degrees and there is never sufficient slack in the leech to allow the battens to bend round the cap shrouds.

Heavy weather

The definition of 'heavy weather' varies considerably from one crew to the next. It is directly related to the seaworthiness of the yacht and the ability of those on board to keep cool and take the appropriate action. Experience is hard to gain in areas of the world dominated by light wind conditions. Thus, the sailor from northern Europe who has been knocked about in the English Channel should be well prepared for anything the Pacific has to offer outside the cyclone season. The sailor from southern California on his first ocean crossing, however, will inevitably have more to learn, but perceptions of what 'heavy weather' is soon shift with familiarity.

This is not to say that strong winds will not be met in the Pacific. Following winds of 35 knots are not unusual, and for the final leg south to New Zealand at least one gale can be anticipated. In the latter case the wind is very likely to be from ahead and the sensible option will be to heave-to and let it pass. One of the greatest advantages that has come from the use of GPS is that there is no longer any concern over the dead reckoning position, which was so hard to plot when any length of time was spent hove-to.

A gale of wind from astern should not be a great worry for a modern, well-designed yacht. Handling characteristics should allow reasonable control at high hull speeds and, although it will be prudent to reduce sail to a minimum or none at all, steering should be within the capability of the automatic systems. There are no continental shelves rising from the deep to put vice into the seas. The chart should, however, be carefully studied for seamounts and isolated reefs such as Beveridge reef and the Minerva reefs. Older yachts, particularly those influenced by the International Offshore Rule, which encouraged distorted lines in the run aft, may not be so easy to control on a run and will have a finite speed, above which steering becomes a problem. These are the yachts for whom heavy weather starts rather sooner than for their more fortunate counterparts.

When the time comes to cut short a sleigh ride that is becoming too much of a good thing, it is time to stream either warps or a series drogue. Each skipper must have in mind a clear idea of what action to take in each possible set of circumstances based on an honest appraisal of his own boat's characteristics. When wave fronts become critically steep and breaking crests are of threatening proportions, then probably the greatest risk arises if the yacht is allowed to lie parallel to the crests, particularly if making forward way. In this attitude the chances of a serious knockdown are at their greatest. The lighter the displacement characteristics of the yacht the less good will be her behaviour hove-to, and these are the types that, if there is searoom available, will have to run off and stream a drogue or whatever. If hove-to, it is vital to keep some sail area aft to create a natural tendency to weathercock and hold the bow up to wind and waves.

One of the least well-appreciated features is the vexed question of stability. From time to time one hears tales of yachts being knocked down by freak waves in unexpected circumstances, and one is bound to wonder quite how much was due to the freak qualities of the wave and how much was due to the faulty seakeeping ability of the yacht. When the advertisements quote the displacement of a design, it may be notoriously understated, in order to enhance the figures for the displacement to length and the sail area to displacement ratios. An optimistic displacement figure also gives an optimistic ballast ratio. The stability of a yacht depends on the shape of the hull, about which little can be done once the choice has been made, and the position of the centre of gravity – not of the ballast alone, but of the whole yacht including the ballast. This may sound ridiculously elementary, but it is amazing how much some owners do on their boats that seriously reduces stability. If you have a shallow-draught boat (less than 2m (6ft) for 12m (40ft) LOA) with a low ballast ratio (less than 30 per cent of the true laden tonnage), then to carry a row of jerry cans of spare water and fuel lashed to the guard rail, together with spare sails, dinghies and spare anchors on the cabin top, is going to reduce the margin of safety significantly. This may sound alarmist, but every owner should consider the stowage of heavy items very seriously and not allow large weights to be stowed higher than is absolutely necessary.

Navigation

Most of what the average sailor crossing the Pacific needs to know to find his way is contained within the instruction manual of the GPS – that is, until it fails! The choice of back-up system, to cope with a GPS that goes down, is either to carry at least one other (preferably on an independent power source) or to carry a sextant and learn how to use it. Taking the failure of electronics to its logical conclusion, if you put your faith in an electronic calculator for the astro workings, how reliable is that if dropped or soaked with sea water! (See Appendix A for a short piece on astro-navigation, to serve as a helping hand when all the electronics have failed.)

The limitations of any form of position fixing system is that it can be accurate within 100m, or whatever is claimed, but that is of no earthly use whatever if the charts are only accurate to the nearest ½ mile or so, which is frequently the case – and will remain so until fresh surveys are made. The overriding strategy should be never to consider making a landfall at night unless you are approaching a high island with a full moon (and radar is also useful), or one of the commercial harbours where the lights can be relied upon. Stay well away, at least 5 miles, from all reefs and atolls until full daylight. So many of the surveys were carried out before the days of radio time signals and the surveyors' longitude was derived from a chronometer whose rate was seldom perfect. Those early surveyors were absolute masters of their trade, but they did not have the facilities that we enjoy today.

Taking a sunsight, using a sextant. Photo Ros Hogbin.

Pilotage

Anyone used to pilotage in the muddy waters of the Solent or the Sacramento river will find a whole new experience when penetrating the passes and lagoons of the Pacific islands. This relies not on charts, but on vision. At first the clarity of the water is quite unnerving, but – with time – a capacity for interpreting the colour coding of the bottom is easily acquired. The technique is for the person in the cockpit constantly to call the depth on the echo sounder to the person on the bows or the crosstrees. In that way, the eye is soon trained to recognise the difference between the shades. Move with the greatest caution to begin with, always with the sun high in the sky, preferably behind you. Feel your way around. There is a certain shade of brown that indicates a genuinely dangerous coral head, but other greys and dark blues are very often no more than patches on the bottom.

Running the passes can sometimes be quite alarming, and when there is a breaking sea close to hand the water will not be so clear. Most passes have daymarks or motus (sand and coral islets) that can be used as reference points from the Admiralty Pilot or other publications. Naturally the passes on the windward sides are always going to be the most hazardous, and sometimes it will be that conditions change while you are inside and therefore leaving should be delayed. The entrance to Maupiti in the Western Society Islands is open to the south-east, which allows the swell to create a most unpleasant approach, but it is easier at high water slack and local advice should be sought if there is a worry. By contrast, at Mopelia, the next stop down the chain, the pass is on the leeward side of the atoll and, even with a massive sea running in the open ocean, the pass is quite smooth but the current extreme.

Where there is a swell running in the pass the yacht will be much safer with sail up and drawing (even though the engine is running). This will steady the roll and keep drive on until the pass is safely crossed. The exciting part is then getting sail off and slowing down before the coral closes in inside the lagoon.

Anchoring

Various accounts of early Pacific cruising have given the impression that the experienced sailor knows how to swim down and lock his anchors into the coral for secure holding – all very macho! Attempting to lock into a coral head *might* be excusable in an emergency, but as a general practice it should be deplored for the sake of the coral. Each time an anchor is dropped onto the coral, damage occurs, and constant damage will harm the ecology for a long time. The lagoons are generally sandy floored with a surrounding wall of coral and, very often, isolated coral heads within the anchorage area (sometimes appearing with much greater frequency). Where these occur, some effort should be made to limit the freedom to range around in varying conditions.

The coral is clearly visible in the crystal-clear water off the Fijian island of Dravuni. Photo Andrew Hogbin.

Quite apart from the desirability of protecting the coral from damage, the free-ranging yacht will wind its chain around any coral head in figures of eight until the scope is seriously reduced. When this happens there is no risk of dragging, but if conditions deteriorate, there is a very real risk of serious snubbing – and this is the surest way to break a chain with disastrous consequences. A snubber with a chain hook will add strength to the chain.

5 Keeping in Touch

Long-range radio by Hugh Marriott
E-mailing by Andrew Edsor

Long-range radio

Ocean voyaging can be a sociable as well as a solitary experience. For both these reasons most people, though not quite all, like to have a radio transceiver on board. VHF is fine for talking with other boats in the same anchorage, but the vast span of the Pacific calls for a short-wave, and therefore long-range, radio for most other purposes.

With a short-wave set, boats can keep in touch with others who have gone on ahead or are coming up astern. Cruising people in different parts of the ocean can exchange positions and fishing stories, arrange to meet, and generally share their joys or frustrations with somebody else.

Radio can be useful, too, as opposed to being merely companionable. It can be invaluable for finding out what the weather is doing just round the corner, what the Customs formalities involve in the next port of entry, where the best fresh water is to be had, and whether there is any room in a marina, or fuel at the fuel dock.

It may, furthermore, be a safety aid – or the source of a false sense of security, depending on your point of view. The yacht *Rabbit* was two days out of Bora Bora bound for Rarotonga. The skipper was worried about a mysterious pain in his chest, but not as worried as his companion. Nobody else was aboard. They came up on the evening radio net and described the symptoms. A doctor aboard another boat making for Tonga was listening in. He made his presence known, asked some questions, gave his opinion, and said he would keep a listening watch. The 'Rabbits' no longer felt so helpless or alone. In the event, the pain subsided. Whether it was an incipient heart attack, or indigestion, or muscle strain, and whether the distant doctor could have done anything about it had the need arisen, must remain for ever uncertain. But for the 'Rabbits', and everybody else who listened in to the conversation, the incident served to justify their faith in radio as an aid to safety.

The minority who do not have short-wave radio, nor want it, believe that it is contrary to the spirit of cruising. Ocean voyagers, they maintain, should be independent and self-sufficient. If they get into trouble, they should be able to get themselves out of it without shouting for help. They should conduct their cruise and their lives without inconveniencing others. And they should not draw attention to themselves. Be that as it may, most cruising people who do not have short-wave radio would like it, and hardly any who have it would

consider throwing it out. So, diehards notwithstanding, here is some background on short-wave radio for yachts.

There are two systems: SSB and amateur radio. Both are distinct from each other, complete with their separate frequencies, radio sets, call signs, jargon, licensing requirements, proponents and detractors, advantages and disadvantages. Yachts can make use of either system, or both.

Single sideband (SSB)

This is the correct and conventional means of communication between vessels at sea via high frequency (HF), long-range, radiotelephony. Very high frequency (VHF) radio waves cannot follow the curvature of the earth, so are for line-of-sight distances only. Medium frequency (MF) wave bands are for ranges up to 200 miles or so. MF sets can only transmit and receive on MF frequencies, but SSB sets can operate on HF and MF bands.

The phrase 'single sideband' refers to the way in which a radio signal is modulated so as to carry audio information. The simplest way of sending information is to interrupt a radio wave intermittently so that it can be heard in the form of dots and dashes. This requires little power, and takes up little space in the airwaves, so it is cheap and efficient. Unfortunately, Morse Code is about as intelligible as Latin or Greek to most people. To impose a voice signal onto a radio carrier wave involves varying either the amplitude or frequency. An amplitude-modulated signal (AM) takes the form of two bands on either side of a carrier wave. Both bands carry the voice information. Since one is unnecessary, AM transmissions are expensive in terms of power and airspace. Radiating one sideband only increases signal strength for a given power output and halves the bandwidth.

If you buy an SSB radio, you will be able to use it for calling other boats on certain authorised marine frequencies, and for making link calls to shore-based telephone numbers via coast radio stations. To do any of this legally, you need both a licence for the operator and a licence for the ship. Acquiring the operator's licence is more or less a matter of applying for it, though in the UK it involves passing a test, to include GMDSS (Global Maritime Distress Safety Systems). It needs some prior instruction, generally a fairly simple three- or four-day course.

The principal requirement for obtaining the ship licence is that the radio itself should be a marine SSB set. This used to be the number one drawback of SSB compared with ham radio. SSBs are designed and built to withstand the marine environment, and for the marine market. For both these reasons they tend to be more expensive than ham sets. However, so many people are buying them these days that the price is coming down.

Having adhered to the formalities and become an officially recognised ship radio station, you will now discover two other drawbacks of SSB when compared with ham. SSB communication is usually (though not always) one-to-one. Ship A calls ship B or coast radio station X. Since there are very few calling frequencies and large numbers of vessels using them, making contact with someone can be as uncertain as shouting to a guest on the opposite side of the room at a successful cocktail party after the third round of refills. Then, even if you succeed in establishing radio contact, you have to switch to a working frequency. This is very likely to be already in use, with several others waiting for it to become free. Your options are to wait and hope that propagation is still workable when your turn comes round, or give up and return to the calling frequency, in which case you'll have to start all over again.

Assuming you do meet up with the other boat on the working frequency and that propagation is good enough for you to understand one another, there will only officially be the two of you in on the conversation, despite the fact that other ears will almost certainly be flapping silently in the background. But what makes long-range radio so valuable to cruising people is the exchange of information among the fleet. For this, it is necessary to have a verbal meeting place, a net, at a fixed time and with a controller. Boat A asks whether you can enter the pass at atoll X at any state of the tide, and boat B chips in and says he tried it at mid-ebb and the outflow was too strong. Boat C hears this, and modifies his plans accordingly. Nets do occur from time to time on SSB, and some of them are beautifully conducted. But they tend to spring up on the spur of the moment, and fade just as quickly. Long-running nets, on the other hand, are the very stuff of ham radio.

Amateur radio (ham)

Ham radio is not, by rights, a means of communication for boats at all. It is a hobby for radio enthusiasts, who are supposed to use it as a forum for discussing each other's signal strengths and comparing notes about antennas. Ham operators are supposed to be able to design and build their own sets, and chat away in Morse Code using minimal power over very long distances. But it seems that radio has much in common with sailing as a pastime. They are both outdated technologies whose dependence on unpredictable natural phenomena, primitive equipment and abstruse nomenclature make them irresistible to people of a technical bent who like to think they are getting something, and

somewhere, for nothing. As a result, the ham radio operator and the ocean cruising skipper are very often combined in the same person.

It is, in fact, possible to use amateur radio purely as a means of communication aboard a cruising yacht. One of the advantages of going down this route is that the set is likely to be cheaper. On the other hand, as it won't be marinised, it will have to be protected from damp sea air, let alone damp sea. You will have immediate access not just to the dozens of nets operated for cruising hams, but will become a member of what is essentially an international club that looks after its own.

US ham operators are able to use their sets to call loved ones at home by means of phone patches. They establish contact with a shore-based ham who has the equipment necessary for linking the transceiver with the telephone. He dials the loved one's number, and then the ham, in the middle of the Pacific, can explain that all is going well. What he can't do is to have a conversation that touches on anything of a business or commercial nature, so this facility is of no use in calling the office or the bank. In England, phone patches are illegal whatever the nature of the message.

There are more ham operators ashore than afloat, which is both a blessing and a curse. A shore-based controller of a net for cruising yachts may well have a powerful beam antenna which can be rotated so as to concentrate the full power of the signal in any given direction. Two yachts that might not be able to hear each other can converse by means of a shore-based relay. Furthermore, shore-based net controllers who never have to interrupt a transmission to go on deck and reef are often able to devote more concentrated attention to a net. It is easier for them to spread charts out and record the positions of the yachts they talk to. And if they should ever need to pick up the telephone to talk to rescue services or relations, that too is easier for them than for a yacht-bound controller. On the other hand, amateur radio is the preserve by right of radio hobbyists, and if one of these should appear out of the ether and cut in on an interesting conversation between you and your best friend who you haven't heard from in two years, you have to welcome him in, and ask him how the weather is and what kind of antenna he is using. Unsociable yachting hams should avoid transmitting on Sundays when shorebound hams in radio shacks all the way from Atlanta to Zagreb will prick up their ears and pick up their mics for the thrill of being able to log a contact (QSO) with a vessel at sea.

Even so, there are fewer ham operators than marine SSB ones, but conversely there are more ham frequencies available. So it is much easier to make contact, and there is less chance of interference. (Note: ham operators never say 'interference'. They use the code letters QRM if the interference is generated by somebody else's transmission, or QRN if it is due to radio static. In fact, ham operators, like sailors, have their own special word for just about everything.)

To be a legal radio ham you have to pass a two-part test. One part is concerned with radio theory, and the other with knowledge of Morse Code. Many people who find one part difficult will find the other easy. Some find them both daunting, though now that the speed requirement for Morse has been reduced from 12 words per minute to 5 there isn't really any excuse for worrying about that. But passing the test is necessary to become legal. Hams are self-policing, because the loss of their licence is a very real possibility if they communicate with an illegal station. So they won't do it. You may think you can invent a plausible call sign, and you might even get away with it for a time. But in the end you will be run off the road. Nor is it a real answer to obtain a licence in one of the countries that issues them in exchange for little more than a cash payment, as many hams will not recognise such a call sign. It is said to be easier to qualify as a ham in the USA than it is in Europe. But the truth of the matter is that anyone who can learn to sail and maintain an ocean cruising yacht has the wherewithal to pass the amateur radio exam in any country.

SSB and ham combined

Since the amateur radio wavebands are interleaved between the marine SSB ones, so that any all-band transceiver will encompass both, it should be possible to use one radio for both systems. And so it is, though not legally. One reason is that ham sets are designed so that they can only transmit on the ham bands, and SSB sets vice versa. However, both can be modified to transmit as well as receive on all bands.

If a ham transceiver is modified and used for transmitting on the marine bands, this is illegal even if the operator has an SSB licence. Using the ham set makes it so. It is perfectly legal to use an SSB set to transmit on the ham bands so long as you are a qualified amateur operator. If not, you are unlikely to succeed. In any case, most SSB sets are insufficiently versatile for ham use. For example, ham operators need to be able to switch between upper sideband and lower sideband, whereas only USB is used when working SSB. The proper solution is to have two radio sets, two call signs and two sets of qualifications. Some do.

What is certain is that those who participate in both ham and SSB usually feel that both are indispensable. On the other hand, those who are restricted to one side or the other usually feel that they are missing out somewhere. Now that e-mail has become so important to most people, the superior e-mailing facilities available to ham operators tend to weight the scales on the side of amateur radio.

Ham nets

UTC	Band	Frequency	Name	Comments
1930	40m	7088	Si/Oui net	Now run from Fiji; named after cruising people's struggle to adjust from Spanish to French when they arrive in French Polynesia from Mexico or Panama
2100	20m	14315	Tony's Net	Run from New Zealand
0000	20m	14320	Rowdy's Breakfast Show	Run from Thailand; covers eastern Pacific rim
0200	20m	14313	Seafarers' Net	Central and East Pacific
0300	20m	14313	Pacific Maritime warm-up	Run from Moorea; chatty precursor of the more formal Pacific Maritime Net
0400	20m	14313	Pacific Maritime Net	Roll call for yachts on passage
1000/2300	20m	14315	Robby's Net	Run from Australia

These nets are run on a regular basis. However, they are subject to change and you may become aware of others as you sail through the region.

SSB nets

UTC	Band	Frequency	Name	Comments
1915	4MHz	4445	Russell Radio	Run from New Zealand
2000	12MHz	12359	Southbound II	Daily weather update, but extends to Panama Canal west
0215	12MHz	12353	Russell Radio	

These nets are run on a regular basis, but times and frequencies may vary. Groups of boats cruising together often create their own nets.

Ham frequencies

Band	Frequencies in MHz	Sideband	Comments
80m	3.5–3.8	LSB	Short range
40m	7.0–7.1	LSB	Intermediate distance to 1000 miles. Worldwide at night
	7.15–7.3	LSB	Reg 2, E Pacific
30m	10.1–10.15	USB	Not much used
20m	14.0–14.350	USB	Long range, and most popular
17m	18 068–18 168	USB	Not much used
15m	21.0–21 450	USB	Less crowded, longer range, less predictable
12m	24 890–24 990	USB	
10m	28.0 – 29.7	USB	Great range with less power

SSB inter-ship frequencies

Frequency Band	Calling/distress	Inter-ship working	Comments
2MHz	2182	2065, 2079	MF, range approximately 200 miles
4MHz	4125	4146, 4149, 4417	4125 available for use by aircraft
6MHz	6215	6224, 6227, 6230	The most popular band
8MHz	8291	8294, 8297	
12MHz	12290	12353, 12356, 12359	Long range
16MHz	16420	16528, 16531, 16534	

Installation of an antenna

Some boats put out a signal which is consistently strong. Their transmissions can be clearly heard while others can hardly be detected if propagation is difficult. The difference is seldom due to the choice of radio, but almost always due to the choice and installation of the antenna. The vagaries of propagation can often make it frustratingly difficult to communicate over HF radio, so the best achievable signal is not a luxury but an essential.

There is a relationship between the desired physical length of the antenna and the wavelength of the transmission. But as it is hardly practical to have a separate antenna for every waveband you are likely to use, the usual practice is to use the backstay as an antenna and to modify its length electronically according to the waveband you want to transmit on. This can be done manually, or with an automatic tuning unit.

One problem with using the backstay as an antenna is that a dismasting will disable the radio, just when you might need it. An alternative is a whip antenna. There is very little difference in cost between an independent whip and a pair of insulators for the backstay. The whip might survive a dismasting, particularly if the mast were to go over the side due to rigging failure in not very severe weather. On the other hand, the shorter physical length of a whip (usually 7m (23ft)) will make it less efficient for the longer frequencies. However, the longer frequencies are those used for the shorter distances, so this is rarely a disadvantage.

End-fed wire antennas like whips and backstays are resonant, or tuned, when their length is approximately a quarter of the wavelength being used. A commonly used frequency band for SSB is 6 MHz. Expressed in terms of wavelength, this is 50m. Most ocean cruising yachts will have a backstay that is 12.5m (41ft) or more in length, and therefore ideal. A whip can easily be lengthened electronically to the required length.

The most efficient antenna available to a yacht is the fixed-length dipole. Its length is matched to a specific frequency band, so it doesn't need to be tuned. It is a balanced antenna, with the transmission wire led to the centre of two wires, so it doesn't require an efficient earth or ground plate. For the ham who likes to work the popular 20m band from his ketch, a 10m (33ft) wire stretched aft from the top of the mizzen mast, linked to a 10m wire stretched forward, will perform wonderfully. It is said that no boatowner ever owns a ketch more than once, but perhaps this does not apply to cruising hams for whom the ketch rig has a peculiar advantage.

A quarter-wave vertical antenna, such as a backstay or whip, is actually half of a half-wave dipole with the missing half being supplied by the earth or ground plane. The most expensive transmitter on the market will be unable to do more than bleat pathetically if it is hitched to an inadequately earthed antenna. Connecting the antenna to the keel is not good enough. What is required is a sintered copper ground plate on the outside of the hull; better still, that and the keel. A web of wires laid in the bilge, equating to a quarter of a wavelength at the centre of the main frequency bands, also helps.

Other uses for short-wave radio

Link calls

Link calls can be made from ship to shore via SSB, though every year fewer and fewer countries offer this facility (many of the shore stations are being bought up by Globe Wireless). To make a link call to New Zealand, for example, it is necessary to go through Sydney Radio, and therefore make an international call, even if you are 20 miles out of Auckland.

Weather

Even if a short-wave transceiver is not aboard, a receiver really should be, if only for the weather forecasts. It could be argued that a yacht cruising tropical waters in the season that is not prone to cyclones has little need of weather reports. Or that the Pacific is so wide, the passages so long, and sailing boats so slow, that forecasts cannot possibly be used, even if heard. But the chances are that Drake, Tasman, Bougainville, Cook and Vancouver would have listened to the forecasts if they had had the option, as part of good seamanship.

A boat fitted with a computer as well as a short-wave radio has no need of a discrete weatherfax receiver. All that is required is a modem and cable to link the two, plus some software. A bonus to this system is that the software may have a Morse decoder included, so that weather forecasts transmitted in high speed Morse can simply be read in plain language from the screen.

E-mailing *by Andrew Edsor*

This section relates solely to the sending and receiving of e-mails. For most of us with finite budgets, it is not currently economical to browse the web when at sea. E-mail is fast becoming the preferred form of communication for the computer-literate sailor – and every ocean cruising yachtsman has the technical ability to become computer-literate. There are a number of available options – depending on your onboard equipment capabilities, whether you require access to your messages at sea as well as on land, and your overall budget.

E-mail by radio

With the addition of a radio modem to connect your set to your computer, you will be able to send and receive e-mail. Your options will be dictated by your licence and your radio set. Boats fitted with SSB transceivers can choose one of the commercial, and more expensive, facilities for radio e-mail, like PinOak (http://www.pinoak.com), which offers Pacific-wide coverage subject to the usual limitations of HF communications; or you can sign on with the non-profit-making SailMail Association, which is designed and operated by yachtsmen (www.sailmail.com) and covers most parts of the Pacific. With SailMail, you don't pay for the time you are connected, or the amount of data you send/receive. Instead you pay a year's subscription in advance. If you use e-mail a lot, it represents very good value. Another possibility is SeaMail (www.pentacomstat.com.au), which is run by Penta Comstat – a private coast radio station near Sydney, Australia; it charges to send and receive e-mails, and there is a monthly subscription as well.

With all of these options, you can send ordinary e-mails (in plain text and with no attachments) to any other e-mail address, ashore or afloat. You can exchange family news, order parts, tell your stockbroker to 'sell, sell, sell', and book airline tickets.

Ham e-mail

If you have invested time in acquiring a ham licence, you will be able to communicate by e-mail from virtually anywhere in the world at no cost at all (see www.airmail2000.com). All you have to do is buy a radio modem – and the smallest, slowest, and cheapest will do for this purpose. After that, there's no charge of any kind, whether sending or receiving. And, unlike SailMail, it's truly worldwide (within the constraints of HF propagation). In the remotest anchorage or the vastest ocean, you will be in touch. But, ham radio is non-commercial and this does have one drawback: you are not allowed to use it to communicate with anyone who is going to have a financial involvement with whatever it is that you're e-mailing about. So you can't legally order parts, sell shares, or book tickets through it. However, since all radio e-mail, even the most expensive option, is painfully slow by comparison with telephone connections, most cruising people prefer to go to a cyber café with floppy disk in hand when there is one within reach. The advantage of radio e-mail is that you are not cut off when there isn't a café within reach.

One of the main drawbacks of e-mail by radio is its dependence on good propagation. There may be times when atmospheric interference or traffic-filled channels prevent clear reception, which can be extremely frustrating when the message you are expecting is urgent.

E-mail by telephone

Web-based accounts

If you have access to the shore, even in some of the most out-of-the-way places, you are likely to find an internet café, where you will be able to send and receive e-mails. The most basic way to do this is to set up a free web-based e-mail account, via sites such as Yahoo, Hotmail, Eudoramail and usa.net. You connect to the

internet to view your messages and you only pay for the time you spend on-line. In fact, any good *free* ISP (Internet Service Provider) providing dial-up access via a modem will also offer management of the same e-mail account via a web browser. This is a flexible solution that is ideal for cruising yachties and much better than mailboxes such as Hotmail. If, for convenience, you compose your messages in advance on a floppy disk to take into a café, be warned that this practice is now severely restricted, due to the risk of spreading computer viruses. When writing messages under these circumstances it is safer and cheaper to draft a message off-line in a simple text editor such as WordPad (Windows) or NotePad (Mac). Then copy and paste into the mail. If you have your own computer, you may occasionally be able to make use of a marina phone socket to access your messages in the same way.

Even without a computer, you can use a hand-held e-mail device called PocketMail (www.pocketmail.com, www.stargate3.co.uk). Once you have written your messages on it, you send them by clamping the device over the handset of an onshore telephone. However, it is not best suited to long messages, and it works via the USA, where it is accessed from an 800 number. Outside the USA, it uses a long-distance call, which limits its usefulness as you travel west.

Internet Service Providers (ISP)

If you have a computer on board, and want a service that provides greater flexibility and facilities, you can subscribe to a conventional ISP either locally or via your home country. If you already have an account with AOL or CompuServe, check whether their international coverage of local dial-in numbers applies to your particular cruising ground.

An example of an ISP that provides local numbers internationally is Easynet (http://www.easydial.co.uk/), which allows conventional dial-up access via a modem and the ability to manage the same mail account via a web browser in an internet café. For a monthly charge, they provide you with a UK telephone number that can receive faxes and voice-mail from anywhere in the world. These calls are converted into e-mails and placed in your mailbox in the normal way. You can also send a fax via the same system from a web browser anywhere in the world, and for a small extra charge they can provide local dial-up access from about 100 countries worldwide. If you are away from home but have dial-up access, you can reach your account via a special roving server like I-pass (www.ipass.com), which connects to the internet via a local number.

E-mail by mobile phone

Logging-in to your ISP via a mobile phone is possible in coastal waters (albeit at a slower data rate than via a land line), provided you can get local dial-in access and as long as you are in range of an antenna. A mobile phone will connect to your onboard computer either via its built-in modem, or using a data-compatible mobile phone, a modem in the phone or computer, and a connection between the phone and computer by cable or infra-red ports. Beware of the problems with different mobile phone standards.

E-mail via satellite-based systems

These include such systems as Inmarsat and Magellan and work by using satellites as the means of data transfer, rather than the phone system.

Inmarsat

The Inmarsat organisation (www.inmarsat.org/via/maritime/index.html) operates four geo-stationary satellites that cover the whole globe. Inmarsat has four types of satellite system: A, B, C and Mini-M. Inmarsat A is the original analogue system still installed on many commercial ships, providing voice and data communication. B is the more modern digital successor to A, with video capability, and used by major racing yacht campaigns to report to media and sponsors.

Inmarsat Mini-M Mini-M provides a cut-down version of Inmarsat B, and is only guaranteed for land and coastal use, although its coverage is being extended and it seems to work some way out into the Pacific. When in range, you can make telephone calls worldwide and connect it to your computer to send and receive e-mails. Its drawbacks, apart from limited oceanic coverage, are that it requires a largish dome and is much more expensive than Immarsat C to buy and operate. Its data transfer rate is slow, and this may affect your choice of ISP. IMC provides a service via the Super-Hub (www.super-hub.com/indexmid.htm). Their software is specifically written for Mini-M and includes cost-saving features such as data compression. This ISP also runs with mobile and terrestrial lines and a local USA number. Further examples of ISPs that work with slow modems are Connect free and Easynet.

Inmarsat C Inmarsat C is a popular choice with ocean sailors (www.inmarsat.org/c_email.html). It is the only Inmarsat system that is part of GMDSS and dedicated to the maritime community. It is a data service, which sends and receives telexes and e-mails, and sends (but not receives) faxes. And it is significantly cheaper than the Mini-M system.

In addition (and for free), it automatically receives regular oceanic weather warnings, forecasts and safety messages for the area the yacht is in. It continuously and automatically reports the yacht's position and provides the facility to declare distress states to the international maritime emergency control centres.

In order to use the service, you must register as an Inmarsat station. You simply add this requirement to your existing ship's telecom licence and the cost is negligible. Once you have received your unique user number (and can thus be charged for calls), you can use every service except e-mail. Charges are levied per message sent via your local telecom operator. Messages go from your yacht to the nearest satellite and on to a ground station of your choosing, in the same ocean region.

To use e-mail you have to sign up to an *Inmarsat Service Provider* – also abbreviated as ISP. For internet e-mail, which seems likely to be the most popular and flexible, you sign up to one of umpteen Inmarsat Service Providers. The Inmarsat website gives its lists for each country (www.Inmarsat.org/Inmarsat/). For a fee, the Inmarsat Service Provider you choose will set up an e-mail box. Then all you pay are the charges per message. Different charging schemes may apply for yacht-bound messages, including 'skipper-pays-all', or incoming messages accepted from designated addresses only, with either the yacht or the originator paying for them. Whichever charging scheme you use, make sure that you understand exactly how the costs relate to your messages, so that you are not unpleasantly surprised when the bill comes in!

Hardware, installation and operation

The two main manufacturers of Inmarsat equipment are Thrane & Thrane (www.tt.dk/3/tt-3020c.html) and Trimble. The hardware components for the C system are very simple and consist of a transceiver, which is smaller and lighter than a hardback book, and a fixed antenna, approximately equivalent in size to a GPS aerial. The antenna weighs about 1.5kg (3lbs) and must be mounted so that it is not obscured in azimuth by more than 2° and can 'see' 15° below the horizontal. The only other installation constraint concerns the distance between antenna and tranceiver, which should ideally be no greater than 10m (33ft).

Most people use a laptop PC for data entry and receipt. It can even be an ancient one as it does not require any horsepower and the software can operate on a monochrome display. The transceiver needs to be fed with a GPS position, either from an existing or integrated source. Inmarsat/GMDSS regulations insist that all severe weather or hazard warnings be printed out directly – the cheapest dot matrix printer will do, but it must be switched on and working. (Hint! Use high-quality glossy paper or otherwise you may suffer feed problems.) The equipment runs on standard 12v, with very modest current usage – much less than HF radio.

Magellan

The Magellan GSC100 combines a GPS with a satellite communicator and uses the Orbcomm satellites (www.magellangps.com, www.orbcomm.com). The unit is as small as a GPS, with its own mini keyboard, and is best for short messages. For a one-off activation fee and a further monthly subscription, you can send and receive a fixed number of messages, within certain size specifications. There have been some queries as to how well this unit operates when a boat heels at sea and also how well it handles traffic.

SMS text messaging

Text messaging can be exchanged between mobiles on the international GSM900/1800 standard. It is a very effective, simple and cheap way of sending a message of up to 160 characters in length. It is instantaneous and, in theory, 100 per cent reliable.

A selection of internet and e-mail links, providing communications information

Address	Subject
www.pocketmail.com	PocketMail
tt@marinecomputing.com	Tim Thornton at Marine Computing in the UK for advice on Mini-M and C, choice and installation
www.kvh.com	Makers of KVH Tracphone for Mini-M
www.thraneandthrane.com	Makers of equipment for Mini-M and C
www.orbcomm.net	Magellan GSC100
www.pca.cc	Marc Robinson at Philip Collins & Associates in Australia for advice on radio choice and installation
www.xaxero.com	Software for SeaMail
www.win-net.org	Ham e-mail shore stations
www.shortwave.co.uk	Shortwave shop for HF equipment
www.hfradio.com	Dealer recommended for all aspects of HF communications equipment, including e-mails

And what of the future?

Satellite communications for small boats are becoming ever more practical and affordable. Mobile phones, like cockroaches, are not only increasing numerically, but threatening with every passing day to take over the world. The time is fast approaching when a cruising boat in mid-Pacific will reverberate to the shrill sounds of a ringing telephone as loved ones call in at 0300 (having mistakenly *added* the zone time difference instead of subtracting it). As a matter of course, a boat with engine failure will call the engine manufacturer for advice and the crew of *Rabbit* will dial their family doctor at home for a consultation. Very soon, the vast majority of us will be on the internet, surfing the web. If this thought fills you with horror, remember that there is always an on/off switch!

Short-wave radio is already looking distinctly antiquated, but it still has its place. Whenever bunches of small, under-crewed yachts set off hesitantly at the beginning of long, lonely sea passages, their crews will usually grab at the chance to be able to talk to one another on an open line as they inch their way across the chart – for mutual reassurance, company, interest and fun, and without paying for the calls.

Contributors

Hugh Marriott is a member of the RCC and a ham operator. His call sign is G0 OWG.

Andrew Edsor is an avionic engineer by profession, and a member of the OCC, who started communicating by HF as a teenager, went on the internet in 1994, and rounded Cape Horn 20 years before that.

6 Provisioning

Provisioning for a Pacific crossing, which may take up to eight months to complete, requires considerable thought on the part of whoever is doing the catering for the voyage. For example, although each leg of a South Pacific crossing may take only a matter of weeks or less, destination ports in mid-Pacific are remote, and the majority offer very little in the way of re-stocking opportunities. Of course, food of one sort or another may be obtained almost anywhere, but the range available in the most distant outposts is often limited. It is important to have some idea about what needs to be purchased before setting sail, and what may be widely available during the crossing.

Storage

Non-perishable goods

The general rule for storing tins is to write the contents on the lids in indelible marker and then to remove the labels (which may otherwise become soggy and disintegrate). They can then be stored low in the bilges or in dry lockers. Dried goods in paper packaging, such as flour and sugar, should be wrapped in plastic before stowage, or decanted into hard plastic containers with airtight lids. The bulk of these basic foodstuffs will often be tucked away behind seats and where space can be found at the back of lockers. It is useful to allocate an easily accessible locker for smaller quantities, so that they are close at hand for day-to-day needs.

Cartons of UHT milk and juice are long-lasting, but take up lots of storage space. Powdered milk is an acceptable alternative. If household consumables can be purchased in concentrated form, this will save on storage space.

Perishable goods

Fresh dairy products can be stored according to the refrigeration capacity on board. Tins of butter may need refrigerating, to prevent the contents turning to oil. Margarine is much more resistant to tropical temperatures. Eggs last for several weeks if they are bought very fresh. If refrigeration is not available, they can be turned at regular intervals to preserve them.

Fresh fruit and vegetables not requiring refrigeration are best kept in netting, to allow air to circulate freely around them. Some may be stowed in the dark, to slow the ripening process until they are required. To maximise longevity, it is important to buy fresh produce that has not been chilled at any stage. At least some soft fruit and vegetables should be bought unripe. All fresh produce requires 'management' – a careful inspection at regular intervals to identify and remove any items that are showing signs of deterioration.

Alfalfa and bean sprouts can be grown on board, but they do need a lot of fresh water and plenty of space.

Stocking up before departure

There are a multitude of excellent provisioning ports on the west coast of America, which will ensure that your lockers are full to bursting by the time departure day has arrived. Those boats that have come from the Caribbean via the Panama Canal may well have already taken on a good proportion of ship's stores in places such as St Maarten, St Barts, Curaçao and the larger ports in Venezuela.

Panama itself provides major provisioning opportunities, particularly in Panama City on the Pacific side. The crime rate here is high, and it is therefore best to take a taxi to the local supermarkets; sharing with other yachting folk is a popular option. Stocking up with fresh fruit and vegetables in Panama makes sense if you want to hold out for the freshest produce available before you set sail. Employing the services of a local taxi driver can be very helpful, since he will take you to the open-air market, guide you to the best bargains, and help with the loading and unloading of sacks of onions, oranges and potatoes.

It is advisable to try out any tinned products that appeal to you *before* making your bulk purchases. This will prevent you from investing in 24 tins of chunky chicken, only to find you can't stand the taste of the stuff one month into your crossing!

Broadly speaking, the provisions that are worth stocking up on before you leave are:

- Tins of meat (and some standby tins of fruit and vegetables)
- Pasta and rice
- Some flour, particularly if *not* standard white flour, which can be found across the Pacific
- Any branded goods that are a 'must have' for your crew
- A few 'luxury' items for special occasions

- Toilet paper, cleaning products and plastic storage containers
- Beverages, both alcoholic and non-alcoholic
- Durable fruit and vegetables, such as potatoes, carrots, onions, cabbages and oranges

It is useful to make an inventory of stocks and their locations in the boat, which can be amended as items are used.

Provisioning during the crossing

The port information in Part III gives some guidelines about shopping facilities in the major centres. However, nothing can beat up-to-date local knowledge from boats ahead of you, which you will acquire naturally as you reach each port of call.

As you travel further across the South Pacific, you will find that some items are easily obtainable in most places. These include standard white flour, sugar, margarine and cooking oil. Fresh bread is available almost everywhere and many destinations house a fresh fruit and vegetable market of some description. Beware of buying the ubiquitous corned beef in the Pacific islands – it is much more fatty than the US equivalent. At the other end of the spectrum, major Pacific centres such as Tahiti stock a wide range of products, catering for the most discerning cruising palate, including delicatessen cheeses and pâtés.

What you buy and where you buy it will depend very much on your cruising philosophy and budget. Some crews stock up on what is cheap and readily available and adapt their menus accordingly. Others allow for the fact that imported products will be more expensive, but include them in their shopping list to add variety to their meals further down the line. For example, fresh yoghurt can easily be made overnight using dried products such as EasiYo (write to EasiYo Products, PO Box 100-371, NSMC, Auckland, NZ for information).

A reasonably well-stocked supermarket will be found at Puerto Ayora in the Galapagos, where most supplies, except fresh fruit and vegetables, can be bought at a price. If you are an early riser, the Saturday market at 6am here is a must for fresh produce. Some fresh supplies can also be purchased in normal hours at the supermarket in Villamil, Isabela, which is a useful last stop before the onward passage. The shops in the Marquesas and the Tuamotus are not quite as well stocked, but most basics can be purchased at a price. Early morning markets exist at main centres in the Marquesas, but be warned that they start at 0430 hours! On some islands, like Fatu Hiva in the Marquesas, it is possible to barter for fruit and vegetables, using T-shirts, cassette tapes, scent, lipsticks, sunglasses, children's clothes, and perhaps odd lengths of rope – most of the local ponies can be seen tied up with ropes from passing yachts. There are very few shops and little to be bought in the Tuamotu Islands. In fact, fruit hanging on deck

Banana and coconut palms fringe a delightful walk from Daniel's Bay, Nuku Hiva. Photo Lisa Shamer.

will be a great treat for the local children if it can be spared, for no fruit trees, apart from the omnipresent coconut palm, grow on the islands.

Papeete in Tahiti is the capital of the Society Islands. It is a fairly sophisticated small city where nearly everything is available for reprovisioning, but at a high price. Meals and drinks ashore are also expensive. Fresh fruit and vegetables are costly in the Society Islands, but can be obtained at a much more reasonable price in the Cook Islands, particularly Rarotonga. The supermarket there stocks a range of products from New Zealand.

Pago Pago in American Samoa has a very good reputation for being an excellent provisioning port for US brands in particular, but there is a port charge for non-Americans. The anchorage itself suffers from the effluent and emissions of nearby tuna factories. In Tonga, the markets in both Neiafu, in the Vava'u group, and in the capital, Nuku'alofa, are well worth a visit. Many familiar exotic fruits – such as papaya, mango, rambutan and passion fruit – are grown there, and then imported into Europe and the USA. The supermarkets also provide New Zealand products. A large amount of New Zealand lamb comes into Tonga, some of it very fatty, but good joints and chops can be found – sometimes at a cheaper price than in New Zealand itself.

Suva, the Fijian capital, has a reasonable selection of food in its supermarkets and also a good fruit and vegetable market. If there are plans afoot to go to the outlying islands, this market is the place to buy the kava

Climbing a coconut palm in search of a drinking coconut. Photo Andrew Hogbin.

'Pick your own' fruit and the humble coconut

A number of Pacific islands, particularly the Marquesas and the Society Islands, have an abundance of fruit trees, sometimes dripping with unpicked fruit. However, just about every tree is owned by someone, and so it is important to ask before you begin picking. Be prepared to offer a small trading item in return for the fruit.

The coconut is an amazing fruit, far more versatile than we give it credit for at home. The green coconut contains a sweet, refreshing drink, enjoyed by many, and it is very thirst-quenching. As the coconut ripens, a white jelly-like substance starts to form and this is delicious eaten on its own. Once the nut is fully mature and ripe, the familiar hard, white 'coconut' as we know it forms inside and this can be grated or eaten in chunks. For the Pacific islanders, this stage of the coconut is 'old' and the water inside is undrinkable – although the flesh is used to make copra. Coconut milk can be made from the grated mature nut and, if this is left to stand overnight, the cream will rise to the top.

There are not many deserted untenanted islands left, but should one be found, the 'heart of palm' taken from the living tree is a rare delicacy.

roots that you will need to present to the chiefs.

For other routes across the South Pacific, the same ground rules apply. Excellent long-term provisioning is usually available at the departure point, be it Australia, Hawaii or Guam. After that, local up-to-date information will prove invaluable, especially from boats ahead of you on the same crossing.

Fish

A freshly caught ocean fish is particularly delicious, and there are plenty to be caught in the Pacific by trailing a line astern. Tuna, wahoo, Spanish mackerel and mahi mahi are reasonably plentiful. Mahi mahi are also called dolphin fish, but are no relation to the dolphins that play under the bows. All these fish make excellent eating. Barracuda may also be caught, but are not as tasty and may be affected by ciguatera.

If your fishing gear is substantial, you may catch some sizeable fish. In this case, it is worth considering how best to use all of its flesh, so as not to waste anything. If there is a freezer on board, then meal-sized portions can be stored over an extended period. Fish

Barracuda

Wahoo

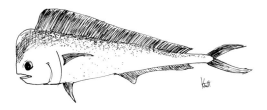

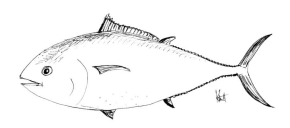

Mahi mahi or dorado

Tuna

Generalised shapes of tuna, wahoo, mahi mahi and barracuda. Sketch Kitty van Hagen.

can be pickled with onions, though this may not last more than a few weeks in the tropics. It is also quite possible to bottle fish at sea, using either Kilner or Mason jars. It is advisable to follow good instructions, but it is usual to pressure-cook for a very long time before screwing down the lids onto brand-new rubber seals, after which the contents should last for months.

Some crews dry fish on racks, particularly if there is plenty of deck space clear of the ever-present salt spray. There are various ways of drying fish: dry salt can be sprinkled onto the sliced-up fish, or, alternatively, soy sauce can be spread on the slices before putting them out in the sun to dry. Laying fish out to dry should not be attempted near to land because of flies.

Another idea is to make your own *poisson cru* by marinating uncooked fresh fillets of fish in lemon or lime juice for eight hours or more. The citric acid breaks down the fibres and the fish 'cooks', tasting very tender, with just a hint of citrus. It is delicious. Flying fish will almost certainly come on board, but their bony bodies make indifferent eating.

Fresh water

Many yachts have watermakers, which eliminate the need to seek out good-quality drinking water. Even so, some crews opt to take on board water to be used for washing, and to use the watermaker (particularly if it is slow) to supply their drinking water only. Rain-catching devices are very useful for topping up the tanks in a downpour.

Fresh water obtained ashore should always be taken from a reliable source. One of the best ways to discover if the local water is safe is to ask the crews of other yachts who have been drinking it whether they are experiencing any health problems. In the Galapagos, desalinated water can be purchased and brackish water is available free. In Hiva Oa there is plenty of fresh water piped to the quay

(as there is in many other Marquesan island settlements), but landing difficulties mean that Atuona is the easiest place to re-fill. Be warned that if leaving for the Tuamotus, the water in Taiohae Bay, Nuku Hiva is tainted. It is better to re-fill in Daniel's Bay, where Daniel's relation Jean Louis is re-establishing the settlement after the recent *Survivors* television series. Like Daniel, Jean Louis appreciates a small gift, and will probably give you pampelmoose if in season. In the Society Islands, the water is generally good, though it is advisable not to take it on after periods of heavy rain; this caution also applies in Tonga, Fiji and the Samoan Islands.

Provision regulations at the end of a crossing

At the end of a South Pacific crossing, most yachts will arrive in either New Zealand or Australia. Both have strict regulations governing what can and can't be brought into the country, and this very much applies to foodstuffs. All fresh and frozen provisions will be removed, as well as some tinned meat and dairy products, depending on their country of origin. New Zealand will also confiscate honey, and both countries will inspect items such as walking boots for mud deposits.

It is a good idea to find out up-to-date information on such restrictions in advance, from other yachts and the radio. It will then be possible to wind down stocks of provisions that would otherwise be removed and destroyed. Both Rarotonga and Tonga operate a very small-scale version of these quarantine procedures, usually applying only to fresh produce.

New Zealand and Australia have an abundance of reasonably priced products from which to re-stock the lockers. In fact, the wide range available, after so many months in mid-Pacific, can at first seem overwhelming!

Cockroaches and other pests

Unlike malarial mosquitoes, cockroaches are not dangerous or life-threatening. However, they are a pest. They are intrusive, multiply rapidly, and are far too easily acquired unless great care is taken to prevent them coming aboard. Never allow cardboard boxes or egg cartons on the boat, for the roaches hide in the seams and lay their eggs on the cardboard. Every tin or packet should be handed aboard separately from the dinghy and no chances taken. Check behind the labels for eggs. Check market-bought fruit and vegetables. If the water is clean, immerse arms of bananas in the sea; the roaches will soon struggle to the surface.

Even after taking all these precautions, some species of cockroach can fly only too well and thus it is incredibly difficult to avoid them landing on deck or below. Should an infestation result, it is perfectly possible to get rid of these insects by spraying with Baygon or a similar insecticide (with due regard to the maker's instructions and warnings) even while living aboard, provided that the insects are not too numerous. Cockroach traps can also be effective, but the key to elimination is to adopt a sustained policy of 'zero tolerance' as soon as they are spotted.

Inevitably, bugs and weevils will be found in flour, cereals and dried beans as you cross the tropical Pacific, but they can be sieved out. If you are able to put these foodstuffs in a freezer for 24 hours, this should kill off the wildlife.

Galley equipment

This is mainly a matter of personal choice. Larger yachts may well have all-electric galleys, including a microwave, electric kettle, toaster and food processor, but they may have to have the generator running to use these items. Otherwise, cooking will be by oil, gas or paraffin. Propane gas is available in the major Pacific islands, but it is a good idea to have at least eight to ten weeks' supply. Butane is not a good choice. It is much less freely available, particularly in northern waters where it is unsuitable in freezing conditions. Butane can be used in propane containers, but the reverse never applies.

Good galley stowage is very important, since it can be an area plagued with rattling plates, mugs and cutlery. This is particularly noticeable sailing downwind, when the boat rolls. A supply of sponge foam or similar is useful for silencing the noise, and promotes better sleep for the off-watch.

It is preferable to have a cooking stove with an oven and to use non-rusting baking tins for making bread, muffins, biscuits and cakes. Bread can be made perfectly well in the pressure cooker, or even in a frying pan on the top of the stove. A pressure cooker is quite invaluable as it is possible to use salt water instead of fresh, and it uses far less heat. Stainless steel saucepans are advisable as aluminium tends to deteriorate with the use of so much salt water for washing up and cooking. Large, sharp knives may be needed if fish are to be cut up for the pot. Spare knives can come in very handy should the others go overboard by mistake.

All opportunities to reduce the amount of heat from cooking below deck should be considered. In the tropics, the deck-mounted barbecue has real merit in this respect. When cooking down below in really hot weather, it helps to set up bulkhead-mounted fans to cool the air. Some people take salt tablets when it is very hot, but remember to take them with plenty to drink at the same time. Vitamin pills are seen on a number of yachts, and can be a useful supplement when fresh fruit and vegetables are unavailable for long periods. Do not forget a recipe book or two for when ideas are needed, and a notebook for swapping recipes with other boats.

Entertaining

One of the joys of a Pacific crossing is the opportunity to entertain on board. It is a wonderful way of making new friends, a delightful way of filling the long dark evenings, and an opportunity to share information and cruising yarns. Many people find that they use their spare time to bake bread, cakes and cookies. They swap recipes with other boats and try their hand at making preserves and other culinary delights, which make excellent presents to take ashore or aboard another yacht. Most crews enjoy making fresh bread on a long voyage, and frequently cakes, scones, muffins and pizzas too. Dried yeast for bread making is easily obtained nearly everywhere and, in the heat of the tropics, bread rises beautifully, taking only half the time it does in colder climes.

7

Health Matters

by Dr Nicholas J H Davies

Good health should be highly cherished. Nowhere is this more true than on board a small yacht in the vastness of the Pacific Ocean, perhaps over 1000 miles from the nearest land, utterly out of reach of any mercy mission. So prevention of disability and disease is all-important, as is the early and effective treatment of common minor ailments. There are relatively few serious hazards to health, but you are so remote from help that it is worth considering them. If you have a short-wave marine or ham radio, you are almost certain to be able to get a doctor's advice, wherever you are on the oceans.

Things to do before you leave 'civilisation'

Before embarking on an ocean voyage, visit your own doctor for a general check-up, and discuss specific needs you may have when compiling your medical kit. There is a checklist at the end of this chapter. Discuss whether any particular drugs you might take (such as anti-malarials) are inadvisable for you, and get a bracelet to warn of important regular medication (such as steroids), or if you have a serious adverse reaction to a particular drug. Long-standing conditions such as high blood pressure, diabetes, asthma, glaucoma etc will need particular care. If you have medical problems, get a doctor's letter that summarises them to take with you. Fortunately, most people feel years younger after a few weeks at sea! It is just as important to get a thorough dental check-up, for to lose a filling may cause you to suffer weeks of toothache. Ask your dentist how to effect a temporary repair to a tooth.

If you are especially worried about coping with illness at sea, doing a first-aid course would give you confidence in the immediate treatment of injuries and common ailments, including serious ones like appendicitis and head injury. You would also learn how to resuscitate somebody with mouth-to-mouth respiration (the 'kiss of life'), although it is most unlikely you would ever need to use this skill. Carry on board a medical book that has been written for yachtsmen, such as *Your Offshore Doctor* by Michael Beilan, published by Adlard Coles Nautical and Sheridan House Inc. You have to pay for medical care in all Pacific countries, so consider medical insurance, including cover for the costs of repatriation if you become seriously ill. Insurance is likely to be expensive, but could buy much peace of mind.

Immunisations

It is essential to protect against **tetanus** and **poliomyelitis** (these vaccines both last ten years). **Typhoid** is uncommon in most of the Pacific, but a single-dose vaccination is probably wise and will last for at least three years. I recommend vaccination against **hepatitis A**, the common form of this debilitating disease, transmitted by contaminated foods. Hepatitis A vaccine provides immunity for up to ten years, but a booster dose is recommended 6 to 12 months after a first dose. An immunoglobulin injection for hepatitis A is of little value for yachtsmen as its effects only last two or three months.

Yellow fever vaccination lasts ten years, and is needed if you arrive in French Polynesia from Panama or tropical South America where the disease is endemic. **Cholera** vaccine is of very limited value, and is not needed in the Pacific. **Smallpox** is no longer required anywhere as the disease has been eradicated. Evidence of negative **HIV** status is needed for long-term stays, or for working in Papua New Guinea.

Any other information on immunisations needed for entry can be obtained from the embassy or legation of the country concerned. It is worth planning several weeks ahead, as immunisations will require more than one visit to the doctor. British Airways Travel Clinics in major cities in the UK give an efficient immunisation service. In addition, excellent advice may be obtained by post from the British Department of Health booklet code T6, *Health Advice for Travellers*. This can be ordered from the UK freephone number 0800 555 777 (24 hours), or read on their website at www.doh.gov.uk/traveladvice.

Common health problems while cruising

Most problems likely to be encountered on a yacht can be prevented by using commonsense.

Injuries

Many injuries can be prevented by safe sail-handling and anchoring practices, and restraining members of the crew from doing particularly stupid things! Sensible footwear should be worn ashore, and when walking in shallow water or on a reef.

Minor cuts and abrasions can be troublesome in the tropics, particularly those inflicted by live coral, as the skin is always damp and so bacteria thrive. If such infections are not treated energetically they may progress to form a tropical ulcer, usually a staphylococcal infection that is difficult to eradicate. Even trivial wounds should be cleaned with a disinfectant such as chlorhexidine and/or the use of a dry powder disinfectant spray such as povidone-iodine (Savlon). The latter is especially good at keeping the wound dry. If there is any suggestion of infection or a tropical ulcer, use a powder or cream that contains antibiotics, such as neomycin, bacitracin and/or polymixin B. Cicatrin is one example. If a wound is still not healing, then give a course of antibiotics (such as flucloxacillin) by mouth; this should eradicate the staphylococcus.

Burns

Burns are a hazard in the galley, often from hot food or water spilling off a cooker, perhaps if the oven door has been opened and the cooker prevented from gimballing. Risks are greatly reduced by the cook wearing a decent layer of clothing to prevent the hot liquid making so much contact with the skin. This is not always a popular suggestion in the tropics!

The burnt area should be cooled with water immediately. This is still worth doing up to ten minutes after the injury, as it limits tissue damage. Burns are probably best covered with paraffin gauze dressings (Tulle Gras), held on with light adhesive tape, and re-dressed every day or two. Other useful dressings, both for burns and other skin injuries, are Melolin. These have a plastic cover on one surface, which is the side to apply to the wound. If you are desperate, any plastic sheeting material (eg clingfilm, a plastic bag) could be used to cover the burn. Covering it helps the pain, and is the most practical option on a yacht. Keeping the affected part of the body elevated reduces swelling. Oral fluids should be encouraged. It should not be necessary to use special creams unless the burn is obviously becoming infected, when silver sulphadiazine cream (Flamazine) could be applied, and ideally renewed twice a day.

Sunburn

This is an obvious hazard, avoided by most yachtsmen, and usually more of a problem for a visiting guest. We all know how deceptively cool it seems when the tradewinds are blowing in your face, and yet there is no escape from the sun, which is either high in the sky or reflected off the water. Use shade, sunscreen lotions and suitable loose clothes to protect the more horizontal parts of the body, ie nose, top of the head (if short of hair!) and shoulders. Ultraviolet rays easily penetrate water to burn the swimmer who is snorkelling over a reef, so a shirt should be worn. The sun can also damage the retina of the eye, so wear sunglasses, preferably polarised to cut out the glare. These concerns are not just for comfort, as it is well known that exposure to the sun hugely increases the risk of skin cancer, including malignant melanoma.

Ears

'Swimmer's ear' (otitis externa) is an inflammatory reaction of the skin lining the ear canal after becoming soggy in tropical conditions. The skin may also be infected with bacteria. If there is much wax, the ear cannot dry out, the situation becomes worse, and may even interfere with the ear-drum and cause deafness.

You could use ear plugs to prevent water getting into the ears while swimming, and always dry the ears carefully after swimming. Some drops containing glycerol or isopropyl alcohol (Auro-Dri) help dry out the skin. Never poke objects into the ear to extract wax. It is much better to soften it with olive oil and let it come out naturally. Otitis externa should clear up after keeping the ear dry, and giving ear-drops containing an antibiotic, often combined with a steroid to help the inflammation. There are many different brands.

Diarrhoea

The many causes of travellers' diarrhoea spring either from contaminated water or poor hygiene when preparing uncooked foods. The worst of these diseases (cholera and typhoid) are fortunately not a significant problem in the Pacific. A common cause is a mild strain of the bacterium E coli. There is no substitute for prevention by careful hygiene. Food should be properly cooked. Uncooked vegetables and salads in restaurants are a hazard, but not on the boat if you prepare them yourself. Wash them thoroughly, and peel any fruit. Water supplies are no problem if you have a watermaker, or rely on catching rainwater. Otherwise choose your source carefully. This is not a major practical problem, although if you are worried you could 'sterilise' the water in your tanks with commercially available tablets that contain chlorine or iodine. The question then is whether you can taste it in your tea or coffee! You will not know where the water came from to make any ice that you buy ashore, so it is most unwise to eat it.

The diarrhoea will get better, and simply needs controlling with loperamide (Imodium) 4mg, and then 2mg doses up to a maximum of 16mg per day, or a combination of diphenoxylate 2.5mg plus atropine 0.025mg (Lomotil) four tablets, and then two further tablets every six hours until things are better. Kaolin mixture may also be useful. The main danger is fluid loss, so encourage oral fluids. An anti-spasmodic drug like propantheline (Pro-Banthine), 15mg three times a day, may help with any abdominal cramp-like pains.

If the diarrhoea persists for more than a few days you need medical help. Amoebic dysentery is rare in the Pacific islands, but common in Central and South

America. Another possibility is infection with another parasite, *Giardia lamblia*, which is widespread throughout the world. Both these are treated with metronidazole (Flagyl), 800mg three times a day for five days.

Seasickness

Anyone voyaging the Pacific will wish to know their limitations. Those setting off from the west coast of the USA should have spent at least a night or two coastal cruising to test themselves. Many will have already discovered the particular form of prevention and treatment that suits them best.

Seasickness is caused by stimuli to the brain from the balancing organ of the inner ear, especially when these conflict with visual inputs. The first night at sea is usually the worst, followed by a gradual improvement. So set sail after an easily digestible, non-fatty meal, with no alcohol. Keep warm and organise watches so that all the crew get some sleep. Getting cold and tired encourages seasickness. Prophylactic drugs are often wise, as the apathy and listlessness of *mal de mer* occur before any nausea.

There are two classes of useful drugs: hyoscine (anti-muscarinic) and antihistamines. Hyoscine is probably the most effective, and can be taken as tablets (eg Kwells 0.3mg three times a day), or as a skin patch (Scopoderm TTS) that lasts up to three days if placed on the hair-free area behind the ear. The latter is especially useful if you cannot keep tablets down. Unfortunately, hyoscine often gives rise to side effects such as a dry mouth, drowsiness and blurred vision. If these trouble you, an antihistamine may be better tolerated, although these also tend to cause some drowsiness. The least troublesome for most people are cinnarizine (Stugeron), 15mg eight-hourly, and cyclizine (Valoid), 50mg eight-hourly, but there are many other antihistamines on the market. All these drugs should be started at least two hours before setting sail.

If seasickness overcomes you despite these precautions, it may be helped by concentrating on helming and looking at a steady horizon, but you may be forced to retire below; if so, keep warm and dry, try to eat a dry wafer biscuit, and lie down with your eyes closed. Do not forget that you may not be able to keep any regular medication down for it to be absorbed into your body. This includes oral contraceptives!

Parasites

If you are cruising with children, then you will know their peculiarities only too well. I suggest that you be prepared to treat infestations of both head lice and threadworms, even if they have escaped these hazards up to now. Head lice respond to malathion or carbaryl 0.5 per cent lotion applied overnight, repeated after seven days to kill lice emerging from any eggs that may have survived the first treatment. This also deals with crab lice. Threadworms are treated in all those over two

years old with a single dose of mebendazole (Vermox), 100mg for all over two years old. In addition, roundworms and hookworms will be cured by the same drug given twice a day for three days.

Rare but serious health problems while cruising

Malaria

There is a high risk of malaria and frequent resistance to chloroquine in south-east Asia, Papua New Guinea, the Solomons and Vanuatu (not Futuna Island). The risk increases as you go west. It is important to get current advice. The rest of the Pacific is not affected.

Prophylaxis: No drug prophylaxis is entirely reliable, so you should try to prevent yourself being eaten by a mosquito in the first place! Use mosquito nets or screens if possible, and lots of insect repellant, which should contain DEET (di-ethyl toluamide). Apply this both to exposed skin and on clothing.

The preferred option for drug prophylaxis is doxycycline 100mg daily. This is a tetracycline, and so must not be given in pregnancy, nor to children under 12 (it affects growing bones and teeth). It may be taken safely for up to six months. In some people it makes the skin very sensitive to the sun, and this would obviously rule it out. Start doxycycline one week before entering the malaria area. An acceptable alternative is Malarone one tablet daily (mixture of proguanil 100mg and atovaquone 250mg). This need only be started two days before entry to the malaria area, can be used for up to three months, can be given to children, but is expensive. The third option, which can be taken for one to two years, is mefloquine (Larium) 250mg once weekly, started at least one week (preferably two or three weeks) before exposure. Unfortunately, resistance to mefloquine has been reported recently, and it is best to get the most up-to-date information. Rare but serious side effects of mefloquine include sleep disturbances, panic attacks, hallucinations and fits. Fortunately, these occur soon after starting the drug, and get better if you stop it. Prophylaxis should always be continued for four weeks after leaving the malaria area, except for Malarone, which needs to be continued for just one week.

Self-treatment: If, despite prophylaxis, you develop a fever of at least 38°C (100.4°F) after you have been in a malaria area for over a week, are getting worse and have no access to a doctor, then you should treat yourself as if you have malaria. This applies even up to three months after you have left the malaria area. In the western Pacific you should take quinine 600mg three times a day for seven days, followed by one dose of Fansidar (a mixture of pyrimethamine 25mg plus sulfadoxine 500mg), three tablets. It would be worth taking a course of these tablets with you, as it could take a while to reach medical help.

Dengue fever

This is a viral infection propagated by a different type of mosquito to that for malaria. It is present in the Caribbean, Asia and the western Pacific islands. There were nearly 2000 cases reported in New Caledonia in 1995. A week or so after the bite there is fever, headache, generalised pains, a skin rash, a tendency to bleed and shock. Dangerous epidemics can sweep through the local population, especially affecting children, but no one is immune. There is no specific treatment, and no vaccine. Get to hospital!

Dangers in the sea

Stings and bites

Much marine life can inflict nasty or even fatal stings. **Jellyfish** are widespread in the Pacific. The **sea-wasp** (*Chiropsalmus quadrigatus*), and especially the **box jellyfish** (*Chironex fleckeri*), are the most deadly. They are found off the coast of Northern Queensland in mid to late summer, especially after rain and away from coral reefs. A specific antivenom is made in Australia. The pain of an extensive sting is excruciating. **Stingrays** are common and can bury themselves in the sand in shallow water, and be trodden on by mistake. They usually have a single venomous spine on the top of their tails, but a sting is very seldom fatal. **Sea urchin** spines inject a venom that causes much pain, but are fortunately very easy to see. The spines should be removed from the skin if possible, although they often fragment. Many **corals** sting, such as the fire coral, a branching variety looking like a red tree. Do not touch live coral. The animals that live inside some attractive **cone shells** such as the textile and geographic cones are highly poisonous. A venom is

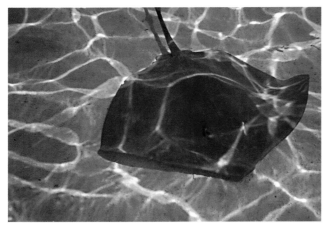

Stingrays are not always as visible as this one. If hidden in the sand, it will inflict a painful jab if trodden on. Photo Annabel Finding.

injected by a proboscis at the sharp pointed end, which can penetrate clothing and be fatal within hours. **Lionfish** (zebra fish), **scorpionfish** and **stonefish** are all widespread in the Pacific, and have 12 or more poisonous spines on their backs. The pain of the stonefish venom is worst, and has been fatal, although there is a specific antivenom. It is also the most readily encountered, as it lurks on the bottom of the sea, looks like a stone, and can easily be trodden on. It is important to wear shoes when paddling in the water, and to shuffle your feet so that you avoid treading directly on a stonefish or a stingray. Stonefish can live for several hours out of water, typically when stranded by the tide, so be careful even if one looks dead on the shore!

All these poisons cause intense pain, inflammation, and possibly death of the body's tissues around the site of entry, and may go on to cause breathing difficulties, fits and even death. Any spines should be removed if possible, and the affected part of the body soaked in very hot water (about 50°C (122°F), a temperature that is almost too hot to bear when tested with an unaffected part of the body). This may denature the venom. Vinegar has a similar effect and is a useful alternative while you heat the water. It is especially good for jellyfish stings. Further treatment may involve injections of local anaesthetics around the most painful areas, antibiotics by mouth or injection, and strong painkillers. Needless to say, the person should be rushed to hospital if possible, if the sting has been a serious one.

Sea snakes have been seen many dozens of miles out at sea, although they normally feed on the bottom. The yellow-bellied variety is the most common, and has a black back. It is probably not naturally aggressive. With most bites little venom is injected, but after a bad bite paralysis and death can follow within a few hours. The bite itself may be painless, and not even noticed! The bitten limb should be immobilised. A tight arterial tourniquet around the upper part of the limb may buy a bit more time, but should be applied for no more than two hours. The patient must get to hospital to have any hope of surviving a serious bite, as artificial respiration may be needed and a specific antivenom is available.

Ciguatera

This is caused by a toxin derived from dinoflagellates found on coral and seaweed, eaten by fish, and passed along the food chain from small fish to bigger fish, and then to man when he eats many common large fish, eg snapper, mackerel, parrot fish and barracuda. You get nausea, vomiting, abdominal pain and diarrhoea, starting between one and six hours (maybe more) after eating the fish. This can get worse, with tingling of the lips, hands and feet, feeling hot objects as cold (and vice versa), and can progress to paralysis and death.

There is no specific treatment, except to make the sufferer vomit to empty the stomach. It is best avoided by asking locally if fish caught over reefs are safe, avoiding eating fish offal, and not eating too much of one fish, especially if it is large. Fish caught away from land are safe to eat.

Conclusions

If you find this account rather alarming, I should reassure you that I have voyaged around the world for six years, mainly in the tropics, and encountered nothing much more serious than appendicitis, burns, ulcers and minor injuries. Of course, if one crew member is ill, a much greater load is placed on the others, who need to be capable of sailing to the security of a harbour several days away while also caring for the sick crew member. This can even apply to the singlehander, a tall order, but cruising yachtsmen are a remarkable species.

I remember a retired couple voyaging from Vancouver to Panama, their first significant cruise. When well off the Pacific coast of Mexico, a large sea knocked the husband off the deck of their 44ft ketch while he was taking an evening star-sight. The wife had to come to terms with the fact that she was unable to retrieve him. I met her just after she had brought their yacht, by herself, 250 miles into Puntarenas, Costa Rica. Even the most unexpected and severe challenges may be overcome with resourceful determination.

Basic medical kit

Equipment

Cotton wool, crepe bandages
Plasters, rolls of adhesive plaster
Sterile gauze, and dressings (eg *Melolin, Tulle Gras*)
Tubigrip bandages
Thermometer
Eye bath and pads
Steristrips
Plaster of Paris
Scissors, forceps, needle-holder
Syringes, hypodermic needles
Needle and suture, sterile gloves
Scalpel and blades
Dental kit and oil of cloves

Preparations for the skin, ears and eyes

Dettol, chlorhexidine, *Savlon*
Cicatrin (neomycin and bacitracin)
Silver sulphadiazine cream (*Flamazine*)
Calomine lotion
Antihistamine cream (eg *Phenergan*)
Sunscreens, lip protection
Insect repellant
Eye drops and ointment:
    chloramphenicol
Ear drops:
    isopropyl alcohol (*Auro-Dri*)
    steroid + neomycin
    (eg *Betnesol-N, Neo-Cortef*)

Drugs taken by mouth

Antihistamine (eg *Phenergan*)
Lomotil
Loperamide (*Imodium*)
Laxative
Kaolin mixture
Popantheline (*Pro-Banthine*)
Antacid (eg *Gaviscon*)
Anti-sickness
Malaria prophylaxis
Vitamins and water-purifying tablets
Painkillers:
    eg paracetamol
    paracetamol + codeine (*Solpadol*)
    ibuprofen (*Nurofen*)
    naproxen (*Naprosyn*)
    tramadol (*Zydol*)
Antibiotics:
    eg flucloxacillin
    co-amoxiclav (*Augmentin*)
    metronidazole (*Flagyl*)

Injections (Note: discuss with your doctor)

Anti-emetic
Adrenaline
Steroids
Diazepam
Narcotic (eg morphine)
Antibiotics

PART II

PASSAGES

8 Choosing the Route: General Considerations

Although the Pacific is huge, the principal routes across it are well defined. Thus the question 'Which way do we go?' can be answered in a straightforward manner, according to whether your starting point is on the east or west side of the Pacific. These routes are considered in more detail in Chapters 9–13.

East to west crossings: the principal routes

Panama to New Zealand

The most popular route across the Pacific is from east to west in tropical latitudes. This well-worn trail, sometimes referred to as the Coconut Milk Run, is in many ways the obvious choice for those crossing the Pacific for the first time. Whether the departure point is southern California, Panama or anywhere in between, the vast majority of crews will elect to call at the Marquesas as their first major offshore landfall. Those leaving from Panama will most probably call in at the Galapagos on the way.

From the Marquesas you either pass through, or skirt around, the northern limits of the Tuamotuan Archipelago on the way to Papeete, the administrative capital of French Polynesia, on the island of Tahiti. This is a calling place that virtually all those passing through French Polynesia are obliged to make, in order to keep their paperwork in order. The natural route is then to follow the chain of the Society Islands until you come to Bora Bora; at this point, decisions need to be made.

The next island group is the Cooks, but they are spread out across a very wide expanse of ocean and the choice of onward route will dictate to a strong degree which, if any, of the Cook Islands should be visited. A yacht heading for Tonga as the next major group to be explored can easily take in the southern Cooks on the way. A yacht intending to call at either American Samoa or Western Samoa will pass much further north and is only likely to call at Suwarrow atoll. The onward passage from Samoa is most likely to lead on to Fiji and, if Australia is the final destination, there is then the option of calling at Vanuatu and New Caledonia. On the other hand, if New Zealand is where you are heading, there is no real reason why, having been to Samoa, a course southward to the northern end of Tonga should not be taken, calling at Niuatoputapu as a first port of call. If one chooses to go via Tonga, then it is possible to head directly to New Zealand from there, or call in at Fiji before turning south-west.

For those leaving the western seaboard of the USA or Canada, the more usual choice is to go south to Mexico in the autumn and depart for the Marquesas in February or March.

Departure points north of San Francisco, travelling via Hawaii to meet the Panama–New Zealand route

Not everybody has the option of starting their voyage in August or September, in good time to head south to Mexico. Some may wish to embark on a crossing in the northern spring. From San Francisco southwards, a direct passage to the Marquesas is an acceptable option. From further north, the distance becomes rather daunting and the Hawaiian Islands are likely to be the more favoured choice. From there, the choice is quite wide. A route to either New Zealand or Australia would probably take in the Line Islands (situated between Hawaii and the Cook Islands), possibly calling at Penrhyn in the Northern Cooks, and then joining the throng in American Samoa or Western Samoa. This route unfortunately misses the whole of French Polynesia, which at least leaves a new experience for the next visit!

If time is limited, then a third option is to press on from Hawaii to the Gilbert Islands or the Marshall Islands, and then on to the Solomons and Australia. Certainly if the Indian Ocean is a primary objective,

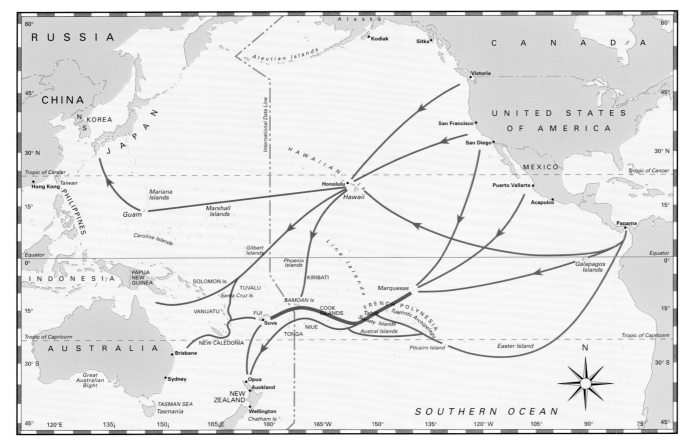

Plan 6 *Principal crossing routes east to west.*

then this route would take you to the Torres Strait in the least time.

Why take the classic Panama–New Zealand route?

There is an understandable attitude of mind that says that if the standard route from Panama to New Zealand is the way everyone goes, then there is a strong case for going somewhere else. Before succumbing to this tendency it is worth considering what you will miss if this is your first Pacific crossing. The concept of 'crowded' is a relative one. Unlike some areas of the Caribbean, the definition of a crowd in the Pacific is still only half a dozen boats in one anchorage. Organised rallies make their way across from time to time and will swell these numbers on specific occasions, but their dates are publicised well enough in advance to avoid them, if you so wish.

French Polynesia is not a remote civilisation and yet it does have some relatively unfrequented corners that are quite delightful. In many ways it would be a mistake to dismiss Moorea and Bora Bora, even though they are such notorious tourist venues. Their remarkable skylines and iridescent lagoons are spectacular sights, and the more so from the water. The lagoon anchorages are usually fairly well away from the crowds. A greater threat would be an increase in 'round the island' jet ski races! There is very little in the tropical Pacific that is

more striking than the Society Islands, so to avoid them is a questionable decision, unless of course you have been there before.

Heading further south: Easter Island and the Australs

The biggest magnet, which may draw you away to the south of the classic route, is the mystery and magic of Easter Island. To sail from Mexico to Easter Island direct is a long haul through quite a windless zone. From Panama, however, the course is an extension of the line to the Galapagos and takes the yacht beyond the Tropic of Capricorn, on a passage of 2750 miles straight from the Canal. It should be appreciated, though, that Easter Island has no safe anchorages and permission may not be given for a yacht to enter the small harbour, for which you will pay a pilotage fee. A small crew may find themselves unable to leave the yacht for long enough to appreciate the sights fully.

Easter Island is at 27°S, and so most available stopovers across the rest of the Pacific are closer to the equator. If the south-east trades are blowing, they will at least provide fair winds for the onward journey. Some 1100 miles further west and only 2° further north is Pitcairn Island, an interesting place to visit but even less restful as a stopover than Easter Island. The anchorages are open and unreliable and all transfers to

Yachts at anchor off the Fijian island of Dravuni. Photo Andrew Hogbin.

and from the shore are only safe in the islanders' longboats or RIBs.

It is, however, only 300 miles on to Mangareva, in the Gambier Islands in the south-eastern extremity of the Tuamotus, where there is a safe and tranquil lagoon and the opportunity to relax at last. From here you have a choice of route: work your way slowly and carefully up the archipelago and then make a short hop to Papeete, or stay south and call at the Australs. From the Australs the obvious next step would be to make for Rarotonga in the Cooks and on to Tonga from there. It should be appreciated that to follow this latter route is to choose to be away from any facilities for a very long time and to have only the most limited of restocking opportunities. Locally grown fresh fruit and vegetables may be available, but mainstream provisions will probably only be found in Rarotonga.

Towards Asia from Panama, via Hawaii and Guam

Before concluding the east to west choice of routes, we need to consider the very small minority whose objective is some point in Asia and who have not the time or the desire to spend much longer by cruising to the South Pacific and then heading north from there. To do this, a cyclone season has to be avoided at some stage. To reach, say, Hong Kong from Panama across the North

Pacific is a daunting prospect, particularly for a small yacht without large reserves of fuel or an above average light wind performance. It is difficult to imagine how this route can be achieved without using Hawaii as a staging post, which will involve a first leg of some 5000 miles with maybe a stopover in the Galapagos. There are endless recorded passages between Panama and Hawaii that have taken 60 days or more. One strategy is to hold a very southerly course close to, or through, the Galapagos, and only turn north when the Equatorial Countercurrent can be crossed at a sharp angle. Some people are of the opinion that this strategy is of little practical benefit and that it is better to head more directly for Hawaii. In either case, the rhumb line can be windless and the established currents are principally contrary. Extra fuel reserves could be considered to help with particularly windless stretches.

From Hawaii westwards it is 3300 miles on to Guam and a further 1800 to Hong Kong. At least between Hawaii and Guam there is a better chance of consistent wind. It is necessary to time this crossing to avoid arriving in Japan too late in the year when conditions offshore will have become unpleasantly cold. Equally, if heading for Hong Kong, due account of the typhoon season must be taken. July to October are the worst months. With so many miles to be covered, a yacht that performs well either under sail or power must be the number one choice.

On a passage eastwards from New Zealand to the Australs, there is a strong probability of quite difficult sea conditions. Photo Annabel Finding.

The crossing from Hawaii to Guam does not have to be made in one jump. It is also possible to travel through the Marshalls and the Carolines before reaching Guam. However, the extra time spent visiting these island groups may mean a wait before the onward journey to Japan and beyond can be completed.

West to east crossings: the principal routes

There are very few yachts travelling against the general westward flow as one sails from Papeete to New Zealand. The very conditions that all those heading west are enjoying so much would create an incredible uphill struggle for anyone trying to go east along the same track. Papeete itself is, however, a crossroads, and those who have left New Zealand and held south in the westerlies to the Australs will pass through Tahiti on their way north.

The two main options for a west to east crossing are either to go north, or to go south and then north, but never across the middle.

Heading south from New Zealand to Tahiti via the Australs

Leaving New Zealand, probably in late May, the first objective is to reach the Australs, a distance of around 2000 miles. Opinions differ on the best course to steer on this passage. The logical and most strongly promoted view is that the yacht should remain below 30° for as long as the crew's patience will allow and then alter for the Australs. However, there are a number of recent passages that have followed the rhumb line and fared very well. Weather conditions are never wholly predictable in these latitudes, and it would be pointless to be dogmatic. Whatever else, strong and difficult conditions are something that must be anticipated on this passage. If they do not occur, so much the better, but be prepared!

From the Australs it is only 350 miles to Papeete where there is every facility, albeit at a price, needed to replenish supplies and prepare for the second half of the voyage. The remainder of the chosen route will depend on the ultimate destination. None of the options is an easy one, and all will involve going further north before heading east. A powerful weatherly yacht will embark on a direct passage to San Diego. The going will be hard in the early stages on a course to the west of the Tuamotus and the Marquesas, but in the later stages the conditions should ease.

From Tahiti to the USA and Canada via Hawaii

From Papeete, the great majority will head north and a little west to the Hawaiian Islands and jump off for the USA or Canada from there. There are two considerations to be borne in mind when tackling the passage to Hawaii. First, the winds are going to turn much more towards a north-easterly sector as the passage draws to an end, so that it is a good policy to maintain an easting

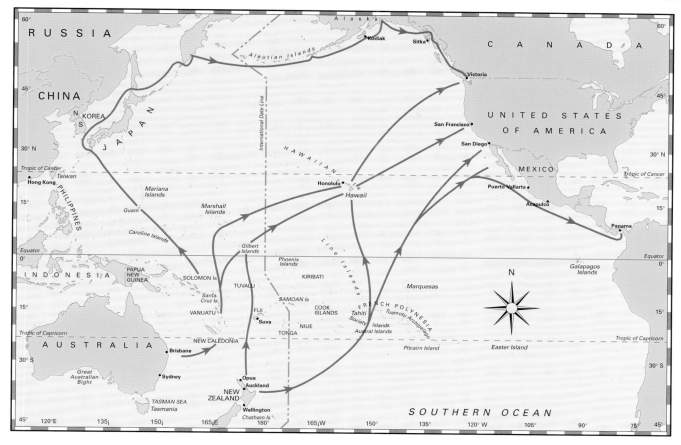

Plan 7 *Principal crossing routes west to east.*

until a late stage when, in addition to the wind heading, the westerly stream will have a noticeable effect. The second concern is that from June onwards the eastern Pacific hurricane season will have begun and a good radio watch should be kept for signs of storms reaching out into the Pacific towards Hawaii.

The traditional course from Honolulu to the Straits of Juan de Fuca is to hold starboard tack northwards until the westerlies are found in about 35°N and then to ride them all the way home. If the high pressure system is behaving oddly, as so often happens, all well-laid plans will be in disarray. Strong winds and big seas are not unusual in the closing stages. This would be a long way round if heading for San Francisco, and for those for whom the Bay is home, probably the only practical solution is to bite the bullet and slog it out to windward.

Heading north from Australia via Micronesia and Japan to Alaska

The northern route is much more attractive to those leaving Australia, or perhaps for those who have gone north instead of south at the beginning of the south-west Pacific cyclone season. Assuming that there is no great hurry, then the chosen route is most likely to pass through the Solomons and the Marshalls or the Gilberts, and from there to the Hawaiian Islands, joining up with those from the southern track.

There are two main alternatives to this route. The first is to follow a circular route north into Micronesia, and from there to Japan and round the northern Pacific rim by way of the Aleutians and Alaska. This route can also be followed, if you are heading east into the Pacific from the Philippines, from where you can sail directly to Japan. For those willing to spend longer in the Pacific, or forgo a circumnavigation, a route around the western rim has much to commend it, particularly now that the eastern Russian ports are open to visitors. This route is an interesting alternative way home for the west-coast-based Canadian or American. The distances are substantial, but no single passage need be longer than about 1500 miles and most can be much shorter. The second alternative is to depart from New Zealand for Cape Horn. This involves an excursion into the Southern Ocean, which is outside the scope of this guide.

Straight to Panama from New Zealand – a difficult option

To reach Panama direct poses real problems. It would be necessary to go reasonably far north initially, but the remaining distance – when the trades are eventually cleared – will be significant. Unless really large reserves of fuel are carried it could be an exceptionally long time at sea before Panama is reached.

Time is an important element in heading towards Panama, as the risk of hurricanes overrunning the Caribbean is a dominant factor (particularly if the yacht has avoided the direct route and is in the final stages of coasting in a south-easterly direction through Mexican waters and past the central states). To leave New Zealand in May and transit the Canal in July, if you could sustain such a pace, would be of little advantage unless you are prepared to run the gauntlet through the heart of the hurricane zone and then clear out into the Atlantic. The alternative, within the Caribbean, is to follow the Colombian and Venezuelan shoreline until November/December – in which case, why all the hurry? Much better to time the Pacific crossing more realistically and reach California in time to join the armada of yachts going south to Mexico in November when the hurricanes have cleared, and then carry on from there.

For the larger yachts in particular, for whom the distances may be acceptable, the really express route to the Panama Canal is to hold south all the way to the coast of South America and ride the Peru Current close to the shore with a fair wind into the Gulf of Panama.

This replica of the Endeavour *was built in Fremantle, Australia. The original scantlings were faithfully followed, but using native Australian timbers. Photo Sepha Wood.*

Captain Cook's Pacific Voyages

No one man has left his mark on the Pacific as indelibly as Captain James Cook on his three voyages of exploration between 1768 and 1780. The more sophisticated our lives and our yachts become, the more difficult it is for us to comprehend the magnitude of his achievements.

On his first voyage in the *Endeavour* in 1768–71 he entered the Pacific, east to west around Cape Horn, and sailed north-west to Tahiti for the purpose of observing the transit of Venus. Having successfully completed the observations he sailed south in search of Terra Australis. This was a mythical land mass that was thought to lie deep in the Southern Ocean and it held out great promise of new wealth. Having no success, he turned north and then to the south-west, eventually reaching the coast of New Zealand. He circumnavigated both North and South Islands, charting incredibly accurately as he went. He then sailed on to make his celebrated landing in Botany Bay on the east coast of Australia.

For his second voyage, departing in 1772, he commanded the *Resolution*, with the Adventure also under his leadership, and was promoted to Captain. This time he sailed by way of Table Bay, near Cape Town, and went deep into the Southern Ocean, actually crossing the Antarctic Circle before passing well south of Australia and returning to his favourite refitting bay in Queen Charlotte Sound, New Zealand.

In June 1773, reunited after being separated in the Southern Ocean, the two ships sailed east into the Pacific in the forties. Again they found nothing and turned north to Tahiti once more. They were separated again as they returned to Queen Charlotte Sound, and Cook sailed alone for a further sweep of the Southern Ocean, this time far deeper into the south; again he found nothing but ice. This time his northerly return to the tropics took him to Easter Island and Tahiti for the third time. Returning to New Zealand he diverted by way of Tonga and the New Hebrides (now Vanuatu). Cook's final sweep of the Southern Ocean began as ever from New Zealand, past Cape Horn, to reach Table Bay once more, before sailing for home.

His third voyage, again in *Resolution*, left Plymouth in July 1776. He was joined by the *Discovery* in Table Bay, and with a brief stop in Tasmania they reached Queen Charlotte Sound yet again. The purpose of this expedition was to investigate the possibility of what we know today as the North-West Passage (the route between the Pacific and Atlantic along the north coast of Alaska and through the Arctic Archipelago). Together the ships sailed north to Tahiti and on to Hawaii. From there they closed the coast of North America, calling at Nootka Sound on the west coast of Vancouver Island. They explored and named Cook Inlet, hoping that it might provide the lead they were seeking, but to no avail. Eventually they penetrated through the Bering Strait until forced back by the ice, and then returned to Hawaii.

Having been welcomed there originally as a god, relationships subsequently turned sour and Cook died at the hands of a native warrior on the beach at Kealakekua Bay on 14 February 1779.

9 South-west from Panama to New Zealand

The classic route across the South Pacific to New Zealand, via the Marquesas, the Society islands and Fiji

The well-worn route across the southern Pacific Ocean, known by some as the Coconut Milk Run, has no single starting point. Yachts departing from as far north as San Francisco and as far south as Panama tend to congregate in the Marquesas and then follow a more or less common route until separating if their final destinations differ. The greater number will be heading for New Zealand, but those who are on a restricted schedule for a circumnavigation will go on to Australia and the Torres Straits.

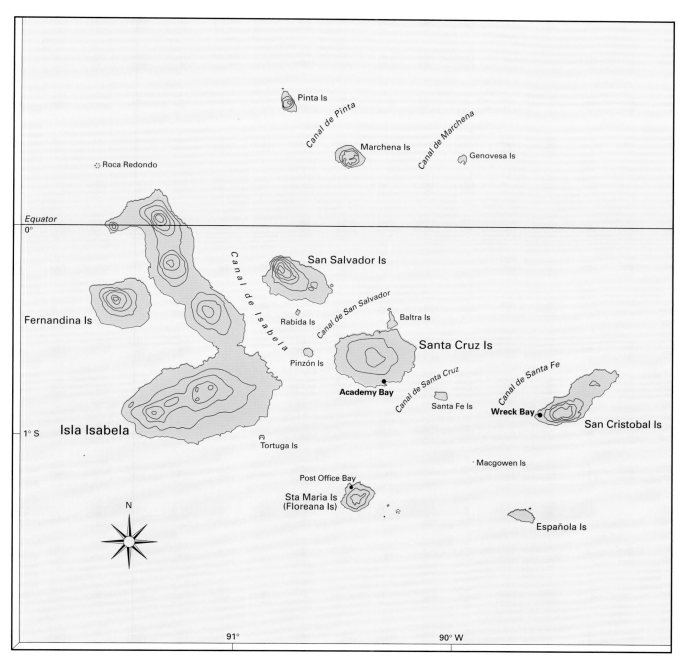

Plan 8 *The Galapagos Islands.*

The Galapagos

Those on passage from Panama are likely to make a stop at the Galapagos Islands, depending for some sailors on whether the high charges are affordable (see Part III, nos 10 and 11).

Bernard Moitessier, in his book *Cape Horn, The Logical Route* (1965), paints an idyllic picture of weeks spent in the Galapagos, living on the fruits of his fishing and turtle hunting, free from official interference and at one with nature. His forays were not sufficient to create any impact on the ecology but, in this day and age, any such freedom would result in large numbers of yachts ravaging the wildlife and causing serious damage. Thus, the passing sailor used only to be granted permission to stay for 72 hours at one or other of the two main ports. In 2001 the regulations were modified to include a 20-day stay and transits between San Cristobal and Santa Cruz Islands, providing permission and clearance had been obtained from the relevant port captain. Visits to Puerto Villamil on Isabela are now possible as well; however, yachts are still not allowed to cruise independently in other areas without a cruising permit. These are expensive to obtain and heavily restricted.

Winds and currents on the way to the Galapagos

For the great majority of passages within the Pacific, it is not appropriate to lay down the law on a strategy for working the winds and streams to advantage. Either the prospects are so simple as to be obvious, or the probability of the conditions being predictable are so unlikely that the advice given would almost certainly be wrong. Leaving the Gulf of Panama and heading west for the Galapagos or the Marquesas is, however, an exception and the established wisdom is worth repeating.

In the early months of the year there is a fair expectation that the Caribbean tradewinds will spill over into the Gulf of Panama and provide good profitable sailing for the first 48 hours or so. Each day thereafter, until west of the Galapagos, is likely to be slower than the day before. There is a temptation to follow the shortest distance and visit Ile del Coco, which is a mecca for keen scuba divers. If this temptation is irresistible, then a large reserve of fuel is advisable because this route is notoriously windless. The favoured route is to hold well south close to Malpelo Rock. The equator should be crossed at around 84°W and a course steered to head south of the track, in anticipation of a north-west stream that is generally very beneficial. In the early stages, the Peru or Humboldt Current, the El Niño and the Equatorial Countercurrents all tend to underrun each other and can surface anywhere. Beyond the Galapagos, the choice, perhaps rather oversimplified, is to go south of 5°S for stronger winds and less current, or stay north and ride the current but in poorer wind.

Those leaving from Cabo San Lucas or Puerto Vallarta in Mexico may call in at the Revilla Gigedo Islands, between 200 and 600 miles offshore. These are intriguing islands, and another excellent scuba diving spot. They are not blessed with a wide choice of easy anchorages, but in the calving season for humpback whales, a visit to Isla Clarion is a remarkable experience.

Pacific Peoples

There, on the horizon, is the unmistakable outline of an island. You have not seen land in the last three weeks, and now your eyes confirm what your navigation has been telling you. You have reached the Marquesas. We all have preconceived ideas about what these remote idyllic places and their people will be like. The climate is tropical, the islands are lush, and the sea bountiful. The Pacific peoples seem to live a luxurious life, indulged by nature. They are an easygoing, proud people, whose forefathers, the voyaging Polynesians, discovered and populated the largest single area of the world. Unlike us, they sailed against the prevailing winds and did not have the benefit of knowing what lay beyond the horizon.

Each Pacific island is a milestone in your voyage. For you it is all a new experience, for the islanders it is the same each year: 100–150 boats parade through during the five months of settled weather. You will be anchoring off their village for a week perhaps, then disappearing over the horizon, expanding your perception of the world. They, however, will remain in their community, on their island. Transient encounters are not part of their culture, as they are in ours. They will not be able to pick up a telephone to contact you. Your letter with photos may not receive a reply, though that is not to say it is not appreciated. On the other hand, you may be rather taken aback, months later, to receive a letter requesting clothing, a camera, money or even an outboard motor! This illustrates the potential misunderstandings that can arise; the islanders sometimes assume that all cruising sailors are millionaires – which of course, compared to them, we are. A reply containing a small gift in kind might be appropriate.

The depth of the relationship between you and the islanders will depend on your sensitivity to their somewhat isolated world and their desire to get to know you. You have an opportunity to develop a relationship in which you may exchange more with this one person or these people in a week, than you do with your friends at home over many years.

If what you are looking for is traditional Pacific island culture, you can still find it. It requires taking some risks, getting off the beaten track, visiting anchorages with less than perfect shelter, and allowing yourself to be open minded about the inhabitants of paradise. It is the latter that many cruisers find most difficult: opening your home as they have opened theirs and allowing your topsides to be bumped by overly enthusiastic canoes. True, the further west you go across the Pacific, the easier it seems to be to find traditional culture along with its crafts and customs.

There are remote atolls in the Tuamotus, the less frequented Gambier Islands, the westernmost islands of French Polynesia, the northern islands in the Cooks, the outlying islands of Western Samoa, the northern reaches of Tonga, as well as the Ha'apai group, the Lau group at the eastern extreme of Fiji, the south-eastern groups of the Solomons, and many more. Sadly, the respective governments have restricted access to some of these areas to special permit holders only, as a result of thoughtless behaviour by visiting yacht crews. There seems to be no limit to insensitivity, including use of drugs, abuse of alcohol, brandishing of firearms, inappropriate dress and behaviour, screening of excessively violent videos; the list goes on. Your actions not only affect your relationship with the islanders, they also affect those who follow in your wake.

In any relationship there will be an exchange. At one extreme it may be strictly a non-verbal nod and a smile, where there is no common language. More often than not, a smattering of English is spoken by many islanders, and even when it isn't, trading and bargaining seem to transcend language. Money is of little value to those who do not depend on it, and in a climate where the food literally falls from the trees, the prevailing sentiment is that money is not used among friends. In a relationship where bartering is the common denominator, then both sides must feel they have received a fair deal. Granted, fruit does not have a long 'shelf life' where there is no refrigeration, but you are not the only game in town; the anchorage is full and more boats are arriving each day. You are not going to trade a few glass beads for a tropical island. On the other hand, a Walkman might be excessive for a pampelmoose.

Even if our perceptions of what a traded item is worth are different, a sense of fairness must prevail. Fairness between the trading partners and fairness for those who come behind. Unfortunately, some cruisers tend to be thoughtless in the way they trade, with the result that the trading scales can be temporarily unbalanced. This makes it difficult for the boats that follow.

In the more remote areas seldom travelled by yachts, one has a rare opportunity to give to the islanders without any material consideration at all. If nothing is 'expected', this is often the time when you receive the most. It is not only repairing an outboard that is important, but showing the fisherman how to repair it in the future, and perhaps leaving them with a feeler gauge or a few wrenches. It is not just applying a bit of topical antibiotic to a festering wound, but showing them the importance of keeping an infection clean; it is not just a matter of assisting in treating a young child's dysentery, but showing the village the importance of a clean water supply. You may not be a mechanic or a doctor, but your life experience may have a lot to contribute to these people. In the same way, you will certainly have much to gain from their life experience. In this context, sharing rather than trading is the most rewarding and memorable for all involved.

Mark Scott

The Marquesas

It is always a sound principle to try to enter any island group at the windward end and explore the islands from there. The Marquesas are no exception, and if one is of an exploring nature and wants to see as much as possible of the group, then Atuona is the obvious entry port and Nuku Hiva is the sensible departure point.

Atuona is on the island of Hiva Oa, which unfortunately is not the furthest to windward. Fatu Hiva is the most south-easterly island and at the same time the most fascinating. As a first taste of a Pacific island it is bound to be an abiding memory both for the spectacular geological formations and for an introduction to Pacific culture. The more law-abiding sailors will stick to the rules and clear into Atuona before heading back out to windward to visit Fatu Hiva. It has to be said, however, that a number of those found in Hanavave Bay, the favourite anchorage on Fatu Hiva, will have made their landfall there and risked the wrath of the gendarme at Atuona. The fact that one has not yet acquired any local currency is of no consequence because the islanders are much more interested in trading for the goodies that are carried aboard yachts and that are not easily obtained locally. Lipsticks, perfume, rock music cassette tapes, T-shirts and odd ends of rope from the yacht are always welcome.

Atuona (see Part III, no 12) is less interesting by comparison and can be plagued by an uncomfortable swell. The lonely, almost deserted bays on the north side of Hiva Oa have much more to commend them. Swell is nearly always a potential problem in the Marquesas, where no island in the group has a fringing reef, and therefore there are no sheltered lagoons. Beach landings can be quite exciting, and any camera equipment needs to be packed in a watertight bag to be safe if the dinghy is overtaken by the surf.

The island of Ua Pou is perhaps the most dramatic, with fantastic immensely tall rock spires reaching up into the sky. There are two anchorages, one on the north side at Hakaitau: here there is a small breakwater where a yacht with modest draught might find space inside; the other is at Hakahetau, further round towards the

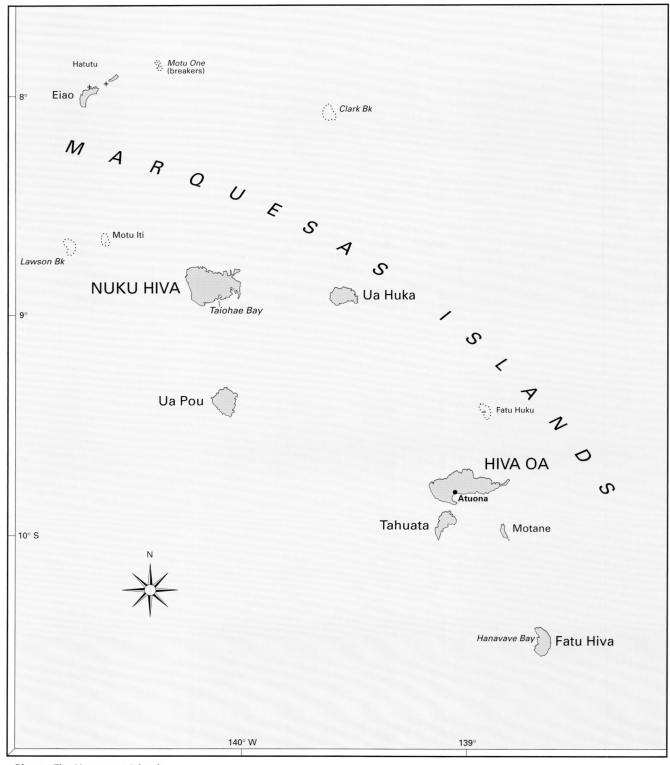

Plan 9 *The Marquesas Islands.*

west side. This is a much more attractive anchorage with stupendous views of the heights, but there are days when landing is very difficult and the roll at anchor rather exhausting.

Taiohae Bay (see Part III, no 13) on Nuku Hiva is the least swell-ridden anchorage in the islands and is the principal gathering place for passing yachts. There are

some fine walks and some good riding to be enjoyed on the island. The walk up the Tipee Valley made famous by Herman Melville can be tackled by anchoring in the central arm of Three Finger Bay. There are tikis to be found in the woods, but it is best to inquire in the village for directions, otherwise a lot of hot and fruitless walking can be endured for nothing.

The towering cliffs surrounding Daniel's Bay, Nuka Hiva, dwarf the yachts anchored there. Photo Andrew Hogbin.

French Polynesia and the Polynesians

For many, the first Pacific islands encountered will be the Marquesas, the easternmost in French Polynesia. The people are Polynesian in ethnic origin, and seafarers by tradition. When the islands were first settled, the villages were established inland at the head of valleys, away from the harbours and landings where raiding parties might attack. It was only after the arrival of the missionaries, who convinced the islanders that they must trade and communicate, that the villages relocated to the coast and harbours where they are today. Along with the physical change there was also the intended social and spiritual change. The latter took much longer to accomplish. Today, you can still find, with the help of a guide from the village, the remains of the spiritual past in the overgrown bush. Stone platforms are generally the only trace of villages or temples. A few stone carvings of gods or idols are still standing, although most were knocked over and remain as a pile of rubble, where the missionaries had them destroyed.

The Polynesians of today must certainly resemble the Polynesians of yesterday. Their bronze-coloured, slight build and straight black hair can not have changed much over the centuries as physical contact with the outside world is still, even now, somewhat limited. The women are a bit less liberated than their sisters in the days when Captain Cook passed through here. He nearly lost his ship when the sailors discovered they could win a girl's favour with as little as a single nail, or so the story goes. However, these Polynesians are very different socially from their ancestors. An observer today might somewhat justly conclude that the land belongs to the Polynesians, the shops to the Chinese, and the power to the French.

Due in large part to the French government, physical survival is less of a concern for the islanders – with subsidies for the cash crop (copra), education, health care, and special low-interest loans. You may be surprised that the 'noble savage' of the Marquesas is wanting to trade videos more than fruit, and uses his air-conditioned four-wheel drive vehicle to haul copra from the hills, instead of a horse. He watches CNN with the help of a satellite dish antenna, and yet his world is his community and his island.

By virtue of having arrived on their island by sailing yacht, you have a far more complete view of the world than the islanders and a wider exposure to different values and cultures. You are a guest and it is important to remember that it is you who must respect their values. For example, there are no fences in the bush or countryside. It may appear at first that the abundance of fruit is free for the taking. However, every tree or bush belongs to someone, including the 'windfalls', and it is an offence to take without asking.

French Polynesia is not like much of the Caribbean where mass tourism is the culture and the prevailing set of values. There are no jump-ups on Friday or Saturday night. But you may be fortunate enough to watch a village group practise and rehearse traditional dance – a skill quite highly prized in competition, culminating at the fête celebrations (Bastille Day, 14 July). Equally beautiful is the harmony sung in the village church on Sunday mornings. In the evenings, a walk along the shore may find a young man playing his home-made 'guitar', constructed with a shaped flat board, a hole with cardboard as a sounding-board, and anything from four to six strings of monofilament fishing line,

tensioned appropriately. It is a tribute to the player how much this actually sounds like a guitar/ukulele, with a passing resemblance to American country and western music. (Popular trading items are country and western or rock and roll cassette tapes.)

Tradition is still very important to these people. It is not uncommon for a group of males in their early twenties to leave the village with a pack of dogs on a Friday afternoon to hunt for wild pig. Easier methods are available, but the young men still prefer to do it as their fathers and grandfathers did, using the dogs to flush out and corner the animal while the hunters go for the kill using nothing more than spears. The casualties may include more than the pig, and more often than not a gouged or wounded dog will retreat to the quiet of the bush to die.

Mark Scott

The Tuamotu Archipelago

When clearing out of the Marquesas, the choice has to be made as to whether to visit one or more atolls in the Tuamotu Archipelago or skirt the north-west corner and head directly for Papeete. The Tuamotus were also known as the Dangerous Archipelago, although the advent of GPS and radar have considerably reduced that danger, but not entirely. In the days when all landfalls had to be made with the help of the sun, the moon

and the stars, a landfall in the Tuamotus was one that was anticipated with more than usual concentration.

All of the atolls are only as high as the tallest palm tree whose roots are only feet above sea level. There is therefore nothing standing more than 14m (45ft) or perhaps 18m (60ft) above sea level, which means that 14km (9 miles) is the maximum range that a visual sighting will be made. This is compounded by the fact that the atolls are not necessarily blessed with waving palms all the way round the lagoon, which is, incidentally, far

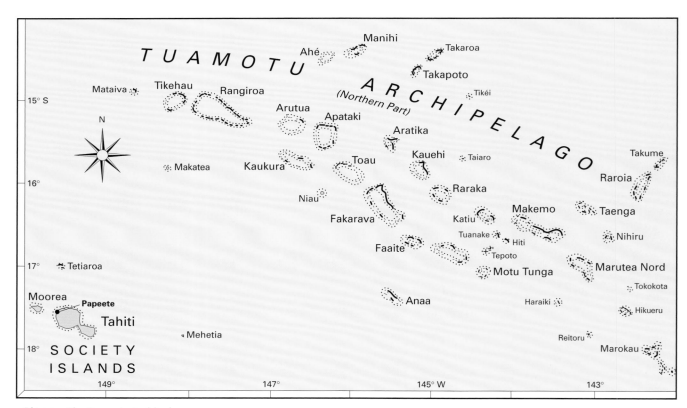

Plan 10 *The Tuamotu Archipelago.*

The windward shore of Toau in the Tuamotus on a blustery day. Photo Andrew Hogbin.

larger than most people imagine. Some 32km x 14km (20 miles x 9 miles) is a fairly average size for an atoll in the Tuamotus. The windward ends are very often nothing more than a reef, awash with perhaps isolated motus with some growth. It pays to make an approach where the villages are on the leeward side and where the palms are tallest.

The general acceptance of GPS as a means of position fixing is a huge advance, but it must not be considered the ultimate answer to safe navigation in the Tuamotus. The indicated position on the screen can be extremely accurate in terms of geographical co-ordinates, but the problems arise when the chart is not to the same accuracy. The available information is very limited in the first place, and all of it is based on surveys carried out before satellite-derived positions were even dreamed of, so that longitude in particular is sometimes seriously in error. During the hours of darkness a wide margin of error must be allowed for, with unpredictable streams to be expected. Radar is of some help, but the echoes are difficult to read clearly and the sensible sailor will stand off until daylight whenever there is the least doubt.

It is worth knowing that the tidal flow in the passes can be predicted from the time of the moon's rising and setting. The full details are given in the *BA Pacific Islands Pilot Vol III*. Briefly, there is slack water 5 hours after moonrise, followed by the inflow, and slack water again 4–4½ hours before moonset when the flow reverses; 5 hours after moonset and 3 hours before

moonrise the pattern is repeated. However, tidal flow can be dependent on swell and wind, and it would be wise to back up calculation for any specific atoll with local knowledge.

Having braved all the hazards and found the pass into your chosen atoll, it is then time to practise your first exercise in eyeball navigation. The chart detail is only so good, and a competent lookout in the bow is an essential aid to safe avoidance of the coral heads – with the light behind you. Once inside, if the atoll is inhabited there will be a warm welcome from the villagers, who lead simple lives – with little to trade – and therefore little anticipation of bounty. There have been instances of shark attacks on the pearl divers, so some inquiry ashore would be advisable. The black pearl industry is a major activity, and visitors should be very careful not to foul the beds when anchoring.

To gain the most from visiting the Tuamotus it is far better to stay away from those few atolls that now have an air strip. The influence of easy access has changed the character of the local culture, and on Fakarava, for instance, there is none of the interest in a visitor that the more remote villages will show. The most commonly visited atolls are Ahé, Manihi, Takaroa and Rangiroa, all grouped in the north-west tip of the archipelago. Exploring further east and calling at, say, Raroia, Kauehi or Toau will take the yacht to less frequented and more intriguing places. Raroia is the atoll on which the *Kon-Tiki* raft was stranded at the end of her voyage from Peru in 1947.

Tahiti and the Society Islands

It is around 200 miles on to Papeete (see Part III, no 14). If conditions are variable, the navigator may change course several times, finally rounding Tahiti clockwise or anticlockwise as appropriate to find Papeete on the north-west corner. It is, however, more likely that the approach will be made anticlockwise around the island. This will entail passing Venus Point, made famous by the then Lieutenant James Cook on his first voyage to the Pacific in the *Endeavour* in 1769. It was here that he set up the observatory to study the transit of Venus.

Tahiti is the largest of the Society Islands, all of which have fringing reefs and beautiful sheltered lagoons. They are the very paradise that all cruising sailors dream about. The water is crystal clear for endless snorkelling – this is superb, with legions of exotic tropical fish, turtles and exquisite spotted rays. The main centres are nearly always on the western, leeward sides of the islands and this is where passing yachts tend to congregate. The windward lagoons may have more exciting passes but, once in, there is every chance of solitude, if that is what appeals, and the swimming will be a rare treat.

Papeete is a throbbing, vibrant centre, very French in culture and the focal point for the whole of French Polynesia. It is a great gathering place for Pacific sailors, although after a week or so the noise and bustle may become too much for some. For these people, there is always the option of exploring the south coast, where there are a few challenging passes to tackle. Alternatively, the island of Moorea (see Part III, no 15) is a very short distance away across a narrow channel with delightful sheltered anchorages, and a ferry service back to Papeete if there is still a need to take advantage of the 'benefits' of civilisation. Papeete is a major staging post for inter-continental air travel, and is therefore a good place for crew changes.

Having escaped from Papeete, the next move is to sail off down the line of the remaining Society Islands and enjoy them one by one. Huahine, Raiatea, Tahaa and Bora Bora (see Part III, nos 16, 17 and 18) are each intriguing to visit, with beautiful lagoons, good walking and friendly people. They are not poor islands; in fact, no one is poor in French Polynesia where child allowances from the government are generous and living costs low. Throughout the French islands, French is taught in school as a second language, so their standards are not all that high, and communication with the islanders is actually easier for that reason.

Should the timing of the voyage be such that Bora Bora is reached in late June or mid-July, you will find that the festivities for the June Independence Day and Bastille Day, 14 July, are celebrated with some spectacular dancing competitions. Teams come from villages on all the neighbouring islands and the standards of presentation are quite dazzling.

Bora Bora is the place for outward clearance and the recovery of the bond for non-EU citizens, but you are permitted to visit two more minor islands as you sail

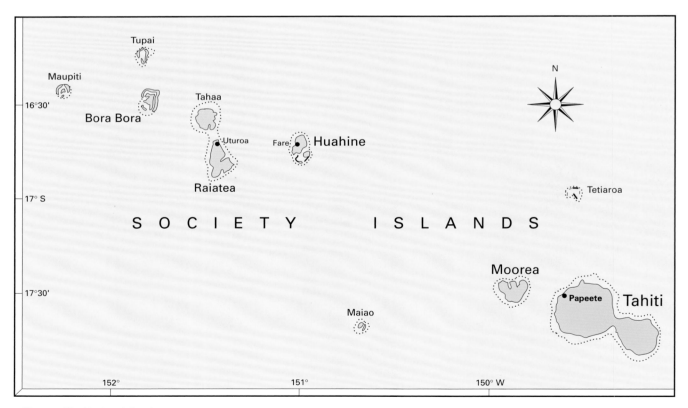

Plan 11 *The Society Islands.*

Sunset over the highest peak of Bora Bora, clearly seen from over 50 miles away, with Raiatea to the left of it. Photo Andrew Hogbin.

away downwind. Maupiti is only a day sail away from Bora Bora, and is a genuine island with a fringing reef and a pass that can be hair-raising on its rougher days. Once in, it is a peaceful spot to lie, and the island is small enough to walk right round quite easily. One hundred miles further on lies little Mopelia which, strictly speaking, is only an atoll. Here the pass is exciting for a different reason. Sited on the leeward side of the atoll, it is relatively free from swell, but it is the only

outlet from the lagoon that is being constantly filled by the breaking swells on the windward reef. The result is an outflow in the narrow channel that can frequently be stronger than a low-powered small yacht can overcome. There are some fascinating nesting grounds on the bird motus, and from the point of view of naval history it was here that Count Von Lucknow careened the *Seeadler* and was driven ashore never to be refloated. There are still parts of the ship to be seen on the reef.

Yachts anchored off the Bora Bora hotel in the south-eastern corner of the lagoon, with the fringing reef of the atoll and Pacific Ocean beyond. Photo Andrew Hogbin.

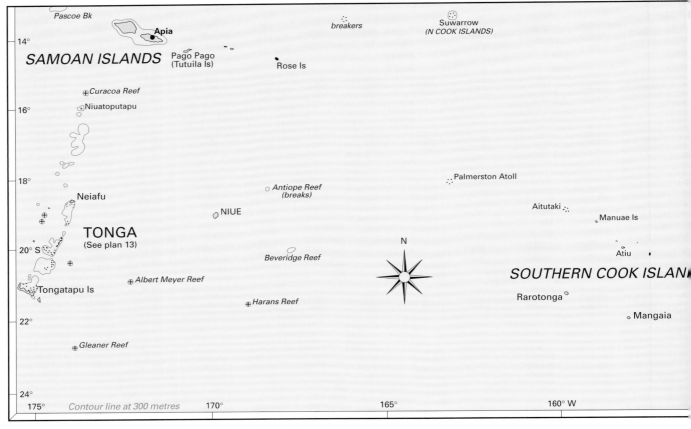

Plan 12 *The Tuamotus to Tonga including the Cook Islands.*

The Cook Islands

As was mentioned in the preceding chapter, when leaving French Polynesia there is a choice of route: south-west to Tonga or due west to American Samoa. Stretched across the path are the Cooks, only five of which are generally visited by yachts. In the south of the group are Rarotonga and Aitutaki (see Part III, nos 20 and 21), of which only the former has a deep enough harbour for the larger yachts. Palmerston Atoll lies on the direct course from Bora Bora to Tonga but, strictly speaking, one should obtain permission to visit from Rarotonga first. Palmerston is an awkward place to call at as there is no pass negotiable by a yacht; therefore the only option is to anchor in the lee of the reef and hope that there is no change in the wind direction. Visitors are very rare and receive an enthusiastic welcome. If sailing from Rarotonga it is quite possible that there will be a request to carry mail or supplies of some sort, and this will of course increase the welcome considerably. Suwarrow lies on the course from Bora Bora to Samoa and was made famous by Tom Neal who lived alone there for many years. Since the advent of satellite navigation it has become a popular stopover, and is regulated by two resident wardens. Penrhyn is a long way to the north and requires quite a diversion from all the regular routes. There is a safe lagoon and a welcoming village. Once again, there is some doubt about the accuracy of some quoted longitudes for this atoll (particularly the Taruia Pass), so extra caution is necessary.

The Cook Islands are a protectorate of New Zealand. The islands do receive some financial assistance from New Zealand, but the islanders are not as materially well off as their cousins to the east, in French Polynesia. Many Cook Islanders have emigrated to New Zealand, were educated there, or have relatives there. On the main island there is plenty of local fruit; this is sold, not traded.

If one is fortunate enough to be in Rarotonga in the first week of August, an Independence Day celebration will provide you with a week of entertainment. Like the French Polynesians, music, song and dance will fill the night air. The dance venue should not be missed. It is said that the French Polynesians used to invite the Cook Islanders to join in the friendly dance competition during fête. The Cook Islanders won the contest several years running and were eventually no longer invited! The best of the rest seem still to come from that small and isolated island of Puka Puka.

Niue

Two days or so short of arrival in Tonga, if sailing from the Southern Cooks or direct from Bora Bora, lies the small island of Niue. It is one of the world's smallest

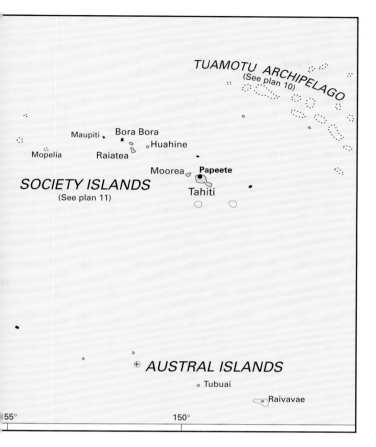

it be your last. A night or two at the yacht club bar speaking to a few ex-pats will unveil some of the 'behind-the-scenes' culture. Unlike the French, the USA treats Samoa more or less as a welfare state. Aside from its small-scale commercial interest as a base for US tuna fishing fleets, it has little military or political value.

Samoans are Polynesian, and large Polynesians at that. Once a year the village chiefs from the island fly to Washington DC and attend the congressional hearings on financial aid to Samoa. They arrive wearing traditional island dress of sandals, lava lavas, and perhaps a white shirt. To the congressmen, this is a striking contrast to the dress-for-success formula of Washington. However, each year the visual impact of the chiefs in their traditional dress brings home a nice cheque for the island. Regrettably, a bus ride around the island will reveal that the money doesn't go much further than the television satellite dishes in Pago Pago. Along with re-broadcasts of American television programmes comes American consumerism and an unquenchable thirst for 'I want it all'.

Western Samoa

Western Samoa, of which Apia (see Part III, no 23) is the capital and only port of entry, is a totally different experience. It is an independent former British territory (German before the First World War), and Robert Louis Stevenson lived there in his later years and also died there in 1894. He wrote about its charm and culture, which is simple and relatively undeveloped. Every morning the capital of Apia wakes up to a parade, as the police marching band leads the corps around government house for the raising of the flag ceremony. To see the real Samoa one must take a local bus or rent a motorbike and get away from the capital city.

The presence of missionaries is obvious as one strolls through the villages. The size of the churches seems disproportionate to the size of the modest homes (falas). Indeed, the unusually large church is a reflection of the pride in a village, not so much the degree of religious commitment.

self-governing states, with a little help from New Zealand. Anchoring off its capital, Alofi, is not a good idea due to a coral bottom with chasms into which the anchor may well get jammed for ever. There are now, however, 16 mooring buoys. In easterly winds the anchorage is quite comfortable, but in south-easterlies yachts will roll. In the event of a sustained westerly it may be necessary to make a quick departure. Dinghies cannot be moored at the jetty, due to the swell, but are hoisted up on an electric crane and parked ashore. The island is well known for its limestone caverns and crevices, and the scuba diving is superb with underwater visibility of 30m or more.

American Samoa

US-flag yachts will probably prefer to take the route through the Samoan Islands in order to take advantage of the re-stocking opportunities at Pago Pago (see Part III, no 22), as well as easy communications with the US mainland. Pago Pago is not the most exciting of stopovers, but for US citizens in particular there are great advantages to be enjoyed. Most cruising boats stop to reprovision and to use the US-trained doctors at the medical centre; they do not stop for the cultural value. If Pago Pago is your first stop in the Samoas, do not let

Tonga

It is a little over 300 miles from Pago Pago to Neiafu in the Vava'u group at the upwind end of the Kingdom of Tonga. However, halfway on this passage lies the isolated Tongan island of Niuatoputapu, familiarly known as 'New Potatoes' by some cruisers, and well worth a visit. It is a port of entry, but formalities will still have to be conducted when arriving in Neiafu (see Part III, no 24).

Tonga is the only kingdom in the southern hemisphere and its reputation as the 'friendly islands' is well

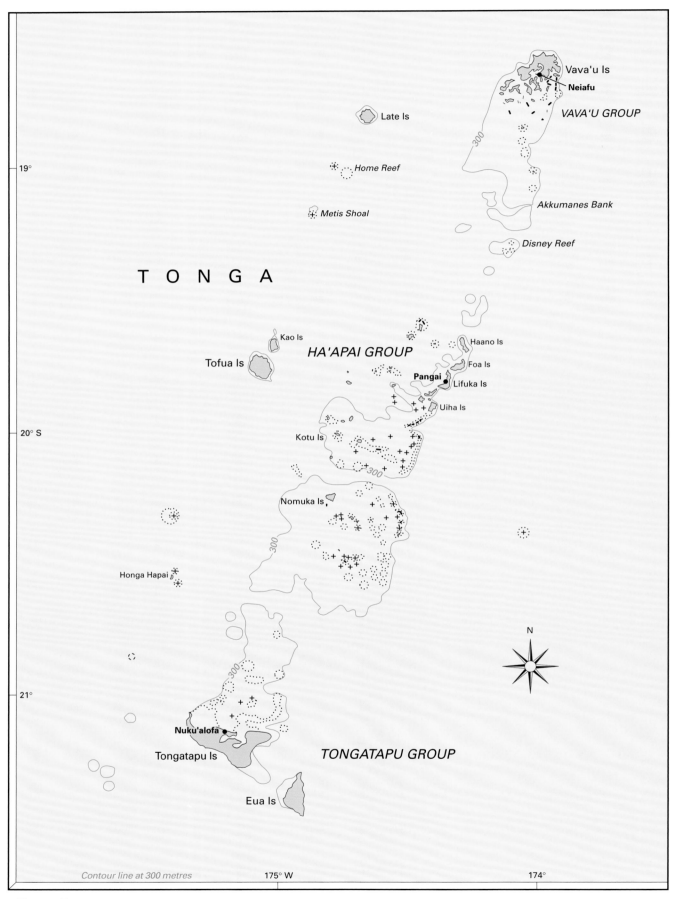

Vava'u Is
Neiafu
VAVA'U GROUP

Late Is

Home Reef

Metis Shoal

Akkumanes Bank

Disney Reef

T O N G A

Kao Is
HA'APAI GROUP
Haano Is
Tofua Is
Foa Is
Pangai
Lifuka Is
Uiha Is

Kotu Is

Nomuka Is

Honga Hapai

N

Nuku'alofa
Tongatapu Is
TONGATAPU GROUP
Eua Is

Contour line at 300 metres

175° W

174°

19°

20° S

21°

Plan 13 *Tonga.*

The contrast between the modern umbrella and the ancient pandanus overskirt, worn as a sign of loyalty to the monarch, is one of the most charming features of the Tongan way of life. Photo Michael Pocock.

deserved by its outwardly amiable inhabitants. Tonga is, broadly speaking, divided into three groups of islands and the Vava'u group is the obvious one to arrive at, being at the windward end and having much more to enjoy than the capital Nuku'alofa at the leeward end. There is some delightful easy cruising to be enjoyed from Neiafu; the presence of a Moorings charter operation has developed the area as an attraction that has served to increase the pilotage information quite substantially, and their chart and guidance notes are well worth using.

There is a very noticeable difference to be found ashore for those arriving direct from French Polynesia. Tonga is without doubt a country of the developing world, very reliant on overseas aid and far less advanced than the French islands. The people are warm and friendly with big happy grins on their faces, but the standard of living is far from affluent. They are expert carvers and the craftwork is excellent and reasonably priced.

For those prepared to tackle the more intricate and less well-documented navigation, the option to call at the Ha'apai group between Vava'u and Nuku'alofa is well worth taking. The islands there are sparsely populated and not much visited, so the cruising is very rewarding for those with a spirit of adventure and a love of more lonely anchorages. The snorkelling is excellent, over some of the most spectacular coral. On a walk ashore, one might find children watching cartoons on a colour television in the shade of a thatched-wall home, roofed in corrugated iron, while their mother pounds taro with an oversized wooden mortar and pestle. Unfortunately, as

we in the western world are all too aware, when the television is turned on, the mind turns off. The visible result of the introduction of television is the decrease in the true crafts of the village, not those produced for the tourist trade, but those produced and used in the home.

The group of islands that surrounds the capital Nuku'alofa is not much favoured by passing yachts as a playground for local cruising. Visitors tend to congregate in the harbour and concentrate on the town before moving on to New Zealand or, if time allows, to Fiji. Tonga is a monarchy and the King's presence is something of which one is bound to be aware. Nuku'alofa is dominated by a variety of massive cathedrals for the denominations that are active locally. It is an enigma as to why the churches extract so much from their congregations for these stupendous buildings when local standards of living are so low.

Fiji

The approach to Fiji is less fraught since the advent of GPS, but the fact remains that the passage is not across open ocean and there are unlit hazards to be avoided. Experience has shown that the one light on the way is not to be relied on, and in the days of dead reckoning and sun sights there were occasionally some very anxious moments. A full moon is a great advantage. The main factor to be recognised is that the temptation

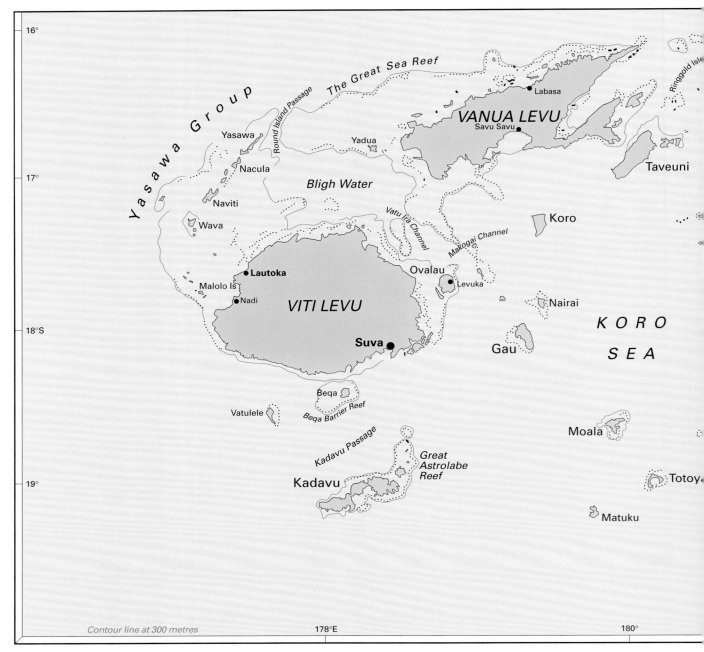

Plan 14 *Fiji.*

to find a sheltered anchorage behind an island on the way must be resisted. The Fijian authorities come down heavily on anyone not proceeding directly to a port of entry. It should at the same time be realised that their information sources from the outer islands are more efficient than one might expect. One consolation is that Suva harbour entrance is well lit, and so a night arrival is for once a reasonable proposition. There are some problems in finding the yacht anchorage once inside, but as clearance will be necessary in the morning, the port radio operator will give good advice and indicate a safe anchorage till daylight.

Those entering Fiji from the Samoan Islands now have a much improved situation because the authorities have introduced a port of entry at Savu Savu on the south coast of Vanua Levu. The distance from Pago Pago to Suva (see Part III, no 26) is 670 miles and the last 150 are within the Fijian Islands – causing much of the same anxiety experienced when travelling from Tonga. Added to all this, Suva is at the downwind end of the archipelago, so exploring the islands to the north-east requires some windward effort. At least from Savu Savu there is more cruising available and the option of going on to Suva on the south coast of Viti Levu or through the Bligh Water to Lautoka (see Part III, no 27) if bound for Australia. The approach to Savu Savu still requires some sailing among the islands in the final stages, but only half the distance of going direct to

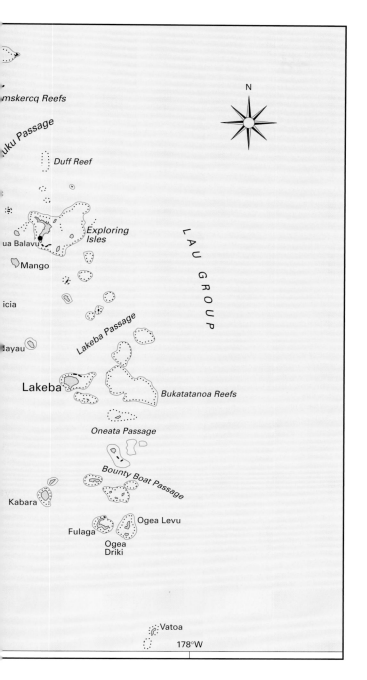

On the map: mskercq Reefs · uku Passage · Duff Reef · Exploring Isles · ua Balavu · Mango · icia · Jayau · Lakeba Passage · LAU GROUP · Lakeba · Bukatatanoa Reefs · Oneata Passage · Bounty Boat Passage · Kabara · Ogea Levu · Fulaga · Ogea Driki · Vatoa · 178°W · N

fairly keen pilotage, which not everyone enjoys. A word of warning is perhaps appropriate with regard to the charts. The British Admiralty charts are undoubtedly the most accurate and reliable. They do, however, show a number of beacons within the reef channels that were maintained in the days of the British administration, but that have since fallen and not been reinstated. It is much better to rejoice when a charted beacon is found than to get excited when one is found to be missing.

The country is made up of two large islands, Viti Levu and Vanua Levu, and a myriad of much smaller outer islands. The climate during their winter is changeable. For the average visitor it is a very pleasant warm temperature, although the Fijians will be complaining of the cold and wearing winter jackets! Suva, in common with the rest of the land on the leeward side of the big islands, attracts an appreciable amount of rain and is often spoken of as 'Soggy Suva'. The northern coastlines are much drier, and these are the great sugar-growing areas that are such a vital feature of the Fijian economy.

The big towns, and particularly those on the north coasts at the centre of the sugar industry, are dominated by the Indian communities that numerically are at least equal to the indigenous Fijians. The Indians are all descended from imported indentured labour brought in by the then British authorities to provide the necessary workers to develop the sugar fields as a profitable concern. The Fijian Indians have a natural sense of business that the indigenous Fijians lack, and their prosperity has precipitated tensions and unrest between the two communities.

The outer islands where the Indian community has not penetrated are being maintained on traditional community lines. There are strict guidelines for cruising yachts, including a rigid standard of dress and behaviour when visiting the island villages. Until one has been to a village and complied with these requirements, which will entail a small ceremony when the visitors present kava roots to the chief, it is difficult to understand the need for such a palaver. In retrospect, most sailors find that they look back on the experience as one that is very rewarding, and one that serves as a delightful introduction to a community that will afterwards make its visitors feel genuinely welcome.

The exception to this rule occurs in the Yasawa group which, from a cultural point of view, has been spoiled by being on the doorstep of Nadi international airport and therefore is subject to a certain degree of tourist fatigue. It is sad that this is the case because these islands are, in all other respects, real gems. Away from the immediate access to the airport and its tourist area the outer islands are quite unspoiled, and for those who are keen to integrate with the islanders the opportunities are endless. An ability to mend anything mechanical, such as an outboard motor, is an excellent introduction. However, having successfully mended one, be warned – there will be a whole batch more appearing next morning!

Suva. The actual entry is probably much better tackled in daylight. While lying in Savu Savu it is worth taking the local bus, an experience in itself, over the hills to Labasa on the northern coast. One goes for the thrill of the journey more than for the destination, but it is an inexpensive day out and a way to see the hinterland.

Cruising in Fiji is a subject that should really warrant a chapter all to itself, if only for the vast area that there is to explore. For those visiting as part of a crossing there may only be sufficient time to get a taste for the attactions and, as is so often the case, crews leave for New Zealand vowing to return next year for anything up to three months' cruising within the archipelago. Exploring the outer limits of the islands involves some

A remote and secluded anchorage in the Lau group of the Fijian Islands. Photo Andrew Hogbin.

Suva, and in particular the anchorage off the Royal Suva Yacht Club, is one of the great gathering places in the Pacific. For the gregarious, this is an opportunity for renewing old friendships and making new ones. On shore, the club provides neutral ground for informal meeting, all at affordable prices. In the town, the mixture of cultures, the well-stocked shops and the unique market are enough to keep many crews happy for weeks.

The Fijian people

This former British Commonwealth country has a very traditional Melanesian culture. Each island village has a high degree of autonomy. There is an elder chief, a 'governing body' of elders, as well as a 'chief' whose role it is to see that the village functions as a whole on a day-to-day basis. The village may have communal gardens or projects that require the partial participation of all the families on a daily basis.

When you anchor off a village, it is important to visit the elder chief as soon as possible. It would be considered rude to go swimming or diving before you have received the 'blessings' of the chief. If you have an audience with the elder chief, it is considered taboo to arrive without an offering of kava, the national drink of Fiji. The ceremony is called sevu-sevu, and you are expected to bring ¼–½kg dried kava root to the chief. Dried kava root can be purchased in Suva at the large market, or in the market of the other towns where you might be clearing in. For the would-be connoisseur of this new drink, some islands will be known for growing

a more powerful species, which will be sought after as a speciality. The chief will bless it and you, and – depending on the time of day or how many visitors they have a week – they may brew some up on the spot, or let you off the hook. In return for your gesture of goodwill, the chief will invite you to be part of the village, to fish in the village waters, to participate in the village social functions, and to come under the protection of the village from 'others'. It is an old custom, and in most parts is still taken seriously by the village chiefs, and should certainly be taken seriously by those cruising these waters. Granted, in some of the villages besieged by cruising yachts, the elder may take the kava and 'run', but in most places the ceremony and the invitation to be part of the village is quite literal.

Kava is drunk casually as a beverage by the men of the village, at least a couple of evenings a week. There is still a degree of ceremony, although it is not as formal as the sevu-sevu ceremony. As an ex-officio member of the village, a visiting man will find a warm welcome at these, generally men only, gatherings.

Fiji is no longer part of the Commonwealth, as it no

longer accepts the directives of a Governor General. Fiji has a dilemma with regard to an introduced culture vying for acceptance alongside the indigenous Melanesian culture. In most cases, outside cultures were introduced by the colonial powers, because there was a difference in their lifestyles. In the case of Fiji, Indian labour was introduced in the latter part of the nineteenth century to harvest the sugar cane. The Fiji islanders were not interested in working in the fields – why should they be? It did not take a lot of effort to live well off the land and sea. It is not surprising that the Indian work ethic has resulted in their dominating commerce and, after obtaining economic power, achiev-

ing political ambitions. General Rabuka, in a bloodless coup in the mid-1980s, stopped the trend by forbidding any Indians from holding elected political office. The Indians argue that after 100 years, and four generations of living in Fiji, they are as much Fijian as the indigenous Melanesians. Britain sided with the Indians, citing discrimination, and Fiji left the Commonwealth. Fiji's dilemma is a difficult one. The indigenous Fijians would lose control and certainly a degree of identity. On the other hand, how many generations must exist before immigrants are integrated and given equal rights? A tough question to answer.

Mark Scott

Passage south to New Zealand

To round off the South Pacific crossing there is the passage to New Zealand, a passage that is more demanding than any other on this route across the Pacific. Although only around 1100 miles long, the tropics will soon be left behind and the latter part of the passage will be sailed in the variables. It is usual to leave in November before the cyclone season begins, but it is still only springtime in New Zealand and a ration of strong weather on the way must be antici-

pated. There are more than 15° of latitude to be crossed, and it will be cold on arrival after six or eight months of tropical heat.

The prevailing winds in the closing stages will be from the westerly sector, and so the perceived wisdom is to make plenty of westing in the early stages until, if possible, one is already in the longitude of the Bay of Islands, and then to relax and head south. This is an easy enough target for those sailing from Fiji, but for those starting further east in Tonga the option to make ground westwards is not so easy. The Fiji contingent have virtually a clear ocean to enjoy, but the Tongan fleet have a number of obstacles to avoid. The Minerva Reefs were previously avoided like the plague, but now that GPS has arrived they have become an attraction, and several yachts at a time will gather in the lagoons. It is said that seafood gathering there is all-absorbing and much enjoyed. The Kermadecs are also on the route. They are manned by New Zealand and can be spoken to on SSB; some yachts anchor off and pay a visit.

New Zealand

Much the easiest arrival port in New Zealand is Opua in the Bay of Islands. The alternatives are Whangarei or Auckland, but the New Zealand authorities are even more strict with regard to anyone who stops anywhere prior to clearance and it really is not worth risking their displeasure. Whangarei is a long way up a river and arriving yachts are very dependent on a rising tide, and Auckland is so much further south. Opua is the favourite arrival port and is geared up to clear the steady flow of yachts efficiently. When the rigours of the passage south have been overcome, then the cruise southwards to either of the other ports can be enjoyed in a relaxed manner. One of the pleasures of being in New Zealand is that once the very strict arrival procedures have been completed, the authorities do not require any further action from their visitors until it is

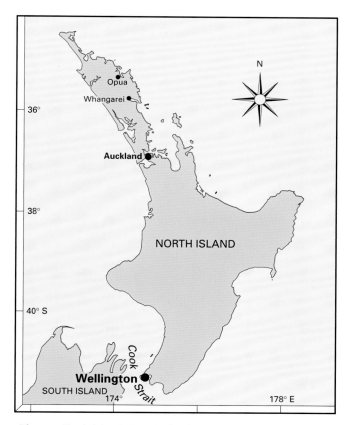

Plan 15 *North Island, New Zealand.*

The beautiful Bay of Islands, North Island, New Zealand. Photo Joanne Gambi.

time to leave. Unless, that is, there are animals aboard and then there will be twice-weekly inspections, all at considerable expense to the yacht.

Arrival in New Zealand is the conclusion of the most exciting chapter of cruising in most people's lives. It is, however, the beginning of a new chapter that will very likely be equally memorable. For those lucky enough to be able to spend six months in New Zealand, there is much to be savoured. Whether the time is spent living ashore, refitting the boat and escaping to explore by road, or cruising the coastline, the experience will leave happy memories of a delightful country with a healthy national pride, a universal love of sport, particularly sailing, and, in the South Island, some really stunning scenery. The sailors who have to lay up and fly away to attend to their affairs elsewhere are sadly the losers.

10 Westwards to Australia or the Solomon Islands

From Fiji via Vanuatu and New Caledonia

While most of the fleet are heading south for New Zealand, another option is to take a more westerly course for Australia, clearing out of Fiji from either Suva or Lautoka. The great majority call in to Vanuatu and New Caledonia on their way to the Queensland coast. Only those who are intent on making an express passage to Sydney or Tasmania skirt south of New Caledonia and remain in open ocean all the way. There is inevitably a wide choice of possible arrival ports, ranging from Cairns in the north (an obvious choice for those whose primary aim is to reach the Torres Strait), to Brisbane, and a number of options further south for those who intend to spend some time in Australia.

This is a good opportunity to repeat a word of warning that is given in Part III with regard to Australian visa requirements. Do not, on any account, leave Fiji without first obtaining a valid entry visa for Australia. It may be possible in Nouméa, but remember that relations between the Australians and the French have been strained in recent years due to the Mururoa atomic testing, and Fiji might be the better option. Anyone arriving without a valid visa will be fined on arrival and most probably be limited to only three months in the country. Australia is a bureaucratic place and the formalities (see Part III, nos 33 to 37) are expensive, and they do not end with inward clearance. At the very least, visiting yachts will have to report at each Customs port throughout their stay.

Vanuatu

It is only around 570 miles from Lautoka to Port Vila (see Part III, no 31) and for most crews it is an easy and, generally, very fast passage. Port Vila is frequently the only place visited before it is time to press on. There is, on the other hand, a whole island group which, if time permits, can be cruised for a month or more.

The Vanuatu Tourist Board promotes the islands as 'the untouched paradise'. As one writer put it, 'how could one fail to be seduced by that title, especially after finding so much of the eastern Pacific decidedly touched'.

Lying between 13°S and 20°30'S and between 166°30'W and 170°30'W, Vanuatu consists of 13 major islands. All are high, well-watered and covered in rain forest. Some are volcanic, some are coral, and others a combination of both. The dry season lasts from May until October. During this time the south-east trades prevail with occasional calms, followed by an east or north-east wind and rain. Lively tradewind sailing is enjoyed between the islands.

For many years the sovereignty of the New Hebrides, as named by Captain Cook, was disputed between the English and the French, both of whom had long-standing interests in parts of the group. In 1914 it was agreed that a condominium government should be set up with completely parallel English and French laws (and native laws) administered by two high commissioners, two police forces, and so on. The similarities between the words 'condominium' and 'pandemonium' were very apt. For the present-day visitor there is a certain fascination in the mixed legacy of the two colonial powers who have since 1978 withdrawn from the scene, leaving the new republic of Vanuatu to fend for itself.

Currently, there are only two ports of entry: Port Vila on Efate Island and Luganville on Espiritu Santo Island. The islands offer a wide variety of anchorages on their leeward sides, with holding ranging from black sand, to sand and coral. Good shelter from the prevailing trades is available, but, as in any island anchorage, one must be constantly alert for potential wind shifts.

Most of the better known anchorages in the outer islands have a small village on the shore and it is here that the real charm of Vanuatu is to be discovered – when you meet the locals. If you do not enjoy or want that contact, then Vanuatu is not the place for you. Local customs should be observed, and it must be appreciated that these are proud and industrious people whose land you are visiting. They will treat you as an honoured guest, and in turn will expect you to respect their way of life. It is worth pointing out that Vanuatu is a malaria zone. Admittedly the risk is much lower in the dry season, but it is still a risk area.

Heading north from Efate there is a convenient overnight anchorage at Laman Bay on Epi; there are times, however, when this anchorage can be very rolly. Within a day's sail from Epi one comes to Ambrym Island, where there are two active volcanoes with smoke plumes that are obvious from seaward. They are clearly the centre of Vanuatu magic! Anchoring is possible at Craigs Cove, Dip Point Cove and Ranon, where the holding is good.

Pentecost Island is the home of the famous land dives that take place in April and May and predate bungy jumping by many moons. Anchorages are at Wali, where the towers can be seen, or at Loltong inside the reef. Maewo Island is particularly rugged and the west coast is covered in waterfalls. There is an anchorage at Asanuari Bay.

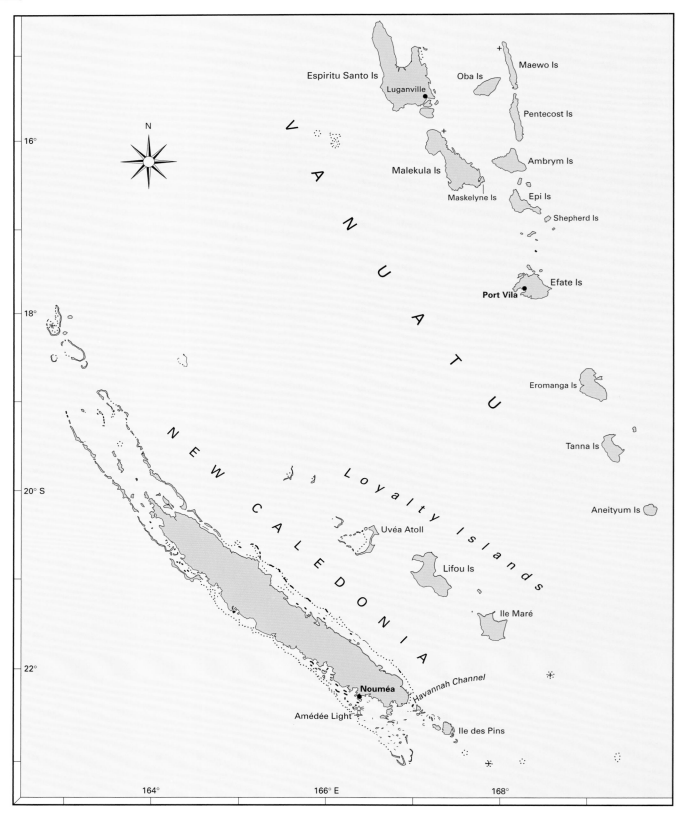

Plan 16 *New Caledonia and Vanuatu.*

Espiritu Santo Island has Luganville as the main town and is the alternative port of entry. It is a mecca for divers, and has some of the best wreck dives in the world. There is an extensive Second World War dumping ground off Million Dollar Point, where US forces offloaded tons of surplus machinery. Palikula Bay is a beautiful scenic anchorage on the east coast.

The Maskelyne Islands at the south-east tip of Malekula Island offer protected anchorages inside the reef area. There is very good diving on the outer reef.

The general belief, however, is that in Vanuatu one should only swim when the water is clear and take local advice whenever possible to assess the risk of shark attack. Port Sandwich, close by, is considered a safe 'cyclone hole', but not safe for swimming.

The beat to windward from Efate down to Tanna is said to be worth the pain. Mount Yasur, an active volcano, provides spectacular entertainment – local guides are available to take you up it. The anchorage at Port Resolution can be rolly. One day there may be arrangements for outward clearance at Tanna, but in the meantime it would be unwise to risk going there, or anywhere else in the group, without having first cleared correctly. There have been instances of yachts being heavily fined for doing so.

New Caledonia

Having visited Vanuatu, New Caledonia is spread across the route to nearly all ports in Australia, and it is only natural to make a stopover there. Nouméa (see Part III, no 32) on the south-western side of the main island is the only port of entry, and if one is going to visit the Loyalty Islands on the way, it would be wise to make some discreet inquiries as to how such a call would be received. The French authorities have a varying degree of security consciousness depending on the activities of certain reactionary groups. Stopping before officially entering may be frowned upon, or it may not be. The SSB or ham nets will be a useful source of guidance.

To reach Nouméa involves entering the Havannah Channel at a distance of 56 miles from Nouméa, and then not being in open water for the rest of the way. The leading lights approaching the channel are quite reliable, but it would be better not to enter before daybreak.

Having crossed the Pacific and become attuned to the low level of affluence and standards of living in the island communities, it is quite a shock to the system to sail in two days from the simple charm of Vanuatu to the sophistication and high standards of a bustling French city like Nouméa. There are well-engineered marinas full of locally owned yachts and the streets are full of new cars and expensive shops. The cost of living is substantially higher than in any country since Tahiti, but it is a change and, apart from the cost, an enjoyable city to visit.

It is worth noting, for any crew who feel they have had enough, that this is the first realistic market for yacht sales that exists in the Pacific, when crossing in this direction. In addition, not having a home product to protect, the import tariffs (particularly for any yacht built within the EU) are not as swingeing as in New Zealand or Australia.

There is immense scope for reef cruising within New Caledonia and the Ile des Pins at the southern tip of the reef is very popular. The Amédée Light, which stands as

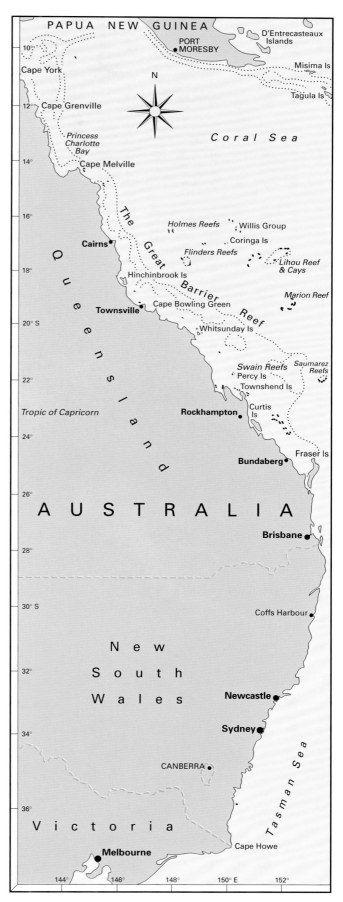

Plan 17 *East coast of Australia.*

a sentinel at the pass by which one would leave from Nouméa, is a magnificent structure. It is the tallest metal lighthouse in the world. It was built in component form in France and shipped out for local assembly.

Onwards to Australia

It can be a slow passage, or it can be a very rough ride, from Nouméa to Australia. Popular entry ports, listed from the south, are Sydney, Coffs Harbour, Brisbane, Bundaberg and Cairns (see Part III, nos 33 to 37). Gladstone, Mackay and Townsville are also Queensland ports of entry, but even Gladstone is just inside the Great Barrier Reef and less easy to approach from seaward. Cairns is the obvious choice if it is accepted that in order to reach Cape York by the most direct route a passage through the Reef must be made somewhere. From Bundaberg south there are no offshore islands to pass on the way in to Australia, until landfall is made. Lord Howe Island is the possible exception which, for those sailing direct to Sydney, would only need a small diversion. Anchoring in the lagoon is forbidden and visiting yachts must take a mooring for a weekly charge. When approaching the continental shelf (approximately 200m deep), one should be aware of the south-running East Australian Current, which can run at 3–4 knots in the Southern summer, especially when the north-east prevailing wind is blowing.

Most sailors spend the southern summer in Australia, biding their time to go north-about towards the Indian Ocean when the cyclone season is over. This probably includes sailing at least as far south as Sydney Harbour, which is a magnificent setting for a big city and should not be missed. Some will go on south to Tasmania, which is a delightful island to visit and has more in common with New Zealand than the rest of Australia.

Going so far south and then retracing the same course in reverse back up into Queensland is the generally adopted option. There is, however, a perfectly reasonable alternative that is seldom considered. The decision to sail west across the Great Australian Bight is not as masochistic as most people imagine. If one sails in February or March, the high pressure systems are well offshore, and following the coastline round the bight it is possible to enjoy a very high percentage of fair winds. There are some interesting stopovers and island groups to explore and, with far less travelling yachts passing, the local yacht clubs are much more likely to extend a spontaneous welcome than anywhere on the Queensland or New South Wales coast. The disadvantages are that it is much colder and the white pointer sharks have a rather evil reputation. No worse, it should be said, than the crocodiles and the box jellyfish of the Northern Territories!

The Solomon Islands

The Solomon Islands offer an alternative option to New Zealand and Australia, particularly for those who wish ultimately to head further north into Micronesia, the Philippines and Japan. The northern part of the Solomons has a low incidence of cyclones and it is therefore reasonable to sail from Fiji via Vanuatu to the islands in the closing months of the year. It is also possible to spend a season in the Solomons and head back to Australia before November, perhaps calling at the Louisiade Archipelago in Papua New Guinea on the way, if time permits.

The Solomon Islands consist of a double chain of six main islands and numerous smaller ones scattered over a huge area extending from 13°S to 6°S and from 167°E to 156°E. Most of the islands are volcanic in origin and

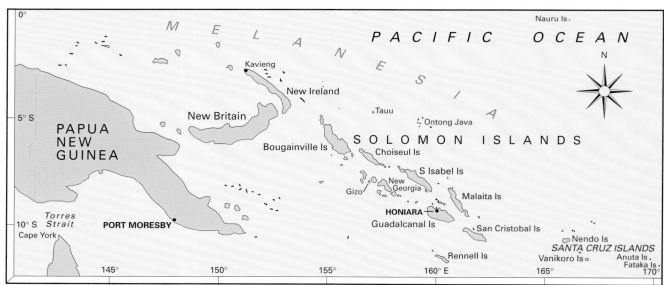

Plan 18 *The Solomon Islands.*

Gizo, Gizo Island, Solomon Islands, with Logha Island in the distance. Photo David Mitchell.

have fringing coral reefs; some are coral atolls. The people are mostly Melanesian, but there are small populations of both Polynesians and Micronesians. The country became a British Protectorate in 1900 and became fully independent in 1978. It is a member of the British Commonwealth and the British sovereign is Head of State. English is widely spoken throughout the islands. Some of the fiercest fighting in the Second World War between Allied and Japanese forces occurred here and the scars and debris of the battles are still evident in many places. Malaria is extremely prevalent and virulent. Visitors should seek medical advice as to the appropriate prophylactics (which are essential), and every effort should be made to avoid mosquito bites.

Entry ports include Ndende on the Santa Cruz Islands, Honiara (Part III, no 38) on Guadalcanal Island, Gizo in the Georgia Group and Shortland Harbour, though this last is not recommended because of the proximity of Bougainville Island (Papua New Guinea) and its separatist movement. Yachts are required to clear in at one of the entry ports before visiting other parts of the country, but those initially calling elsewhere and reporting to the local police or village headman have been tolerated in the past. There is an entry fee charged in Solomon Island dollars, but many of the entry ports have no banks, so it is worth trying to acquire some local currency before arrival in the country. It is probably best to avoid Malaita, due to the civil unrest that occurred in 1999 between the local inhabitants of Guadalcanal and the Malaitan settlers there. At this time, Honiara also

effectively shut down, yachts kept clear, and the fledgling tourist industry collapsed. However, there are about 1000 islands, cays and atolls to choose from, so there is plenty to see in other parts of the Solomons. It is possible to visit 'tabu' sites, where sacred skulls of chiefs and captives are kept, along with 'kastom' money.

The climate is tropical and the rainfall is heavy, so the islands are covered in dense forest, much of which has, so far, escaped the attention of the logging companies. Cyclones can occur in much of the territory during the season from about late November to April, which is also the period of the north-west monsoon. During the rest of the year south-easterlies predominate. Apart from tropical storms and short-lived squalls, winds of over 30 knots are rare; they are usually between 5 and 10 knots. There are numerous potential 'hurricane holes' where a yacht should be able to ride out the severest weather. For greater peace of mind, however, anyone waiting out the cyclone season will be even safer closer to the equator.

The country offers wonderful cruising for the self-reliant, and particularly for those who are prepared to navigate in poorly charted places. Most of the islands are covered by charts on 1:300 000, from which it is difficult to identify potential anchorages, but the local Land Survey maps, on a larger scale and available in Honiara and Gizo, are helpful. When approaching the shore, conning from aloft is often essential and it is sometimes necessary to examine potential entrances with a lead line from the dinghy or by snorkelling before proceeding.

The country is not much visited by yachts mainly because it lies a little to the north of the obvious circumnavigation route, and those that do tend to remain in the southern chain where the famous Morovo Lagoon lies. The people are extremely friendly, and in many places a newly arrived yacht will quickly be surrounded by canoes, usually with goods for barter or, more rarely, for sale. (Most business, apart from in Honiara and Gizo, is conducted by trading.) T-shirts and shorts, fish-hooks and line, batteries, sugar, tea, coffee, sweets, washing powder and soap are much in demand in exchange for fruit and vegetables, crayfish, exotic shells and carvings. Petty theft is not unknown, but the obvious precautions should be sufficient to avoid trouble. In the more sparsely populated northern chain of islands it is possible to spend weeks without seeing another soul. The waters are mostly extremely clear and the snorkelling and diving (only possible if you have your own compressor) are excellent in many places. The fish life is abundant and little skill is needed to secure regular meals.

Solomon islanders

Ninety-five per cent of the 400 000-strong population are Melanesians who moved westwards from Papua New Guinea and, arriving first, settled on most of the islands. The Polynesians, who account for about 3.75 per cent of the population, came from the east and found only a few atolls at the eastern end of the island chain on which to settle. Some 4500 Micronesians arrived in the 1960s from Kiribati, when they were resettled because of the overcrowding and inability to produce enough food on Kiribati. Minorities include Chinese, who run most of the trading and shops, and a small white population involved in businesses such as tourism; 96 per cent of the population are Christian and 10 per cent of those are Seventh Day Adventists.

Most people live in traditionally built houses in very small villages. They cling to a lifestyle that has barely changed for centuries. There are more than 125 languages and dialects, but everyone speaks Pijin and many speak English. People are always smiling and solicitous in this country that they call 'The Happy Isles'. There is little concept of time. There is no word in Pijin for tomorrow and a wristwatch is regarded as a prestigious wrist ornament.

The Malaitans are, by contrast, the only islanders with any drive. They have therefore ended up running important parts of the government as well as most of the business. Some see Malaitans as the aggressive playground bully who snatches rather than asks, and pushes rather than waits. As some say, 'Malaitans don't even like each other'!

As a whole, the Solomon Islands remain 'islands adrift in time' and the people are very special. But a successful visit depends largely on a consideration for, and an understanding of, local culture and values.

David Mitchell

Mention the Solomon Islands and cruisers will describe the marvellous wood carvings with mother-of-pearl inlay. Many of the trained carvers today come from the 'trade schools' set up by the Seventh Day Adventist missionaries. Known to observers as the 'fast-faith', many of the congregation seem to be members who gain immediately by joining the church – ie if you have children approaching secondary school age and the Seventh Day Adventists happen to have a secondary school in the area, open to all church members. After secondary school there is an opportunity to attend Brigham Young University in Hawaii, for those who are committed to the goals of the church. So it is not too surprising to find the wood carvers want to trade only for money – in other words, sell their carvings.

The Solomon Islands cover such a large area that one still finds traces of somewhat esoteric religions such as the Shark Worshippers Cult found in the Langa Langa lagoon. In the south-easternmost islands you can still find an old sea canoe rotting under the dried brown palm fronds of a chest-high canoe house, left unattended for the last 20 years.

It is from these isolated islands, by necessity, that seafaring canoes were still plying the waters in the mid-1960s, using traditional Pacific navigation techniques as described by David Lewis and others. On one such island, we sat under the shade of a palm tree showing two octogenarian brothers our charts of the Solomon Islands, an area that they had navigated several decades before. They looked on in confusion, not due to their age, but to the orthogonal relationships depicted on this sheet of paper. We might as well have had a chart of the moon. Their spatial concept was the relationship of star paths, wave patterns and bird sightings indicated on their reed and stone star 'charts', and in the verbal directions handed down by generation after generation. When the government outlawed offshore voyaging passages between islands in the mid-1960s, the verbal lore died with those who carried it. Now, armed with few navigation skills, traditional or modern, islanders have found that the introduction of outboard engines has not yielded any greater freedoms.

Mark Scott

11 Westwards from the USA and Canada

*Via Hawaii south to the Line Islands and the Cooks or to Kiribati
and the far western Pacific*

The Hawaiian Islands are well placed in the northern Pacific to act as a focal point for those departing from the western seaboard of the USA or Canada. A direct passage to the islands provides the fastest route to the tropics. It is traditionally a downwind ride and should be quick. The further south such a departure is made, the more the wind will broaden on the quarter, making for some exciting sailing in the last week if the trades are fresh. Routes onwards from Hawaii then either head west towards Guam and on to Japan or the Far East, or south to join the main South Pacific crossing to New Zealand and Australia.

The Hawaiian Islands

For those arriving from the east or south, there are three ports of entry to choose from: Hilo (Part III, no 45) on the island of Hawaii to the south-east, Honolulu (Part III, no 44) on the island of Oahu to the north-

west, and Kahului on the island of Maui midway between the two. The latter is not much favoured. It is right in the middle of the windward coast of Maui and not hugely attractive as a stopping place, having few facilities for yachts. Although overrun by popular tourism and short on natural beauty, Oahu offers the only place in the islands for a serious pit-stop.

As a cruising area the Hawaiian Islands group is not rated very highly among the ocean cruising fraternity. This is almost entirely on account of the paucity of good secure anchorages. The winds are sometimes very strong, particularly between the islands, which are nearly all quite high, accelerating the tradewind in the channels between them. Whereas the ocean swells create some of the finest surfing in the world, they can make the search for a safe anchorage a real problem. Often the swell comes from the south, and the tradewinds blow from the north-east, so that any roadstead that is open in either direction is affected.

Having said all this, these are exciting, dramatic volcanic islands – well worth exploring when the oppor-

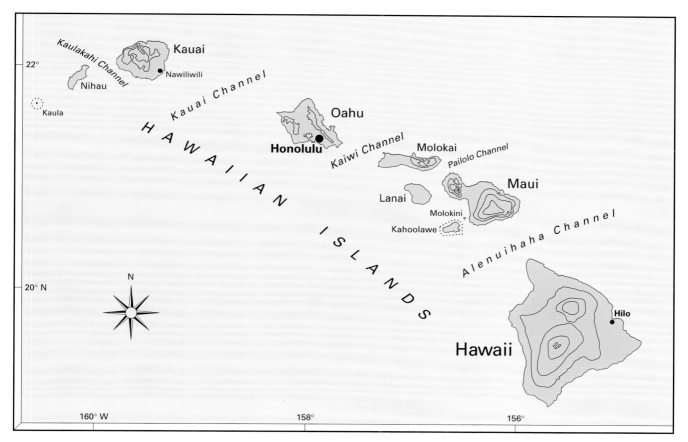

Plan 19 *The Hawaiian Islands.*

tunities are there. There are some who will find the intense tourist activity a trifle overbearing, but this must be accepted. In the spring, the humpback whales are a unique attraction. To see them breaching, leaping almost clear of the water and then crashing back in, is a spectacle never to be forgotten.

Hawaii, the big island, is the first in the chain starting from the south-east. Radio Bay in the port of Hilo is the only secure place to stay. The various bays on the south-east and west coasts are only attractive when the swell is not running. Captain Cook lay more than once in Kealakekua Bay and was eventually killed there in an angry confrontation with Hawaiian warriors.

The next island to the west is Maui with the port of Kahului, which is an entry port on its north-east shore. The popular resort and yacht anchorage is at Lahaina on the south-west shore. The tiny harbour is always full to capacity with tourist boats, and visitors are restricted to anchoring in the open roadstead. The holding is indifferent and, if there is any swell, the passage into the landing may need a tender with enough power to outrun the breakers.

Lanai, which is one of the smallest islands, has a delightful little protected harbour at Manele. If one is lucky enough to find space available, it is well worth a visit.

Molokai, one step further west, is sometimes thought of as the forgotten island that the mighty wave of modern tourism has failed to notice. As such, there is a low-key atmosphere that is a positive relief to find. There is an anchorage at Kaunakakai with some facilities, or another in a deserted quarry port at Lono towards the western end of the island. This is a

well-protected anchorage, but there are no facilities whatever.

Oahu is the most sophisticated island of the group. Honolulu, on its south coast, is the state capital of Hawaii and the focal point for the holiday and yachting industries. There are alternative anchorages in Kaneohe Bay on the north-east corner of the island, which require more than average nerve to enter if the trades are blowing hard, and also one at Pokai Bay on the west coast. The latter is a simple and attractive spot, which is an ideal jumping-off point for an overnight crossing of the channel to Kauai, the last visitable island in the chain.

Kauai has a popular haven for yachts, named Nawiliwili, which is a protected harbour with an inner small boat basin providing alongside facilities for visitors. It is also a Customs port and a suitable place for departure for those heading north or west. Hanalei Bay on the north coast is a favourite anchorage for yachts, but it may be less comfortable in the early part of the year when the trades are still at their freshest.

For those who have set off from the western seaboard at the very beginning of a much longer voyage, it is a relief to be able to call at such a sophisticated place as Honolulu. The resources of the city are quite extensive, and dealing with teething problems should not be difficult with regular flights from the mainland and only internal conditions operating. It will save a lot of hassle and expense to clear the jobs list really thoroughly before departure.

Beyond Kauai, the remainder of the Hawaiian chain all the way to Midway Island is not a practical area for cruising yachts. The islands, atolls and reefs between 161°W and 176°W form a wildlife refuge. Entry is

When approaching Honolulu, the curtain of high rise hotel development on the beach at Waikiki is an unmistakable feature. Photo Michael Pocock.

prohibited except by permission of the US Fish and Wildlife Service based in Oahu. Midway Island itself is controlled by the US Military and is out of bounds except in a real emergency.

From Hawaii south: the Line Islands

The Line Islands are a seldom visited collection of islands and atolls, very thinly spread over 20° of latitude straddling the equator, approximately between the Hawaiian Islands 1000 miles to the north and French Polynesia and the Cook Islands to the south. If the intention is ultimately to join the main body of yachts on the standard South Pacific route, they provide a useful route through to the Cooks. (They also provide a stepping stone westwards to the main islands of Kiribati, before turning south.) To visit or pass through them, the best available chart is British Admiralty No 4617 at a scale of 1:3 500 000. The appropriate large-scale charts will be required if one is planning a stopover: DMA 83158 for Tabuaeran, NOAA 83157 for Palmyra, and DMA 83130 for Kiritimati.

The Line Islands, with the exception of Palmyra, which is privately owned and formerly part of the Hawaiian group, are part of Kiribati. Entry is possible at Tabuaeran (formerly Fanning Island) and Kiritimati (formerly Christmas Island).

Palmyra atoll was originally claimed by the Kingdom of Hawaii in 1862. However, it was not included in the group when Hawaii achieved US statehood and it is now privately owned by the Nature Conservancy. It is managed as a nature preserve and its surrounding waters were designated a National Wildlife Refuge in January 2001. Enquiries as to the possibility of visiting Palmyra would need to be made in Hawaii or Honolulu before sailing. This unpopulated island is a major tropical gem. For cruisers visiting only one place in the area and not requiring shoreside facilities (except water), this is the one to visit.

Tabuaeran atoll was only discovered in 1798, by the American explorer Edmund Fanning. It was annexed by Great Britain in 1889 and became a part of the colony of the Gilbert and Ellice Islands in 1916. Fanning Island was renamed Tabuaeran when it gained independence as part of Kiribati in 1979. Residents of overcrowded islands in Kiribati have been resettled here. There is a settlement at English Harbour in the middle of the south-west side. The lagoon is entered through a narrow pass 50m (164ft) wide.

Kiritimati is the largest atoll in the Pacific and 152 miles south-east of Tabuaeran. It was formerly named Christmas Island by Captain Cook because he spent Christmas Day there in 1777. There was a US Air Force staging post on the island during the Second World War

and in 1956–64 it was used by Britain and the USA for nuclear testing. The only remaining settlement is London, on the north side of the entrance to the lagoon. Deep-draught yachts may be severely restricted in their ability to enter the lagoon, and the latest information should be obtained. There are prolific seabird colonies, and access to certain areas is controlled by the authorities to protect the nesting sites.

The Northern Cook Islands

Penrhyn Island is the obvious first stop in the Cook Islands, lying about 660 miles due south of Christmas Island. The Taruia Pass on the west side leads to the principal village of Omoka where clearance will be given. If the tradewinds are at their strongest, there is a much more satisfactory and more sheltered anchorage off the village of Tatua on the other side of the lagoon. The passage across is far from simple, so local advice is worth seeking. From Penrhyn, the standard route across the western portion of the South Pacific may be taken, via Suwarrow or directly to Samoa, then Tonga, as detailed in Chapter 9.

Whichever route is followed from the Hawaiian Islands, the ITCZ must be crossed sooner or later. Sailing down through the Line Islands is in the 'sooner' category and by the time Tabuaeran or Kiritimati is reached, assuming it is still the northern summer, the zone should be losing its influence and the south-easterly will become predominant. This will probably mean that the leg to Penrhyn will be on a reach and the opportunity to run will be reserved for the onward passage to Samoa.

Westward from Hawaii

The Republic of Kiribati (pronounced 'Kiribass') consists of a number of island groups scattered across 2400 miles of the Pacific near the equator. The Line Islands, at the easternmost end, are discussed in the preceding section. The Phoenix Islands are a group of eight islands, which were visited by British and American explorers between 1823 and 1840. Both countries exercised joint control over the group for a 50-year period from 1939 and colonised some of them with people from the overcrowded Gilbert Islands. However, these settlements eventually failed and the islands now have virtually no permanent population. The Gilbert Islands are at the western end of the Republic of Kiribati.

Some may wish to make a quick crossing to the Torres Strait on their way to the Indian Ocean. In this case, the most direct and fastest route would be through Kiribati, the Solomons and across the Coral Sea, south of Papua New Guinea. The main route westwards from Hawaii, which remains almost entirely in the North

Pacific, calls at the Gilberts and/or the Marshall Islands, before heading through the Caroline Islands and on to Guam in the Federated States of Micronesia.

The Gilbert Islands

Sailing from the Hawaiian Islands to the Gilberts or the Marshalls will delay the crossing of the ITCZ and bring the wind closer to the stern for most of the way. A close study of the current distribution chart is important. It should be possible to gain some advantage by staying north of the rhumb line rather longer than might appear correct. You will thus ride the North Equatorial Current as far as possible before dipping south across the Equatorial Countercurrent at a steep angle. Once Kiribati is reached, the South Equatorial Current will be established and a west-going stream will persist for the remainder of the crossing.

Kiribati straddles the equator, with winds that are governed very largely by the seasonal location of the ITCZ. The prevailing winds are easterly and light. The dry season is from March to November when the tradewinds are blowing from the north-east, or more easterly with some calm spells. November to March is the wet season; however, the rainfall is not very great. Winds at this time are between north-east and south-east, but there can occasionally be quite strong westerlies which may last for a few days. Gales are infrequent. When they do occur they are more often associated with the westerlies and are strongest in February.

Tarawa (Part III, no 39) is the port of entry for the Gilberts and it is inadvisable to risk calling elsewhere in the group before completing a formal entry. There is little on Tarawa itself to attract the visitor. But, having cleared in, there are a number of interesting atolls with sheltered lagoons that are worth exploring. Only 5 miles to the north is Abaiang Atoll and 64 miles further north is Butaritari Atoll. To the south-east is Abemama.

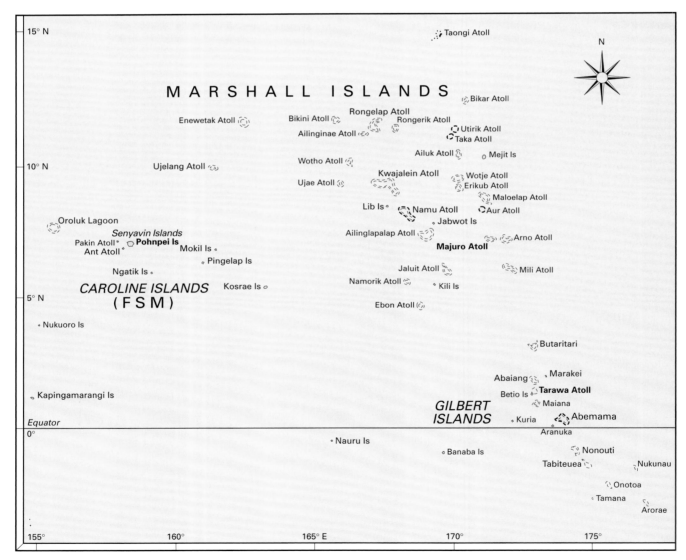

Plan 20 *The Gilbert, Marshall and Caroline Islands.*

Maneaba or village hall, Tabuaeran, Line Islands. Photo Noël Marshall.

The passage from Tarawa to Abemama is a full 75 miles, with the current setting the yacht to leeward all the way. All of these atolls have strong streams in the approaches to their passes, so some intelligent anticipation is called for and undoubtedly some power.

The Marshall Islands

The Marshall Islands are made up of two major groups, the Ratak Chain in the east and the Ralik Chain in the west, with a total of 34 atolls. Majuro (Part III, no 40) is the capital and the only port of entry, but is of little interest except as a practical pit-stop. Permits must be obtained from the Ministry of the Interior for visiting outer islands, and each island may levy its own fee established by its chief. Some may be as high as $150 (such as Mili). Others require no fee. Those wishing to visit Mili and other islands en route to Majuro from the Gilberts may be able to obtain permits from the Ministry of Foreign Affairs in advance. Otherwise, it is necessary to clear your itinerary with Outer Islands Affairs in Majuro and make sure the cruising permit is properly endorsed for the islands you intend to visit. The advice is always to anchor off the principal village, which will be the one with the same name as the atoll. The chief will want to see the permit and, providing it is in order, the yacht will then be made welcome.

The Caroline Islands (FSM)

The Carolines (apart from Palau, which is a separate independent state) now make up the Federated States of Micronesia (FSM). Any vessel arriving in the FSM is expected to obtain an entry permit in advance. A three-month permit may be arranged in a matter of days by fax from a previous port of call – see Pohnpei (Part III, no 41) for details. A permit may also be obtained from FSM Embassies or Consulates, but this has been known to take several months.

The first port of entry from Majuro is Lele Harbour on Kosrae Island, the most south-easterly of the group. Other ports of entry are Pohnpei (Part III, no 41), the capital of FSM, Chuuk and Yap (in the far western corner of FSM). It would be wrong to visit any other island before clearing in. It pays to be careful with regard to dress when ashore in these islands. Modesty is expected in all villages except Pohnpei, where the expatriate population have created a more relaxed approach. Long sleeves and trousers, to cover bare flesh, are advisable if one is going to avoid causing offence.

If cruising in remote areas it is as well to remember that all territory is owned by someone, and therefore a small gift to the village headman will smooth the way for a more enjoyable relationship before you explore ashore or fish in the lagoons. Sundays are very keenly observed, and for the islanders all activity other than church attendance is banned on Sundays.

Kosrae is a high island, densely forested and with fringing reefs. It is visited by a few tourists, attracted by the diving and to see the remains of the medieval city of Insaru. Lele (or Lelu) is not the only harbour, but one must go there first for clearance. There is room to anchor in 10–12m off the south-west shore with good holding in mud. Call Marine Resources on channel 16 to arrange for clearance. It is said that the manager of the Ace Hardware store is the friend of all visiting sailors and that his waterfront is the place to moor a dinghy. Lele also has a supermarket and a number of small stores. Two miles up the road in Tofol there is a post office, a bank and several small restaurants.

Propane is not available, and it would appear that diesel has to be bought by the barrel. The water is suspect and should be boiled before drinking. Rubbish disposal is not something that is understood locally, beyond throwing it all in the sea!

Palikir is the capital of the FSM on Pohnpei Island. For the visitor, apart from the normal facilities of a tropical island, Pohnpei has a major historic site at Nan Madol. The ruins of the medieval city are built of huge basalt blocks and cover several square miles.

From the Caroline Islands, Guam in the Northern Mariana Islands is the only major stopping-off point before moving north to Japan or west to the Philippines.

12 The North-west Pacific

Routes to Guam, then northward to Japan, or back to Hawaii via the Marshalls

The far west Pacific, north of the equator, is subject to typhoons. Unlike cyclones south of the equator, which conform to a well-defined cyclone season, the behaviour of typhoons further north is less predictable. In general, typhoons are active after the end of the northern spring until December. Some may occur after this, but their incidence in the northern spring is low. As described in Chapter 9, yachts crossing the South Pacific move out of the cyclone belt either to the south or north at the end of the sailing season. In the same way, yachts working their way north from the Antipodes need to time their arrival in Guam and further north to coincide with a low risk of typhoons. This may involve waiting near the equator (approximately 5°S–5°N), where tropical revolving storms are rare at all times of the year, until it is safe to continue. In addition to cyclone activity, the NW monsoon affects an area from the equator to about 20°S and west of 150°E from October onwards, and this narrows down the location of suitable waiting places. Such places include Tarawa (the Gilberts), Funafuti (Tuvalu), Ontong Java (Solomon Islands) and the north-eastern end of Papua New Guinea.

Just as Hawaii provides a major focal point for connections between the west coast of the USA and the south and west Pacific, so Guam offers a smaller staging post in the far western Pacific. It provides access to the west coast of America, via Japan and the North Pacific rim. In the other direction, Guam can also provide a route via Palau to the Philippines, for those heading further west towards the Indian Ocean.

Guam

Guam (Part III, no 42) is the largest and most southerly of the Mariana islands, with a population of more than 150 000. It is governed from Agaña and maintains a large US naval base at Apra, the port of entry. The southern part of the island is mountainous and much of the interior is jungle. Most villages are located on the coast. Guam was visited by Ferdinand Magellan in 1521, and belonged to Spain before being taken by the USA in 1898. It was captured by the Japanese in 1941 and re-taken by the USA in 1944. It is now an unincorporated territory of the USA. Subsistence farming is still practised, but Guam's major industry is concentrated in the goods and services sector, supplying the huge military base. Tourism, particularly from Japan, is also important and very much in evidence on the island.

A dozen or more yachts arrive early each year before moving north to Japan in March–April or going west to the Philippines. Most reach Guam from the south, but a few arrive directly from Hawaii, or stop at the Marshalls on the way. Many take the opportunity to work on their boats in Guam before they leave. The Marianas Yacht Club is welcoming and most American facilities are available, although some may be widely scattered in the town.

From Guam, it is possible to head west to Palau and the Philippines, which are most easily reached during the NE tradewind season, in the early part of the year. However, typhoons may occur in any month of the year (particularly later on in August and September). It is therefore imperative to monitor weather reports for some time before setting off. Plenty of information is available by weatherfax, radio and the internet, including the US Navy's Typhoon Warning Center in Apra.

Japan

Most yachts travelling to Japan arrive from the south. However, it is also possible to make the long passage of over more than 3500 miles directly from Hawaii. Japan itself extends over 1500 miles from just above the Tropic of Cancer to beyond 44°N. This richly interesting and beautiful country has much to offer as a cruising desti-

The monument to Magellan, Guam. Photo Noël Marshall.

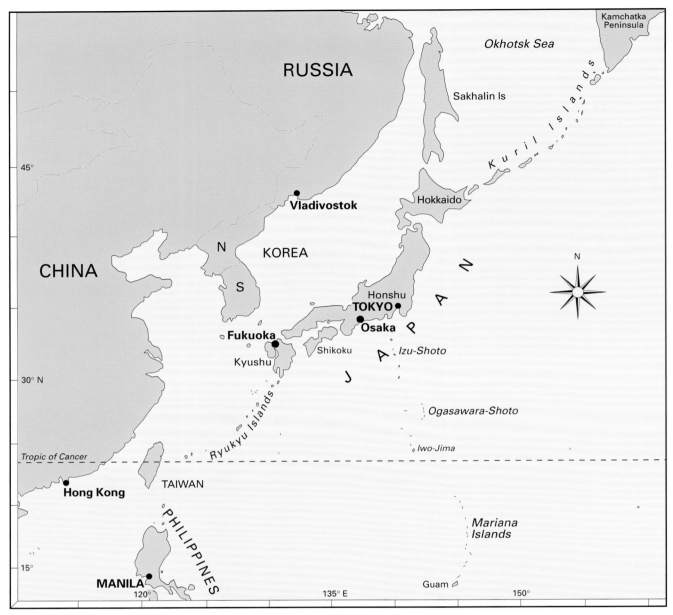

Plan 21 *The north-west Pacific.*

nation in its own right, although the area is not readily accessible. Very few yachts cruise Japanese waters. No doubt partly for this reason, the people you meet will seem uniquely pleased to see you and show you their country – often showering you with hospitality and assistance. It is as well to remember this when considering the more difficult aspects of visiting Japan.

Weather

Typhoons occur in all Japanese waters, but are least prevalent from January to May, and fewer hit the west coast than the east. In southern Japan they are infrequent either side of the period from July to September. Off the east coast, most come through in August and September, and at the latitude of Tokyo, it is unusual, though not unknown, for a typhoon to hit outside these two months. On the west coast, particularly at the south-west end, they can track through earlier. Modern weather forecasting has greatly helped in assessing typhoon hazards. Although Japanese forecasts are broadcast only in Japanese, the radio weatherfax service from Tokyo is excellent, and when in port it may be possible to get weather information from coastguard stations. There is also a six-hourly audio HF broadcast from Guam, which is useful for monitoring typhoons.

Most of Japan is well outside the tropics. While Hokkaido and northern Honshu are cold and windy from October to March, from Tokyo southwards, sailing on the eastern side is possible through much of the year, depending on one's resistance to the drop in temperature. Winter depressions do track through Tokyo, but are not usually as frequent or as long-lasting as those found in the UK. The strongest winds come from the west and the north. Few yachtsmen arrive before April, or stay much into October. Even in the absence of tropical storms, the weather can be unpredictable and often foggy. However, there is still a summer season ample for those on passage north to Alaska or Russia. Winds around the Japanese coasts in late spring can blow from any direction, but there are fewer gales in the Sea of Japan than in the waters to the east of the country.

Currents around the Japanese islands mainly flow along the chain from south-west to north-east, more strongly to the east than on the western side. There is also, however, a pronounced south-westerly current, the Kamchatka Current, running past Hokkaido on the south-east side and continuing south down the east side of the northern part of Honshu (see Plan 5, Pacific Ocean currents). It meets the main Japan Current a little north of the latitude of Tokyo, and this current then heads off to the north-east. Its average speed is 1 knot. Currents can flow at up to 8 knots between some islands, and good tidal information is essential.

The coasts are generally well lit, but offlying dangers are not always marked with buoys or beacons. The fishing industry is colossal. At night, when small fishing craft often show high-intensity lights powered by noisy generators, they can give precious little attention to navigation. In addition, extensive fixed nets are widely set and not necessarily lit at night. The shoreline and small bays are cluttered with a variety of fishtraps and pens. Radar is therefore particularly useful in the area.

Local yachts are not allowed to use VHF, and many vessels do not have it or do not maintain a watch on channel 16. Furthermore, the language barrier may make radio communication difficult – many Japanese people understand English, but are reluctant to speak it.

Formalities

Crew members need visas for Japan, but no advance documentation is required for the boat. Entry from abroad (and exit) must be made at one of the 117 ports where there are Customs offices, known to the Japanese as 'open' ports. The bureaucracy, although scrupulously polite and correct, is ponderous and involves filling in several forms. In a marina or yacht club, the manager will make the arrangements. Foreign vessels are also cleared in and out of ports when moving within Japan, and carry papers in a sealed envelope addressed to the offi-

cials at the next port of call. In principle, foreign vessels are only supposed to visit 'open' ports. In practice, it seems that these restrictions are not always enforced.

Facilities

There are few cruising yachts in Japan and most seem to be used for local racing, so that facilities for yachtsmen, although expanding, are very limited. Busy commercial/fishing harbours will usually be as helpful to a foreigner as they can, but they are not welcoming – and anchorages can be hard to find. All around the Japanese coast, marinas are under construction, some of them very grand and most of them expensive. They tend to incorporate yacht clubs, but not all can accommodate offshore keelboats, so it is advisable to get a Japanese person to make enquiries before heading for an unknown yacht basin. Marinas are recommended, even for those who normally prefer to avoid them. It is here you will meet members of the Japanese sailing fraternity, who will be astonished and delighted to see you. There is a widespread custom of offering foreign yachts free berthing, usually for one or two weeks, or agreeing to handsome reductions in berthing fees (charges can otherwise be the equivalent of over £50 per day).

Facilities for haul-out and general yacht work exist in Japan, but chandleries are sparse or non-existent. Basic yacht supplies (shackles, rigging, fuel filters, chain, etc) are available at reasonable prices in areas that have a fishing fleet. Specific yacht items such as sails, engine parts, winches, etc are more difficult to find, except in major yachting centres on Honshu (eg Tokyo or Osaka). It may be easier and cheaper to contact West Marine in California for anything listed in their catalogue, which will arrive by courier within a few days. Sailmakers are few and far between and it is best to arrive in Japan with all gas cylinders full.

Provisioning conforms to the general principle that goods supplied locally are much cheaper than imports. Therefore fish, local vegetables and noodles are affordable, whereas meat, western canned and packaged foods, imported vegetables, cookies, flour, etc are much more expensive. The conspicuous anomaly is rice, which enjoys a protected high price; so stock up well beforehand.

The Japanese people

The pride of the Japanese in their country, and their tradition of hospitality to strangers, seems to surmount their natural diffidence and the language barrier. You will be befriended by people providing hospitality and assistance of all sorts on a scale that is embarrassingly generous by our standards. The Japanese also love to give small presents at almost any social meeting. In addition, you will need to seek help from people – for

example, in yacht harbours – that goes beyond the call of their normal duties.

You will want to do something in return. It is probably not a good idea for a passing visitor to try to return favours in comparable substance by means of meals out or expensive locally bought presents. And if you do, your Japanese friend will turn up the next day with a whole carton of drink in order to get in the last word!

It is, however, essential to be well supplied with small but interesting gifts of some kind. Traditional 'yachtie' goods such as T-shirts, caps and small items displaying the ship's logo are acceptable – and also pennants. We found that good photographs of the boat, some of them mounted and/or framed, were well received, eg by a harbourmaster who would display it in his office. For more sophisticated use we had a few good-quality leather items, silk scarves, etc brought out from home by our joining crew. In the absence of such things, a nicely wrapped bottle of whisky – which is of course obtainable locally – is acceptable as a seri-ous gesture by any Japanese person. Try to take some amusing gift wrap with you.

The language problem, however, is formidable. Presumably for lack of practice, very few Japanese seem to retain anything of what they learn in several years of studying English at school. But one can not but be anything other than grateful for their efforts. In daily life it helps that more and more public signs are now also written in Roman script or actually in English.

Noël Marshall

Heading north to Russia

Now that the ports of eastern Russia are open to visitors (though securing visas is time-consuming), there is much to be said for working one's way up the Sea of Japan and leaving Hokkaido in late May. This should provide enough time for a brief stop in Russia before setting out for the Aleutians and Alaska. The Okhotsk Sea has usually melted by May, but its icy waters affect the sea around the Kuril Islands and Sakhalin Island. Anyone making this passage in May/June will therefore have to accept that it will be cold and often foggy. A cabin heater is very desirable! Further east, the effects of the warm Japan Current make conditions more bearable, even in the higher latitudes of Alaska.

An alternative route to the north-west coast of America

Most boats in the western Pacific, wishing to cross to the north-west coast of America, will follow the route through Japan and the Aleutians around the North Pacific rim to reach their destination. It is also possible to part company at the Marshall Islands with those heading for Guam, and instead head north directly to Hawaii. From Hawaii, passages to Alaska or British Columbia can then be made.

It is possible, but it is not easy. This passage north, then east, is a daunting prospect if the yacht is not a good windward performer. A long windward leg is very demanding on sails, gear and crew, and this factor must be considered before taking this route. The distance to Honolulu is approximately 2000 miles and there are no usable stopping places on the way, unless there is a major emergency – in which case help may be available at Wake Island or Midway. Those with the capacity to do so may very well consider a liberal use of power assistance. The North Equatorial Current has to be crossed sooner or later, and the obvious strategy must be to limit the time taken in the adverse stream. If on departure the winds are north-easterly, then there would be an argument for taking a long port tack, dipping into the favourable Equatorial Countercurrent, and looking for a shift to the south-east so that the foul stream can then be crossed more nearly at right angles. Once committed, the policy should be to carry the starboard tack well to the north until the latitude of Hawaii is reached, where the rate should at least slacken. Whichever way one looks at this passage, the only really enjoyable part is going to be the arrival at the other end!

All the comments on the Hawaiian Islands made in Chapter 11 are equally applicable to those arriving from the west. The islands lie in the north-east tradewind belt and the rhumb line to the western seaboard is another windward leg. Those heading for the Strait of Juan de Fuca (at the Canadian/US border) will opt for a long passage to the north, in order to find their way onto the top of the high pressure system and then ride home in the westerlies. The trades should weaken and reverse on or around 40°N in summer, and much further south in winter. However, any passage made in the winter months will usually include some strong weather north of 30°N and all the way into the Strait of Juan de Fuca.

13 Across the North Pacific to the Western Seaboard of the USA, Canada and Mexico

Via the Aleutian Islands or returning via Hawaii

Around the North Pacific rim via the Aleutian Islands

Passages eastwards around the North Pacific rim, leaving from Japan or Russia, are usually made in May–June, when gale frequency in the area is tolerable (as it is from June–August along the Aleutian chain and in the Gulf of Alaska). During the summer, gales are less frequent in the Bering Sea than the North Pacific, so it is probably worth keeping north of the Aleutian Islands. The winds in this area are created by the passage of successive lows and are predicted to be westerlies. However, passage-makers may encounter gale force winds from any direction. Cloud cover in these more northerly regions is usually much greater than in the tropics, so radar and other electronic navigational aids are invaluable.

The Aleutians, a part of Alaska, are a chain of rugged volcanic islands extending eastwards from the Kamchatka Peninsula to the tip of the Alaska Peninsula, separating the Pacific Ocean to the south from the Bering Sea to the north. They are made up of four main groups: the westernmost Near Islands, the Rat Islands, Andreanof Islands and Fox Islands. Like Prince William Sound further east, they are a spectacular area of Alaska and very much in the wilderness.

A visit to the Aleutians may include long periods of isolation, similar to those on an offshore passage. Self-reliance is important, and restocking opportunities are infrequent and expensive. If arriving via Japan along the Aleutian chain, Dutch Harbor, Unalaska, will be the first real provisioning centre. Not officially a port of entry, Dutch Harbor is none the less designated as a US Customs station and vessels may be cleared here. Yachts that call at islands further west in the chain should, properly, make arrangements for a Customs official to meet them at Attu Island in the Near Island group at their own expense.

From Hawaii back to Alaska

As mentioned at the end of Chapter 12, the passage from Hawaii to the western seaboard is a windward one in the north-easterly trades. The passage further north to Kodiak should be timed to arrive around the beginning of June. The course is northerly, with light, fair winds for the first part of the trip, until the westerlies are reached at approximately 35°N. There is a high chance of encountering strong to gale force winds. In May, the weather in Alaska is still cold, especially at night. Poor visibility is also very likely to be encountered on approaching Kodiak. For those aiming for Juneau or Vancouver, the route heads north and then east, skirting the top of the North Pacific High. The depressions during the summer are less intense and head into the Gulf of Alaska, where they dissipate as they move inland. Continuous marine weather forecasts from Canada are excellent, giving plenty of notice in advance of approaching weather systems.

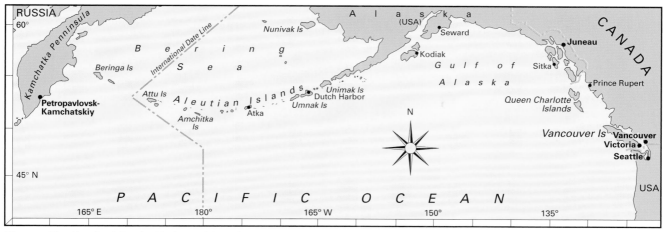

Plan 22 *The Aleutian Islands, Alaska and Canada.*

Heading south-east along the western seaboard

Although for some a Pacific crossing officially ends once the coast of Alaska has been reached, there is merit in including a section about landfalls along the coastline heading south-east into Canada, the USA and Mexico. In effect, this 'closes the loop'. Those completing a crossing around the North Pacific are presented with some ideas for extending their cruise southwards. Similarly, those based on the western seaboard at the start of a planned crossing through the South Pacific (see Chapter 9) can follow the coast down towards departure points in Mexico and Panama.

Most sailors would agree that the preferred way to travel is south-easterly from the north-west – ie starting in Alaska or British Columbia and ending up in Mexico rather than the reverse. In general, both the wind and stream favour progress in this direction. If, however, Alaska is the priority destination after having passed through Panama, then an offshore route would be the most effective way of reaching it – out into the Pacific via the Galapagos and Hawaii, then on to Alaska as described above.

Alaska

From a cruising point of view, Alaska may be divided into three parts heading south-east: (a) the Aleutian Islands and the rest of the Alaska Peninsula towards Kodiak (Part III, no 2) (b) the northern part – which, broadly speaking, is from Kodiak to Prince William Sound, and (c) the Panhandle, 500 miles across the Gulf, which stretches from Cape Spencer to the Canadian border.

For those with little time to spare in the region of Prince William Sound, there are similar features to be marvelled at in the Panhandle further south, but without the same degree of remoteness. Entry from the Pacific in these circumstances will most probably be made at Sitka (Part III, no 3). The glaciers of Glacier Bay or the Tracy Arm are quite splendid, but you are more likely to share your enjoyment of them with other boats than you are further north.

Throughout Alaska and British Columbia (except in the big towns) yacht chandlery is sparse, but electronic equipment repair is available in many small towns where there is a fishing fleet. Thanks to the high tidal range, drying out is possible in many Alaskan and British Columbian ports, which maintain grids for the purpose.

Canada

From Cape Spencer and Icy Strait it is possible to travel all the way to Vancouver or Seattle with only a very short hop in open water. The inside waters are, in the summer, tranquil to a degree and very beautiful. However, tranquillity and wind are contradictory, and anyone bound by a strict schedule will be forced to motor for a high proportion of the time. Entry to Canada is easily completed in Prince Rupert and, for those who feel that the motoring is getting just a little bit too much, there is the option of standing out across the Hecate Strait to the very beautiful Queen Charlotte Islands. The finest cruising in these islands is in the inlets on the east side of Moresby Island.

Heading down the inside of Vancouver Island, there is a very handy restocking stop at Port Hardy. There are also useful air connections to Vancouver for any crew changes that may arise. Good tidal predictions are very important in these waters. It should be realised, however, that the very fast streams for which the area is well known are restricted to the rapids. These only occur where the channel is crossed by a shoal that accelerates a slow, deep watercourse into a shallow, dangerous 8–10 knot turbulent stream for a short distance. These rapids are very well documented and, provided there is good forward planning so as to pass at slack water, they should not present a problem. The fastest and most straightforward route is down the Johnstone Strait and Discovery Passage to Campbell River. There are, however, various options by smaller backwaters which are great fun. Desolation Sound is very popular with those cruising north from the Vancouver area, and therefore does not live up to its name!

Duet in front of a spectacular glacier at Tracy Arm Fjord, Alaska. Photo Simon van Hagen.

Plan 23 *The Pacific coasts of the USA and Mexico.*

The USA

Having passed through into the Straits of Georgia, you are now in the same waters as those who may have made a landfall by way of the Juan de Fuca Strait that separates Vancouver Island from the USA. In this case, a convenient port of entry is obviously needed and the choice is dictated by whether it is more desirable to enter Canada or the USA. For the total stranger, Victoria (Part III, no 4) should not be missed and is an easy solution. For entry to the USA, clearance is obtainable in Port Angeles, just across the water from Victoria, or in Port Townsend, another 30 miles or so further in at the entrance to Admiralty Inlet. The latter is a great centre of yachting facilities, with large areas

devoted to dry land storage. It is a very popular place for those needing a major refit and wishing to do most of the work themselves. Seattle is another day's sail further up into Puget Sound. It is a major city and a major yachting centre. Seattle probably has the most attractive choice of flights to Europe in the area. There are excellent marina facilities both on the Sound and above the locks on Lake Union. Equally, it should not be forgotten that any visit to this part of the world would be incomplete without a week spent in the heart of Vancouver, which is a very fine city indeed.

Local opinion is that, for those heading south and east down the US seaboard, departure should be made before the end of August to be ahead of the autumnal gales. While this is sound advice for those whose experience has been limited to local conditions, those with more offshore mileage behind them can probably afford to linger a week or two longer. At the far end one should not cross the US–Mexico border before early November for fear of a late Caribbean hurricane overrunning the Gulf of Mexico. This means that there are up to two and a half months to be spent on the western seaboard of the lower forty-eight (this is an expression used mainly in Alaska to identify the original States below the 49th parallel) which, for the more restless of sailors looking for interesting waters to explore, can be frustrating.

Providing the bar is passable, the Columbia river is a possible distraction. It is big and broad all the way to Portland, Oregon, and gives an opportunity to penetrate well inland. San Francisco Bay (Part III, no 5) is a rewarding area to spend some time. Within the bay there is nearly always some wind, which makes a change from the situation offshore. Fog is a hazard to be contended with, and for those unused to strong tidal streams there is a new dimension to be recognised. The delta region up the Sacramento river is intriguing, and a pleasant interlude could be spent exploring its backwaters. In the anchorage at Sausalito and in the marinas there is the opportunity to fall in with other crews heading south and a chance to meet some kindred spirits.

As one heads further south and east, approaching southern California, the chances of a brush with authority increases. Understandably, so close to the frontier, the fight against drug importers is increasingly intense and the Coast Guard are taking no chances. The best advice is to toe the line to the letter and keep a low profile while presenting a clean image. In the bigger cities like Los Angeles, crime is a problem. It can be a shock for the visiting yachtsman to find the marina staff armed. It makes sense to be on your guard and very careful after dark. San Diego (Part III, no 6) marks the end of affluent civilisation, and the accepted jumping-off point for heading into Mexico. The chandlers are well equipped to serve the departing armada that sets off each November and the prices are extremely competitive. At least one chandler, Downwind Marine, runs a courier service into Mexico, thereby bypassing the Mexican mail, and monitors SSB radio channels to pick up orders.

Mexico

Cross the border into Mexico and you are entering an altogether different world. It is convenient to enter at Ensenada and then feel free to stop where the fancy takes you on the passage down the outside of the Baja, that long tongue of land that contains the Sea of Cortez on its inner side. However, Mexico is one of those countries where you endure a longwinded clearance procedure in and out of every Customs port. Customs, *Migracíon*, the police and the port captain all have to be visited on arrival and departure, armed with endless

The frigate bird is a striking feature of the Mexican coastline. Breeding colonies can be seen at close range on Isla Isabella. Photo Michael Pocock.

paperwork. Rubber stamps are liberally spattered over these forms, and woe betide the skipper who reaches the end of the line without the correct total of stamps! The Mexican Navy, heavily armed, will sometimes insist on coming aboard in intervening anchorages using steel lifeboats without fenders and a gung-ho approach to boat handling. It can be a bruising encounter, although done with plenty of good humour on their part. It is not always easy to reciprocate!

At the southern tip of the Baja is the glitsy tinsel city of Cabo San Lucas. This is the area's chief tourism hot spot and has an air of affluence and high living entirely in contrast to the rest. Cruise ships call regularly and there is a large fleet of sports fishing boats ready to take the passengers out to plunder the deep. How long the stocks will last is not a question that is addressed very seriously.

As the season progresses, this rather inadequate basin becomes distinctly crowded, with very close anchoring the only option. On Saturday mornings the harbourmaster may order everyone into the rolly bay outside, but his orders are not universally obeyed and the space soon fills up again. In December and January the Baja is quite chilly, but Cabo San Lucas seems to be the exception, with a much hotter microclimate all of its own.

Turn the corner and head up into the Sea of Cortez and you meet the cold north wind that is coming down from the Colorado mountains. This makes for windward sailing around the Cape to La Paz, which is the principal town of the area. By comparison with Cabo San Lucas, it has a much more genuine Mexican feel to it. The wind-over-tide condition that occurs on the ebb gives rise to what is known as the La Paz waltz, so close-quarters anchoring is definitely to be avoided. There is a popular marina in the town, and several boatyards with slipways that can be booked for a haul-out.

As you cruise further south, so the temperature rises sharply and the winds decrease. There are plenty of small anchorages between the towns and many US yachts enjoying the scene. Puerto Vallarta (Part III, no 7) and Acapulco (Part III, no 8) are useful stopovers, and for quite a number of yachts one of these will be their chosen springboard for taking off across the Pacific.

PART III

PORT INFORMATION

Selection

The ports in this section have been chosen either as departure and arrival ports, or as principal ports of call within an island group. They are nearly all Customs ports of entry for their respective countries. The exceptions are places where entry can be acknowledged by the authorities on the spot, to be confirmed at a subsequent, more important, port within the same country.

Co-ordinates

The co-ordinates given for each port are taken from whatever chart has been available for the preparation of this guide. They refer to a general position within the place described and they are given only to enable readers to relate the information to a small-scale chart, for example when passage planning. **They are emphatically not a waypoint for the approach**. Within the Pacific, navigators must realise that satellite-derived positions may frequently be at variance with the chart by appreciable margins. GPS should thus never be used in an inshore situation without also undertaking a conventional check on distance off.

Local time

The times given for each port are related to UT (GMT). An asterisk by the time indicates that daylight saving time is added during the summer months. Local information on the dates that apply will need to be sought.

Tides

The information given is for the range of tide at springs and neaps (MHWS–MLWS and MHWN–MLWN). In mid-Pacific the range is so small that it is hardly worth thinking about unless there is a very critical situation to be planned (such as the entry to Aitutaki). For a very large area of the Pacific, high water occurs at noon every day. As with any large ocean, the greatest rise and fall will always be found around the perimeter.

Chart numbers

Chart numbers have been taken from the British Admiralty catalogue, the US National Imagery and Mapping Agency (NIMA) lists, or the US National Oceanic and Atmospheric Administration (NOAA) chart catalogues. Some numbers may be withdrawn as time goes by, and there may not be 100 per cent availability of the charts listed. It has not been possible to examine each chart listed, and readers would be advised to go into great detail to compile a suitable portfolio at a reasonable cost. In particular, those listed as general charts will very likely overlap with others listed elsewhere, and to order both could be both impractical and unnecessarily expensive.

Buoyage

In general, all the North American seaboard and the US-dominated island groups will adhere to IALA B (red right returning) and the remainder to IALA A (red to port and green to starboard and cardinals).

General and harbour plans

The accuracy of the charts and plans in this guide is not guaranteed and they should *not* be used for navigation. They are provided as an illustration to the text and should be treated as such and no more. Every effort has been made to keep abreast of new developments, but at such long range this is not easy. Allowance must always be made for new features that have arisen since this edition went to press. Where given, soundings are in metres, and bearings are in true notation from seaward. The scale of each chart should be obtained by reference to the latitude divisions on the margin of the plan.

Caution

Navigators must never rely on a listed light being in a functioning condition. Standards of maintenance may not be as high as expected, and those beacons powered by solar energy may well be running below their best.

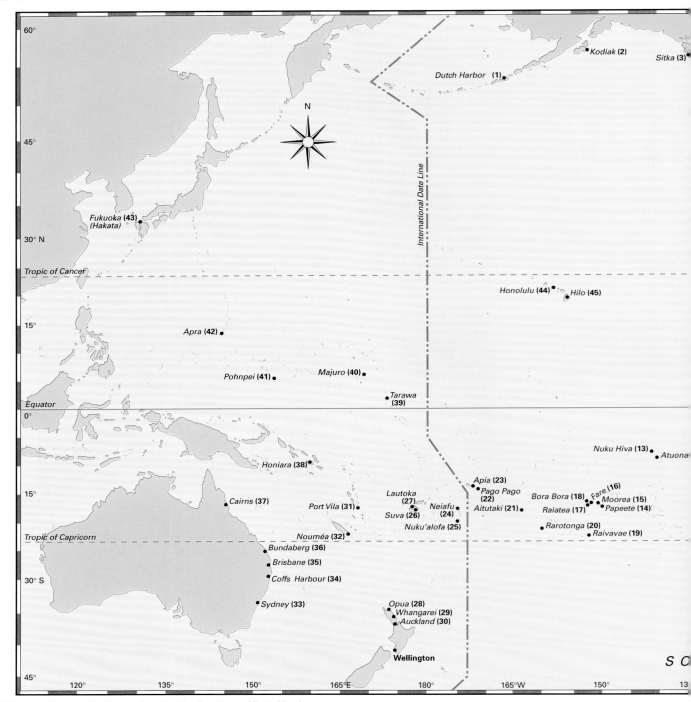

Plan 24 *The Pacific Ocean showing the location of listed harbours.*

Key to ports and harbours listed

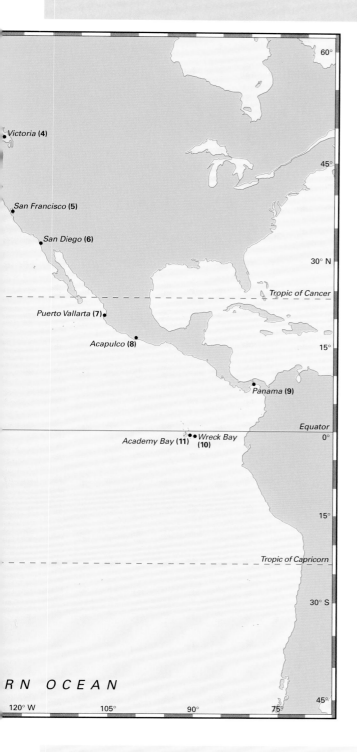

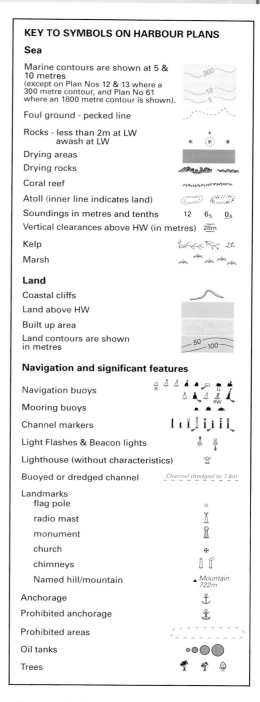

KEY TO SYMBOLS ON HARBOUR PLANS

Sea

Marine contours are shown at 5 & 10 metres (except on Plan Nos 12 & 13 where a 300 metre contour, and Plan No 61 where an 1800 metre contour is shown).

Foul ground - pecked line

Rocks - less than 2m at LW
     awash at LW

Drying areas

Drying rocks

Coral reef

Atoll (inner line indicates land)

Soundings in metres and tenths   12 6_5 0_6

Vertical clearances above HW (in metres)   28m

Kelp

Marsh

Land

Coastal cliffs

Land above HW

Built up area

Land contours are shown in metres

Navigation and significant features

Navigation buoys

Mooring buoys

Channel markers

Light Flashes & Beacon lights

Lighthouse (without characteristics)

Buoyed or dredged channel   *Channel dredged to 7.6m*

Landmarks
    flag pole

    radio mast

    monument

    church

    chimneys

    Named hill/mountain   ▲ Mountain 722m

Anchorage

Prohibited anchorage

Prohibited areas

Oil tanks

Trees

Key to symbols on harbour plans.

1 Dutch Harbor, Unalaska, Alaska, USA

53°53'N 166°31'W UT-9

Springs: 1.82 m	Flag: USA	
Neaps: 0.76 m	Currency: US dollar	
Charts	Admiralty	US
General	3336	16500
Approach		16528
Harbour		16529

General

Dutch Harbor, part of Unalaska, is a natural gateway to Alaska, for those crossing the North Pacific via the great circle route from Japan, and may be used as well for those arriving from Hawaii. Unalaska Island is one of the Fox Islands, the nearest of the Aleutian range to the mainland. To arrive at Dutch Harbor earlier than May is probably not feasible if one has taken the time to visit Japan or explore the Aleutians. On the other hand, if exploration of other parts of Alaska is the objective, then it is easy to underestimate the time

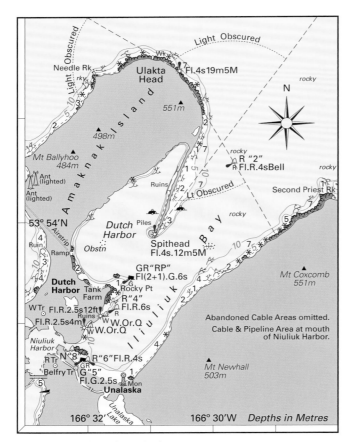

Plan 25 *Dutch Harbor, Alaska.*

needed to cover the miles to Kodiak, Prince William Sound or Sitka. An early arrival will provide time to sit out the bad weather that is inevitable on occasions in the unpredictable Gulf of Alaska, with travel only when conditions are suitable.

Although not as 'wild and woolly' as in the past, Unalaska is still a frontier town. Tourists arrive by the planeload, but Dutch is predominantly a fishing harbour, and you will probably jostle for a berth between the smaller boats of the fishing fleet. Like the fleet elsewhere in Alaska, the fishermen are likely to take good care of you, since yachts, in their scarcity, stand out.

Approach and entry

Visibility can be a problem because of fog, so radar and GPS are invaluable aids. The approach to Dutch Harbor from the west is via Unalaska Bay, which opens into the Bering Sea between Cape Kaletka and Cape Cheerful on the north side of Unalaska Island. Keeping Amaknak Island to starboard, head for the flashing red bell buoy at the entrance to Iliuliuk Bay. Call the harbourmaster on channel 16 – he will direct you to a berth either in outer Dutch Harbor or the Unalaska small boat harbour in the inner basin of Iliuliuk Harbor. Follow the well-buoyed channel. Remember that if arriving from offshore, you are entering the USA and the buoyage system will be IALA B. The *US Coast Pilot Vol 9* is an excellent aid when cruising the area. *The Alaskan Harbor and Boating Facilities Directories* can be obtained from the Department of Transportation and Public Facilities, Maintenance Operations, Southeast region, Box 3-1000, Juneau, Alaska 99802, USA. Both publications are invaluable guides to the area.

Radio

The harbourmaster monitors channel 16, and will request a transfer to a working channel. The Coast Guard also monitors channel 16.

Anchorage and moorings

Request a berth in the small boat harbour if possible, as the berths at Dutch Harbor are a long way from town. Crowding is likely in the summer due to the fishing fleet, and rafting up may be required. Water and power are available on the dock. There are showers at the fish plant. A laundry service is available in the old town of Unalaska, or at the Bunk House Lodge on the Dutch Harbor side.

Formalities

Unalaska (Dutch Harbor) is a Customs station, not a port of entry. However, the officials at Dutch Harbor will either clear you in or issue instructions for Customs clearance via telephone with Anchorage, Juneau or Sitka. Immigration clearance is available.

Facilities

Unalaska has several chandleries, and has good resources for mechanical, electronic and refrigeration repairs. There are no grid facilities, slipways or haul-out facilities. Some yacht items are available at the chandleries, whose supplies are geared to the fishing fleet. Speciality items would be ordered elsewhere, and flown in. The airport has one scheduled flight daily; there are, however, many days without service due to bad weather and fog, as the short take-off and landing strip is not equipped with radar, and planes do not land without clear visibility.

All essential supplies are obtainable. There are three grocery stores, a bank, a hotel, several restaurants, several lodges, a gift shop, community centre, health centre, museum, post office and library. Unalaska is developing rapidly.

Communications

There are daily flights (if the weather is good) to Anchorage and a ferry service once a week in the summer. Internet facilities are available at the library, free of charge, for a maximum of 1 hour per day usage.

2 Kodiak, Alaska, USA
57°45'N 152°3'W UT-9

Springs: 2.5m	Flag: USA	
Neaps: 1.5m	Currency: US dollar	
Charts	Admiralty	US
General	1499	531
Approach	1454	16594
Harbour	1454	16595

General

Kodiak, Alaska's largest island, is mountainous and heavily forested in the north and east. Most of it is a national wildlife refuge, with sheltered anchorages, free of ice. The island was the scene of the first permanent Russian settlement in Alaska, and Kodiak village became the centre of Russian fur trading. Kodiak town, the largest on the island, is a busy fishing harbour, and your first sight of the very highly mechanised and capitalised fleet is quite an eye opener. Salmon fishing is the major industry here. Kodiak has now lost its 'frontier' feel, with the steady development of the town. However, a warm and helpful welcome can still be expected for visiting yachts.

Approach and entry

Like Dutch Harbor, visibility in Kodiak can be hampered by low cloud and misty rain, so electronic

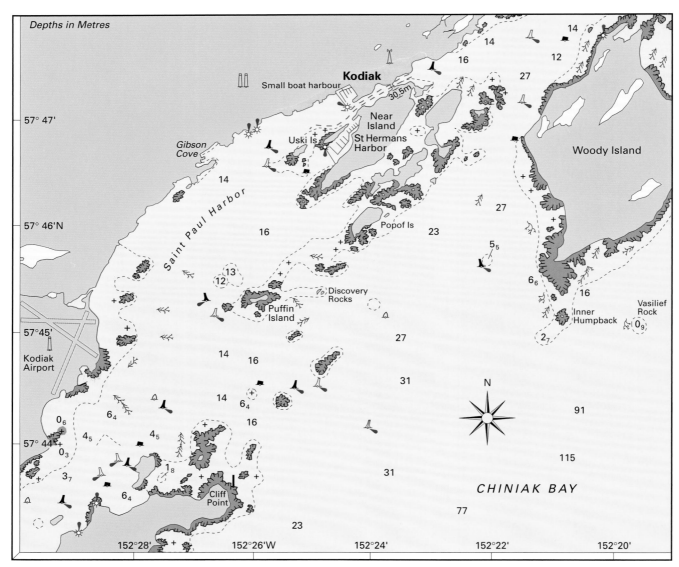

Plan 26 *Kodiak, Alaska, USA.*

aids are helpful. At the same time, although the standard of chart survey is first class, the earthquake of 1964 caused subsidence or upheaval of about 1.75m (6ft), so soundings may vary from those charted. The approach to Kodiak from seaward is through Chiniak Bay. The best option then is to enter Saint Paul Harbor (recently re-built) by the marked channel north-east of Cliff Point and west of Puffin Island. The *US Coast Pilot Vol 9* is an excellent aid when cruising the area. *The Alaskan Harbor and Boating Facilities Directories* can be obtained from the Department of Transportation and Public Facilities, Maintenance Operations, Southeast region, Box 3-1000, Juneau, Alaska 99802, USA. Both publications are invaluable guides to the area.

Radio

The harbour authorities monitor channel 16 and will request a transfer to 12 or 14 as a working channel. The Coast Guard working frequency is channel 22A.

Anchorage and moorings

Try to moor in the Kodiak small boat harbour on the port hand at the head of Saint Paul Harbor. This is so much nearer to the centre of town than St Hermans small boat harbour situated between Uski and Near Islands, which is a bit less than a mile away, across the bridge.

These are boat harbours principally for the fishing fleet, which in this area is dominated by 13m (43ft) seiners. The harbours are laid out like marinas, and in the season are generally fairly full as the 'open' fishing days are nowadays fewer than the 'closed' ones. It may well be necessary to double up alongside a fisherman who will, in all probability, be a first-class source of useful information.

Formalities

Kodiak is not, as it happens, an official port of entry; however, experience has shown that, particularly for those arriving from Hawaii, the process is fairly low key and can be negotiated on the telephone to Anchorage.

Facilities

As a major fishing harbour Kodiak has very good resources for mechanical, electronic and refrigeration repairs, although generally on a scale rather larger than the average yacht requirement. There is a 50-ton travel hoist at a boatyard to the east of the town and, as a high proportion of the fishing boats are GRP, repairs in glass should be possible. Specialist yacht items are obtainable from Seattle, but would have to be flown up. In the town all essential supplies are obtainable – albeit at a price. Internet connection is available at the local library, with no charge for 1 hour's use.

Communications

In Alaska, four wheels go very little distance out of town before they reach their limit. Marine Highway ferries and the ubiquitous floatplanes form the local transport system, and for longer hauls there are air connections with Anchorage for international flights.

3 Sitka, Alaska, USA
57°3'N 135°21'W UT-9

Springs: 3.9m	Flag: USA	
Neaps: 1.7m	Currency: US dollar	
Charts	Admiralty	US
General	4971	17320
Approach		17324/5/6
Harbour		17327

General

It is all too easy to arrange a route that misses out Sitka, and this is a shame. If you have come south from Prince William Sound it is natural to cross the Gulf to Cape Spencer and Icy Strait for an opportunity to visit Glacier Bay, and equally sensible to go into the leads calling at Juneau, maybe the Tracy Arm, and then go south by the inner channels. Sitka, on the ocean side of Baranof Island, is the original Russian capital dating from the days when the fur trade was at its peak. It is therefore the centre of Alaska's short history, and is intriguing for this reason if no other. Sitka is a port of entry, and as such is very popular with yachts arriving from Hawaii that do not have the urge or the time to go further north. If the glaciers are not a priority, then a cruise through Peril Strait, down Chatham Strait, and around the west coast of Prince of Wales Island is worth a whole summer. At times, the salmon fishing can be very rewarding.

Approach and entry

Sitka can be approached from three different directions, hence the need for a choice of charts for use in the approach. From the north you will pass inside Kruzof Island and through the Neva Strait. Otherwise, you will either come in from seaward using the unmistakable Mount Edgecombe, a miniature Fujiyama, as a landfall, or come up the shoreline from the south. Sitka Sound is well charted and well marked and, given reasonable care, should not present a problem. The town lies inshore of Japonski Island where the airstrip is situated; and because the bridge has a limited clearance (15.8m (52ft)), some consideration may have to be given at an early stage as to whether you are going to seek a berth north or south of the bridge.

Radio

The harbour authorities monitor channel 16 and will request a transfer to 12 or 13 as a working channel. The Coast Guard working frequency is channel 22A.

Anchorage and moorings

Now that the New Thomsen Harbor and its nearby breakwater have been completed, facilities for anchoring within reach of the town have improved. Many people anchor just inside the new breakwater. There are also many anchorages in the nearby islands, which are just 5 or 10 minutes fast dinghy ride away, in calm conditions. Otherwise a berth in one of the small boat harbours is a good choice. The most popular and convenient is New Thomsen Harbor, which has been expanded to form the largest harbour in Alaska (and one of the largest on the North American West Coast). It is situated at the north end of the channel inside Japonski Island on the town side. This harbour is occupied by a mixture of commercial and pleasure craft that all seem to coexist quite amicably. *The Alaskan Harbor and Boating Facilities Directories* are invaluable guides when cruising in Alaska and can be obtained from the Department of Transportation and Public Facilities, Maintenance Operations, Southeast region, Box 3-1000, Juneau, Alaska 99802, USA.

A faithful replica of the Russian Orthodox Church in the centre of Sitka (the original was destroyed in a fire). Photo Michael Pocock.

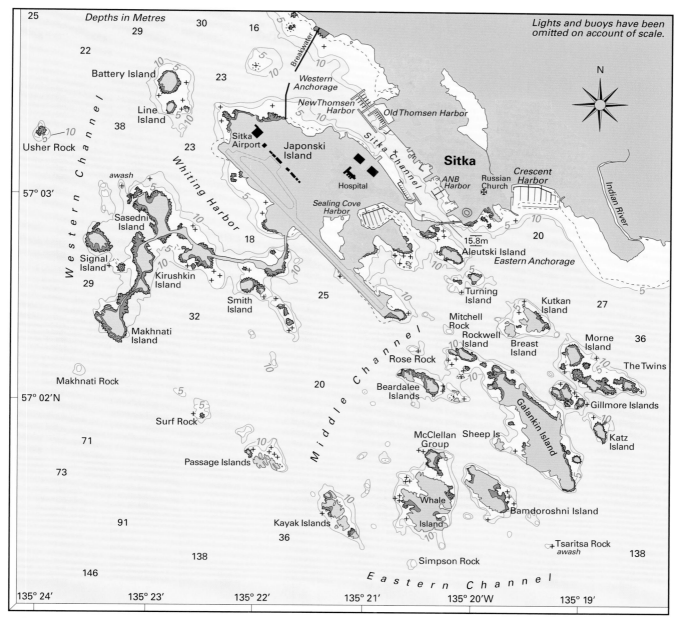

Plan 27 *Sitka, Alaska, USA.*

Formalities

Sitka is an official port of entry. The Customs officer will deal with all aspects of entry, calling first at the yacht, and then probably completing the formalities at his office in the town.

Facilities

As a major fishing harbour, Sitka has very good resources for mechanical, electronic and refrigeration repairs. There is a sizeable sports fishing contingent for whom

small boat service is available, but relatively little specialist sailing gear.

Communications

Sitka has no road connection with the rest of the world, as is the norm in most of Alaska. There are, however, regular passenger connections to Seattle, Juneau and Anchorage, via Alaska Airlines' jet plane service or ferry.

4 Victoria, British Columbia, Canada
48°25'N 123°23'W UT-8*

Springs: 1.8m	Flag: Canada	
Neaps: 0.3m	Currency: Canadian dollar	
Charts	Admiralty	US
General	76	18416
Approach	77	18416
Harbour	1897	18419

General

Victoria BC is the first Canadian port of entry for those arriving from the Pacific by way of the Strait of Juan de Fuca. Although Vancouver, on the mainland of Canada, is a far bigger city and the commercial capital of the west coast, Victoria, which is on Vancouver Island, is the administrative capital and seat of government for British Columbia. None of this should belittle the standing of Victoria, which is a fine city with an imposing waterfront and an established reputation for welcoming visiting overseas sailors. From Victoria one can go north through the inside waters, south into Admiralty Inlet and Puget Sound to Seattle, or enjoy local cruising in the Gulf Islands or the US San Juan Islands. Victoria is intensely British – with well-known tourist attractions such as the world-famous Butchart Gardens.

Approach and entry

Arriving from offshore, the approach from the Strait of Juan de Fuca is very straightforward, and those with good charts can take a useful short cut, given a fair stream, inside Race Rocks. This shortens the distance across the bay to the entrance to Victoria Harbor, between Macaulay Point and Ogden Point. The final stages of arrival can be enlivened by the close proximity of landing floatplanes and passenger ferries, both of which are using the same stretch of water. There are strict traffic separation zones during daylight hours, particularly in the floatplane take off and landing zone. Three white strobe lights located at Shoal Point, Laurel Point and Pelly Island are activated by the flight service station up to 60 seconds prior to a seaplane taking off or landing.

Radio

Call the US or Canadian Coast Guard on channel 16. Traffic is heavy in the approaches and can be monitored by listening to Tofino Traffic (governing the Strait of Juan de Fuca) on channel 74, Seattle Traffic on channel 14, and Vancouver Traffic on channel 11. Pleasure craft should not call on these frequencies except at night or in poor visibility.

Anchorage and moorings

There are no facilities for anchoring in Victoria Harbor, and proceeding under sail in the harbour north of a line drawn between Shoal Point and Berens Island Light is prohibited. Call the harbourmaster on channel 73. The most convenient berths are alongside the Government Floats by the Empress Hotel and off the end of Fort Street, a short distance further north. These floats are right in the centre of the city; they are not necessarily the quietest place at night, but are close to the shops and handy for the excellent bus service. There is a choice of commercial marinas both within the harbour and in Oak Bay about 3 miles to the east of the centre. The Erie Street Government wharf (also known as Fisherman's Wharf) is 0.1 miles east of Shoal Point, and James Bay (Victoria inner harbour) is 1.2 miles NE of the harbour entrance. Even further out is the Royal Victoria Yacht Club, in Cadboro Bay, with its own private marina where visiting yachts from other clubs will be made very welcome for short stays depending on space. Anchorage is possible both in Oak Bay and Cadboro Bay.

Erie Street Government Wharf
Wharf Street
Tel: 363 3273
Fax: 363 3224
VHF 73

This view across the harbour in Victoria, British Columbia, shows yachts moored in front of the Empress Hotel. Photo Michael Pocock.

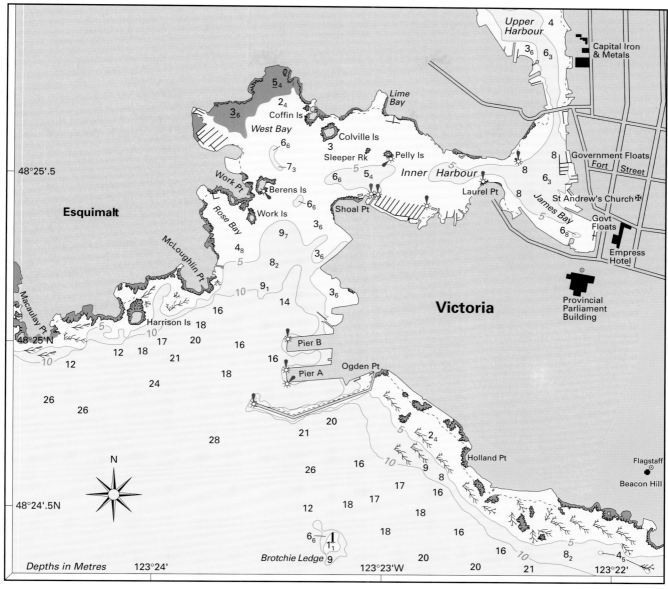

Plan 28 *Victoria, British Columbia, Canada.*

Formalities

If clearance is required there is a Customs wharf on the east side of the inner harbour just south of the Fort Street floats. There is a direct line telephone on the dock (Customs free phone: 1 888 226 7777) and a call will promptly bring an officer who will deal with clearance swiftly and easily. The Customs office is nearby at the corner of Government and Wharf Street. Any fresh fruit or vegetables will be confiscated, so eat it all before you dock.

Facilities

The sailing community of Victoria is very keen and active and well served by chandlers and sailmakers. The Erie Street floats have power and water (showers and laundry in the summer months), washrooms, a chandlery, charts and propane. Fuel is obtainable nearby at the Esso barge (tel: 388 7224). Yard facilities are widely dispersed, and all are actually in Sidney about 15 miles north of Victoria. Sidney is now the major centre for marine-related businesses and all facilities are available. One of the easiest places for the visiting sailor to spend money is in Capital Iron, a large store offering chandlery, hardware, fishing and camping equipment, and only a short walk from the downtown floats. Thrifty Foods, 475 Simcoe, is open seven days a week and delivers free to your boat. There is a chandlery at 60 Dallas Street. Don't miss the Maritime Museum.

Communications

From Victoria it is possible to travel to the mainland by conventional domestic flights or from the heart of the city by floatplane or by coach and ferry. By any of these you can connect with international flights in Vancouver or Seattle. The latter is sometimes more convenient and less expensive.

Harbourmaster
Tel: 363 3578

5 San Francisco, California, USA
37°48'N 122°38'W UT-8

Springs: 1.62m	Flag: USA	
Neaps: 0.61m	Currency: US dollar	
Charts	Admiralty	US
General	2530	18645
Approach	229	18649
Harbour	591	18650, 18653

General

San Francisco Bay is more than just a halfway house between the Juan de Fuca Strait and San Diego. It is a very fine bay in its own right and a rewarding place to spend a protracted stopover. It is far enough south for those heading for Mexico to feel that they are ahead of the autumnal gales off the Washington and Oregon shores, so that a few weeks relaxing around the bay is an attractive proposition. As a departure point for a Pacific crossing it is ideal, with the distance to, say, the Marquesas being barely any less from any of the alternatives further south and east. In contrast to the prevailing conditions offshore, there are regularly good sailing breezes inside the bay, thus making daysailing a pleasure and providing spectacular yacht racing – particularly during the Big Boat Series in the fall. The Sacramento river leads to the delta region with miles of navigable waterways, warm weather and swimming.

Approach and entry

San Francisco Bay is entered by passing under the spectacular Golden Gate Bridge. The pilotage is entirely straightforward and movements within the bay should follow well-marked channels with reference to the appropriate chart. Care should be taken not to obstruct commercial ship traffic and to anticipate the actions of racing classes so as to avoid interference. The clearances on the three major bridges vary between 70m (231ft) for the Golden Gate and 40m (132ft) for the Richmond to San Rafael Bridge, so there are few yachts that need be concerned!

Radio

All the authorities monitor channel 16 and will request a transfer to a working channel. The Coast Guard working frequency is channel 22A. San Francisco Marine Operators monitor channels 24, 86 and 87.

The Golden Gate Bridge. Photo Kitty van Hagen.

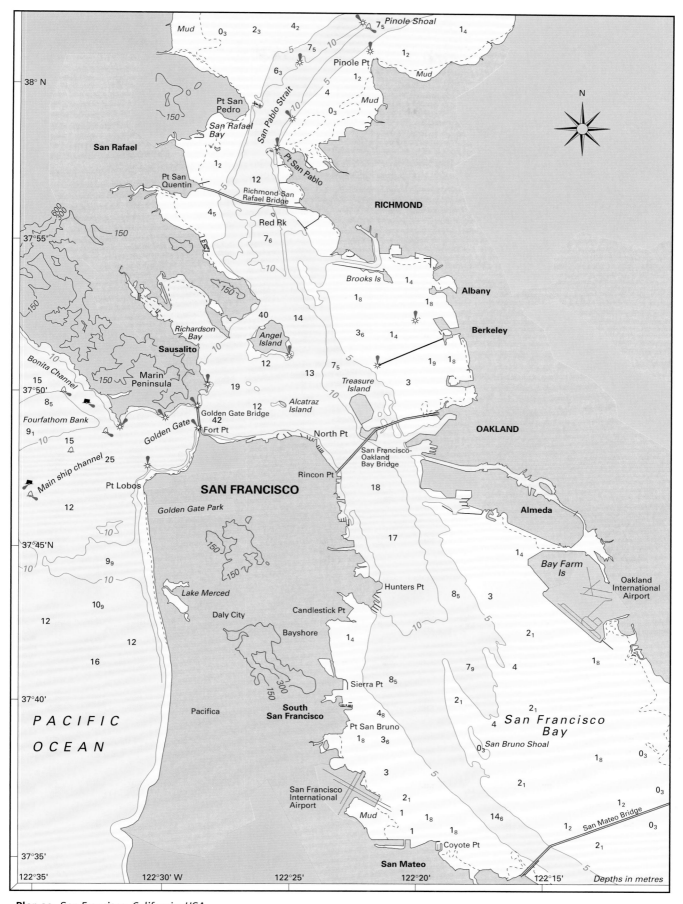

Plan 29 *San Francisco, California, USA.*

Anchorage and moorings

There are innumerable marinas within the bay, but rather fewer opportunities for anchoring. Most transient yachts seem to congregate at anchor in Richardson Bay off Sausalito, in particular off Schoonmaker Point, with a mud bottom – not always giving an absolutely reliable holding.

The best position is off the Horizons Restaurant immediately south of the ferry dock in Sausalito. At peak times the preferred area on the town side of the channel can be quite crowded. It is possible to anchor in the Aquatic Park by the Maritime Museum which is convenient for buses or cable cars into the city. You are, however, required to manoeuvre your boat only under sail and there are no facilities or dinghy security ashore beyond a beach landing.

There is also a fairly popular anchorage by Treasure Island, but it is a long bus ride from anywhere. Of the numerous marinas, the South Beach Marina just above the Bay Bridge on the starboard hand is perhaps the most convenient to the city and the coaches to the airport, and the Coyote Point Marina 13 miles above the Bay Bridge is one of the least expensive – and ideal if leaving the yacht and taking a rental car (from the airport) to travel inland. Coyote Point Marina is extremely noisy, being immediately below the approach flight path, which undoubtedly contributes to the low level of charges!

Formalities

San Francisco is a port of entry. A call to the US Coast Guard in the approach will obtain directions for a clearance berth if arriving from foreign parts. If arriving from another US port, a foreign-flag vessel should report by telephone on arrival. San Francisco is the centre for the Northern California Customs area, and one reporting should suffice from Crescent City in the north to Morro Bay in the south. Foreign yachts will need a cruising licence, if eligible. There is normally no difficulty except for certain nationals whose countries, such as Switzerland, have no reciprocal arrangements.

Facilities

This a major yachting centre with a high level of sophistication and all needs are catered for. For chandlery, West Marine in Sausalito will be hard to beat.

Communications

With direct flights in all directions, San Francisco is an ideal place for crew changes. There is a wide choice of locations where one may leave a yacht in order to travel inland, or fly home should that be necessary.

6 San Diego, California, USA

32°43'N 117°10'W UT-8

Springs: 1.79m	Flag: USA	
Neaps: 0.76m	Currency: US dollar	
Charts	Admiralty	US
General	2530	18765
Approach	3056	18772
Harbour	2885	18773

metropolis has a large US Navy presence, and until very recently was strongly dominated by the San Diego Yacht Club's grip of the America's Cup, which in 1995 did a Pacific crossing to New Zealand after a famous victory for the Kiwis. San Diego Bay is a major yachting centre – despite a significant lack of good wind and beds of kelp that are a hazard for the unwary. As a final stocking-up port it is superb, with every conceivable item freely available – from chandlery to Mexican visas and fishing licences.

General

San Diego is traditionally the last stop before leaving the USA, and all its civilised benefits, before crossing the border and heading south on to the relatively undeveloped Mexican coastline. This vast and throbbing

Approach and entry

If approaching from the west it is not worth cutting the corner round Point Loma as the kelp beds shown on the chart are much better avoided. Look for Nos 5 and 6 buoys and then follow the channel inwards. When No

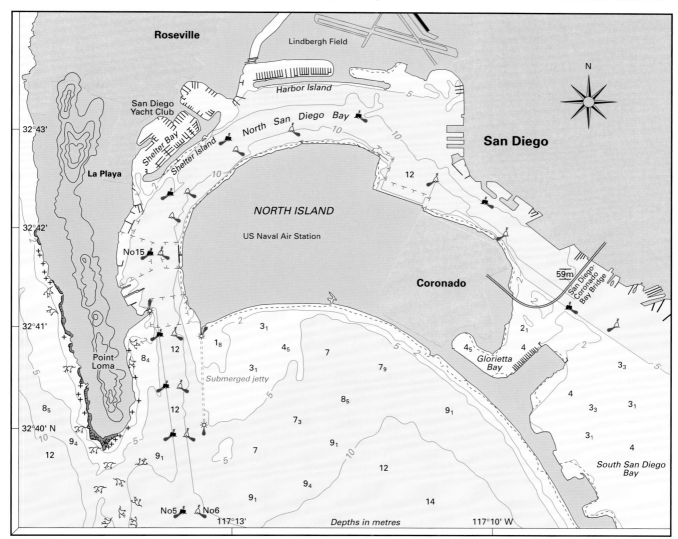

Plan 30 *San Diego, California, USA.*

15 has been passed to port, the entrance to Shelter Bay will be seen fine on the port bow. Overseas visiting yachts, whether entering from abroad or from within the USA, should go direct to the police dock on the south-west tip of Shelter Island.

Radio

All the authorities monitor channel 16 and will request a transfer to a working channel. The Coast Guard working frequency is channel 22A.

Anchorage and moorings

The bay inside Shelter Island is almost entirely ringed by yacht clubs and marinas. Guest berths are maintained at many of the clubs, and a reciprocal arrangement is a great advantage – but unlikely for a yacht whose home base is outside the Pacific. The Silvergate Yacht Club has been very welcoming to strangers in the past. Visitors can remain on the police dock for up to ten days at a very reasonable charge, or alternatively lie to an anchor in Glorietta Bay – which is quite pleasant and convenient for bus services into the city. It is also possible to anchor in a restricted area inside Shelter Island, but a police permit is required.

All anchoring facilities are subject to limitations on length of stay, normally 72 hours, and the harbour police have a policy of rigid law enforcement that is aimed at preventing visitors taking root. It is advisable to exhibit a black ball by day and a riding light at night, and to paint some official-looking number on your dinghy. If you are using an outboard on the dinghy after dark, red and green lights must be shown. You have been warned!

Formalities

All foreign-flag vessels must report immediately at the police dock on arrival irrespective of their last port. San Diego is a port of entry and, being the front line in the war against illegal drug imports, the authorities take their duties very seriously; therefore it is wise to recognise this and behave accordingly.

Facilities

The facilities in San Diego must be the major reason for visiting yachts to call. There are a number of excellent chandlers, at least one of which runs a courier service into Mexico, thereby bypassing the pilfering that is apparently rampant in the Mexican mail service. Arrangements can be made before leaving for goods to be charged to credit card accounts, and orders can be placed direct through SSB radio nets. There are a number of first-class yards with excellent haul-out facilities.

Downwind Marine Chandlery
Tel: 619 224 2733
Fax: 619 224 7683

Communications

San Diego has a major international airport with direct intercontinental flights. It would be an ideal crew change-over stop. Fax, telephone and internet access are as easy as you would expect them to be in a top-ranking modern city. If heading south it is as well to make the most of the opportunities, for the same can hardly be said for Ensenada, the first available stop south of the border.

7 Puerto Vallarta, Mexico
20°39'N 105°14'W UT-6

Springs: 0.8m	Flag: Mexico	
Neaps: 0.4m	Currency: Peso	
Charts	Admiralty	US
General	2323	21017
Approach		21338
Harbour		21338

Paradise Village Marina
Paseo Cocoteros 001
Nuevo Vallarta
Nayarit
Mexico CP 63731
Tel/fax: 52 322 66728
Tel: 52 322 66773
e-mail: marina@paradisevillage.com

Marina Vallarta
Tel: 52 322 1027
Fax: 52 322 1072

General

Puerto Vallarta, or PV as it is familiarly known, has been chosen for inclusion in this guide because it is a popular jumping-off point for those who, having spent the winter months in the Sea of Cortez, are taking off into the blue yonder at the start of a Pacific crossing. The passage to the Marquesas is 2650 miles, which can be broken by a stopover in the Revilla Gigedo Islands. PV is a vibrant resort town with, by Mexican standards, better than average supplies. The bus service is cheap; it is also a unique experience, with every driver attempting to gain maximum revs from unwilling machinery!

Approach and entry

The approach is straightforward once the features of the town have been properly identified. There is a lit transit on 053° that leads into the main basin off the Terminale Maritime.

Radio

Channel 22A in US mode, known in Mexico as the cruiser channel, will probably produce a more useful response than channel 16. The two marinas monitor channel 6.

Anchorage and moorings

There are two main marinas. Marina Vallarta is in the main harbour, but has now been superseded in popularity by Paradise Village Marina. This marina is situated in Nuevo Vallarta, a few miles up the coast from the town. It has excellent facilites and actively welcomes visitors, although it is wise to book in advance. It is still possible to anchor with a shore line from the stern on the port hand in the main harbour. Across the bay at Cruz de Huanacaxtla there is a pleasant, quiet (except for the Saturday disco) anchorage, which provides an alternative to the noise and dirt of the Terminale Maritime.

Formalities

Formalities in Mexico are still a nightmare, regardless of whether you are entering or leaving the country or just travelling from one port to another. The officials are quite courteous, but they have a set of rules and their procedures must be followed exactly. Immigration will supply you with a six-month visa. Customs will authorise temporary importation of the boat (to avoid import tax). Finally, the port captain will clear you in (at a cost of 140 pesos in 2000). On departure, all departments must be visited again and additional charges apply. Marina staff may offer to do the paperwork for you, but at an extra charge. Office hours are Monday to Friday 0830–1600 (be aware that the authorities keep to Jalisco time, an hour's difference from local PV time). New clearance rules were applied in January 2001 stating that you are supposed to clear in and out of any place that has a port captain (even anchorages off beaches where there is a village!).

Facilities

There are now several chandlers and a boatyard with a 35-ton travel lift. A fuel dock is planned at Paradise Village Marina. Closest fuel supplies are 5km (3 miles) away from the marina. Propane and kerosene are available. The marina organises a propane run every Wednesday. The facilities for topping up the yacht's stores in Puerto Vallarta are reasonably good on account of the resort trade that the town has attracted. Chandlery items can also be ordered from West Marine (www.portsupply.com). Local chandlers will import these items for you, with a surcharge of 10–20 per cent.

Communications

Local air services are constantly improving to serve the tourist trade, but all internal flights are expensive. Local

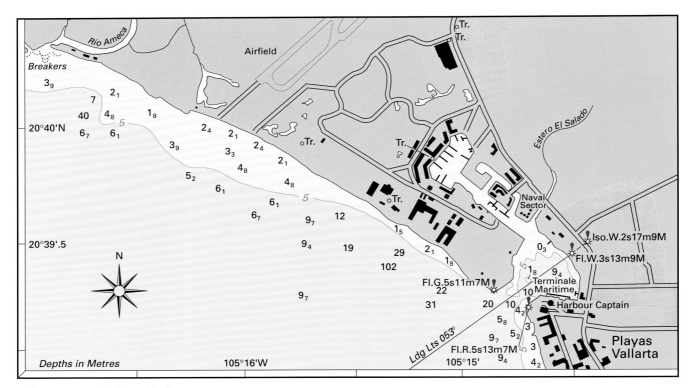

Plan 31 *Puerto Vallarta, Mexico.*

bus and coach services provide a cheap and reliable way of getting around, and car rental is possible. American Express or Paradise Village Marina are useful mail drops, but it is probably unwise to have any valuable packages sent through the Mexican mail service. It is safer to use Fedex or DHL. Mexican payphones are prohibitively expensive for all overseas calls. A cheaper option is to use

your credit card with a service such as Primus Telegroup (tel: 0500 789 800 from the UK, or 1-888 550 6072 from the USA, or e-mail: tgservice@primustel.co.uk). There are plenty of internet cafés in town. Local information may be obtained via the Cruiser's net on VHF channel 22 at 0830 Monday to Saturday.

8

Acapulco, Mexico

16°51'N 99°54'W UT-6

Springs: 0.9m	Flag: Mexico	
Neaps: 0.5m	Currency: Peso	
Charts	Admiralty	US
General	1051	21020
Approach	1944	21441
Harbour	1944	21441

General

Acapulco is a buzzing, lively city that has long been a tourist centre. It also has its own commercial and industrial life, and exploring the city for yacht necessities – or simply for pleasure – is a delight. It is a popular stopover for US and Canadian yachts, and for many it is their ultimate destination before either returning to the north or departing for a Pacific crossing. It is a good base for taking a side trip inland. Visits to Taxco and Oaxaca are easily arranged. The main Mayan sites are situated in the south and east of Mexico and involve travelling first to Mexico City. The Copper Canyon in the north-east is well worth a detour and the train trip from Los Mochis to Creel is spectacular – and worthwhile for the journey alone.

Approach and entry

Acapulco is unmistakable from seaward on account of the prominent high-rise development. Together with the rocky coastline immediately to the north and south, it is the only interruption of the endless sands that stretch for over 160km (100 miles) from Papanoa to Punta de Acanama. Roqueta Island lies off the western headland

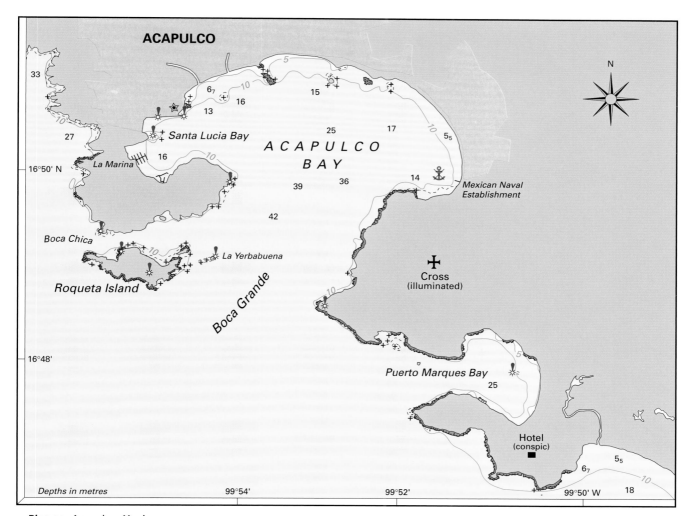

Plan 32 *Acapulco, Mexico.*

and the inshore passage, Boca Chica, appears to be a clear and useful short cut to the Boca Grande and Acapulco Bay. However, there is considerable small craft and ferry traffic, and the best advice is to take the offshore route and enter the Boca Grande well clear of foul ground off La Yerbabuena. Yacht facilities are in the western part of the bay, and easily found to the left of the commercial facilities that occupy the central area.

Radio

La Marina will respond on channel 16.

Anchorage and moorings

The main facility for yachts is La Marina, which has 296 berths and dry storage for 150 yachts, as well as a wide range of marina facilities. La Marina has a beautiful swimming pool on the roof of the single-storey building, complete with sun loungers, palm trees, fountains and a poolside bar. The location is easily identified by the lighthouse-style tower. The Yacht Club (almost next door) will accommodate visiting yachts if it has room. There are also moorings to rent, or you can drop an anchor clear of the moorings in a little over 10m (33ft). Anchoring is prohibited on the east side of the bay where there is a Mexican naval establishment.

El Club de Yates de Acapulco
Gran Via Tropical y Tambuco
Acapulco
México 39390
Tel: 52 74 82 3859

Formalities

Clearance procedures in Acapulco, in line with other Mexican ports, are not very easy. However, if the yacht is in La Marina then the staff will see to the whole business for a fee. Otherwise, the procedure is long-winded, with the authorities some distance apart across the town.

Facilities

You can find almost anything you need in Acapulco, with the exception of chandlery items. The extensive market areas are a delight.

Communications

Air services are constantly improving to serve the tourist trade. Local buses are cheap and frequent: a journey downtown takes about 15 minutes. Taxis are cheap and plentiful. Mail can be addressed c/o Marina Acapulco, Costera Miguel Alemán 215, Fracc, Las Playas CP 39390, Acapulco, Gro, Mexico, but it is probably unwise to have any valuable packages sent through the Mexican mail service.

9 Panama Canal

9°N 79'W UT-5

Flag: Panama	Currency: US dollar	
Charts	Admiralty	US
General	396	26060
Approaches	1400/1401	26066/21603
Transit	1299	21604

General

A transit of the Panama Canal should be a memorable experience and, barring accidents, a very enjoyable one. However, it is difficult to be quite so enthusiastic about the preliminaries in either Colon or Balboa. There is a distinctly tedious bureaucratic paper chase to be endured in crime-ridden surroundings and persistent heat. Once this has been completed and the necessary extra crew enlisted, there is far less horror to the passage through the Canal than is widely believed.

From the Atlantic side, vessels rise through the three stages of the Gatun Locks to the manmade Gatun Lake, 26m (86ft) above sea level. The axis of the Canal is from the north-west to the south-east so that you emerge into the Pacific at a lesser longitude than you left the Caribbean. The descent to the Pacific starts with the single Pedro Miguel Lock and a mile further on the two-stage Miraflores Lock completes the transit.

For some years now the arrangements have been that yachts leaving the Atlantic take two days to complete the transit, and those leaving the Pacific go through in one day. However, currently, about half the yachts travelling to the Pacific now transit in one day. The overnight stop is spent lying to an anchor off the mouth of the Gamboa River. Line handlers and the pilot go ashore and return in the morning.

It is essential to have adequate power to maintain at least 5 knots and four 38m (125ft) strong warps are mandatory. There must be four able-bodied persons on board, who act as line handlers in addition to the helmsman and the Canal adviser. There is a tradition of mutual aid between crews to solve this problem, the return overland journey being reasonably easy. It may be wise to include at least one professional line handler (at $55 per handler). These are arranged by the taxi drivers at Panama Canal Yacht Club. Have sealed bottled water on board for the pilot to prevent extra charges for delivery by launch.

Before your transit, it is worth visiting the viewing gallery at Gatun, to watch the big ships locking

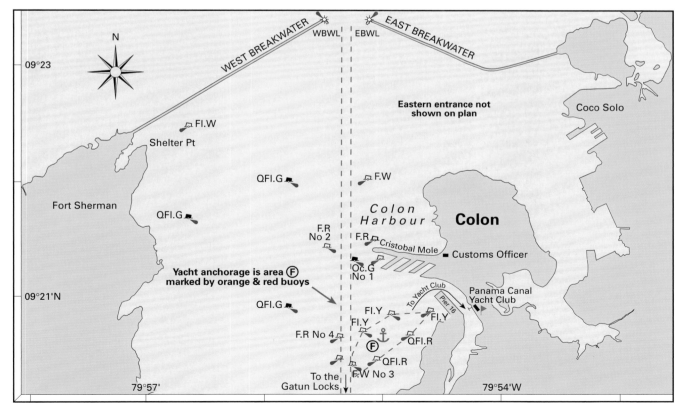

Plan 33 *Panama Canal, Colon, Atlantic approach.*

Yachts in a raft of three moving together between stages of the Gatun Locks. Photo Bill Perkes.

facilities. At Balboa there is no option but to pick up a club buoy off the site of the former Balboa Yacht Club building (Balboa Yacht Club still operate from a temporary office on their pier). A club launch may guide you in. On the other hand, if the transit is completed early in the day, there is no need to remain in Balboa, when it is possible to continue to a quite pleasant anchorage off the island of Taboga. From there it is still possible to spend a day in Panama City by using the ferry. With the appropriate consent it is possible to break your transit at the Pedro Miguel Yacht Club just below the lock where a haul-out can be arranged; and a number of crews have used the facilities to complete a mini refit before tackling the Pacific.

through. Particularly in Colon, it is considered decidedly unwise to go anywhere on foot, and taxis are cheap and plentiful.

Approach and entry

From the Caribbean you enter Colon Harbour, preferably via the eastern entrance (not shown on plan), having first received clearance to do so on VHF channel 12. The fairway up the harbour lies true north and south, and once you are past the Cristobal Mole and No 1 buoy to port, then anchorage area 'F', to which one will most likely have been directed, is less than 1 mile ahead on the port bow. The designated anchorage areas are clearly shown on the large-scale chart. To move in to the yacht club leave Pier 16 to starboard, and the club is on the port hand a short distance up the channel. When approaching Balboa from the Pacific, yachts are advised to stay clear to the north-east of the ship channel until they reach No 14 buoy, and then pass No 14½ and No 16 close to starboard before turning to starboard into the recommended anchorage off the former Balboa Yacht Club building (destroyed by fire in 1999).

Radio

Call Cristobal Signal on channel 12 in the approach for clearance to enter.

Anchorage and moorings

At Colon there is a choice between lying at anchor on the flats, area 'F', which is cooler but a long dinghy trip to the club, which is the only viable landing place, or moving to the club marina. The latter is infinitely more convenient and more convivial, with very welcome

Formalities

On 1 January 2000, responsibility for the Panama Canal reverted back to the Panamanians. The former Panama Canal Commission is now known as the ACP (Panama Canal Administration). Immigration paperwork is completed in the Panama Canal Yacht Club. Then enlist the help of an English-speaking taxi driver to take the captain to visit Customs and the port authority. All other crew members remain on board. The continuing paperwork includes (depending on nationality) the purchase of a tourist card, and a visa. The port authorities will issue a mandatory cruising permit, costing $69 for three months, whether you transit the Canal or not. If you do not intend to stop in Balboa, outward clearance can also be accomplished in Colon. All formalities may be handled by the taxi driver, for a fee, which may be worthwhile to speed up the process. Seek recommendations from another yacht first.

Preparations for transit require a further set of procedures. The boat must be inspected by the Admeasures Office. Call the scheduler (telephone number at club office). An admeasurer will then come out to the boat. Fees charged relate to LOA. The minimum fee in 2003 was $600 for boats up to 15m (50ft). A deposit of $850 must also be paid (which should be refunded in six weeks). All fees can be paid by credit card. They are no longer paid direct to the Panama Canal Commission at their offices but are now collected only at Citibank in Cristobal (or Balboa) before 1400. Then ring the scheduler after 1800 to obtain your transit day and time. Those who want to visit Pedro

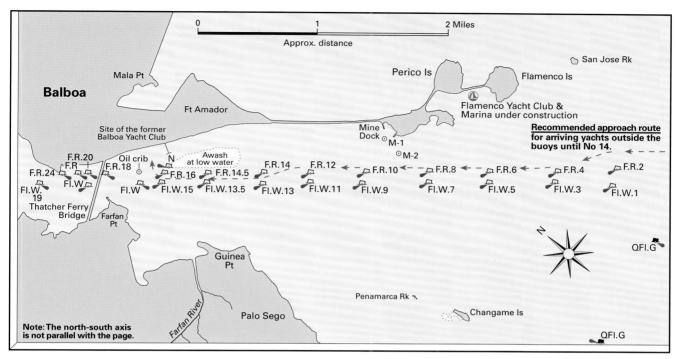

Plan 33 *Panama Canal, Balboa, Pacific approach.*

Miguel Yacht Club mid-transit must inform the authorities when making initial arrangements.

The transit of the Canal

Yachts usually transit the Canal with other shipping, and the lock chambers are shared. A yacht will usually transit centre chamber – either alone or rafted to one or two other yachts. Sometimes it is also possible to travel down alongside a tug. The admeasurer will ask for your preference, but a final decision will be made by the authorities on the day. Sharing the lock increases the problems of turbulence when the ship ahead begins to move and, if moored centre lock, places great strains on warps and cleats. Be warned that if you are rafted with other yachts, it is a failure on the other side of the raft that puts your own topsides at greatest risk. The best position is in the middle! If formed up as a raft, a skippers' union is worth forming to help ensure that manoeuvres are agreed by all. At the same time it is vital to check water pump impellers and alternator belts before the day of the transit to ensure that the engine will not object to a long period of sustained effort. Fees for breaking down while transiting can run into thousands of dollars.

Facilities

Haul-out is possible in Colon, but the facilities at Pedro Miguel and Balboa are better. The Pedro Miguel Yacht Club is situated on Miraflores Lake between the two sets of locks leading down to the Pacific Ocean. Although a visit to the yacht club means a diversion mid-transit, it is a very welcoming place, with electricity, water, laundry and showering facilities, as well as haul-out capabilities. Mail can be sent to all three yacht clubs. Flamenco Yacht Club and Marina are under construction (see plan). Buoys are already in position and are very popular. It is expected that a wide range of facilities and services will be available on completion.

Communications

Panama City is well served by international flights. Crew changing is easily organised here.

Panama Canal Yacht Club
Box 5041 Cristobal
Colon
Tel: 507 441 5882
Fax: 507 441 7752

Pedro Miguel Yacht Club
Tel: 507 232 4148/4509

Balboa Yacht Club
Tel: 507 228 5794

Flamenco Marina
Tel: 507 314 0665

10

Wreck Bay, Puerto Baquerizo Moreno, Isla San Cristobal, Galapagos Islands
0°54'S 89°37'W UT-6

Springs: 1.8m	Flag: Ecuador	
Neaps: 1.0m	Currency: US dollar	
Charts	Admiralty	US
General	1375	22000
Approach	1375	22521
Harbour	1375	

General

In recent years, the Ecuadorian central authorities have restricted visiting yachts to a single location for a few days at most. The accompanying charges have also been high. However, these rules have now been relaxed, so that a stay of 20 days is possible (as of 2001). Yachts may also transit between Isla San Cristobal (Wreck Bay) and Santa Cruz (Academy Bay), and are able to visit Puerto Villamil on Isabela – all without a cruising permit. However, permission and clearance for such transits must be obtained from the port captains in either Puerto Ayora or Puerto Baquerizo Moreno. Failure to observe these rules may result in a heavy fine or the impounding of one's yacht. Yachts may not cruise independently among the islands without a cruising permit. These permits are heavily restricted and may only be obtained at great expense in money, time and effort. It would be best to use a local agent for this purpose.

Wreck Bay is the less active centre of organised tourism, and as such has a certain simple charm. Sea lions are to be seen sprawled out in the sun on the decks of the local fishing fleet, and within walking distance of the anchorage there are pools where it is possible to swim with them; marine iguanas are easy to find among the rocks.

Approach and entry

If arriving from Panama, your landfall will most likely be on the south coast of Isla San Cristobal. Rounding the south-west tip of the island is the shortest approach to Wreck Bay, which is easily identified from seaward – there being no other comparable settlement on the island. Care should be taken to avoid the Arrecife Schiavoni. Approaching from the west it is possible to pass inside. Otherwise, approach from the north in deep water and follow a bearing of 155°T towards the piers at the head of the bay.

Radio

Channel 16 is monitored, but replies will only be given in Spanish.

Anchorage and moorings

Visiting yachts anchor off the beach to the west of the local boats on moorings. The naval headquarters occupy a prominent position on the same side of the bay and will probably send a boat out as soon as the anchor is down. The most convenient landing is on the beach and the dinghy is very likely to be escorted in by some fascinating rays. It is best not to leave anything loose in the dinghy, such as snorkelling gear; there have been reports of disappearances.

Formalities

At Wreck Bay you can expect the port captain to board the yacht on arrival, but it is necessary to visit Immigration ashore. In 2001, there was an anchoring cost of $1 per tonne per day and a single payment for 'lights and buoys' and immigration. Cruising permits are difficult to obtain (see 'General' section), but essential for cruising further afield in your own boat. There is a National Park charge of $100 per person, but reports vary as to whether it is always collected. The port captain and other officers, who are all navy personnel, are courteous and friendly – but usually speak limited English.

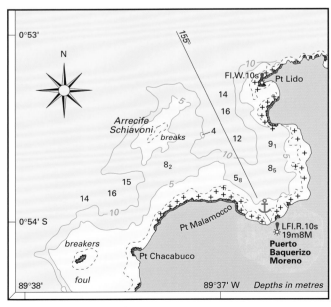

Plan 35 *Wreck Bay, Galapagos.*

Sea lions sun themselves on a convenient deck in Wreck Bay. They often take up residence in yacht tenders. Photo Michael Pocock.

Facilities

Diesel is available at the petrol station, a short taxi ride out of town. It can also be brought out to the boat. Gustavo from Rosita's Restaurant may visit your boat on arrival and offer to deliver diesel, arrange tours, help with repairs, etc. Gas is not available. Drinking water is available but does not have a good reputation, and is best kept separate from the rest of the yacht's supply. There are several laundrettes in town, which offer good, reasonable service washes. A range of staple fruit and vegetables are available when the supply ship arrives. The Panaderia sells good bread rolls; and flour, rice and pasta are available in the small grocery shops. However, Panama is the place to stock up with these items in advance. Ice blocks are sold in some waterfront shops.

Communications

There are ferry and local air services to Isla Santa Cruz and connections to Quito. The post office will hold mail addressed 'General Delivery', but it is not recommended as a mail drop. There may also be long delays for outgoing mail. There is a DHL courier office on the main street. However, import duty is 40 per cent and 'Yacht in Transit' is not recognised. There is an internet café off the main street and the local telephone company offers reasonable phone rates. The Panama Net operates on 8107 MHz at 1330 UT.

11

Academy Bay, Puerto Ayora, Isla Santa Cruz, Galapagos Islands

0°45'S 90°18'W UT-6

Springs: 1.8m	Flag: Ecuador	
Neaps: 1.0m	Currency: US dollar	
Charts	Admiralty	US
General	1375	22000
Approach	1375	22528
Harbour	1375	

General

For 'General' and 'Formalities' details, which are similar to those for both Wreck Bay and Academy Bay, please see the relevant paragraphs in the Wreck Bay entry. Both Puerto Ayora and Puerto Baquerizo Moreno are the official ports of entry for the Galapagos Islands. Although Puerto Baquerizo Moreno is the administrative capital of the Galapagos, Puerto Ayora is the established centre for tourism in the islands. It is therefore much better served with facilities, although the bay suffers from serious crowding at times from large numbers of small cruise boats and visiting yachts.

Since the collapse of the Ecuadorian economy in 1998, costs for passages on local cruise boats have fallen markedly (approximately $75–85 per person per day in 2001 for a modest vessel). A number of agencies in Academy Bay will arrange cruises. Berths on the top-quality cruise vessels attract a premium and may require booking with travel agents in one's home country.

Approach and entry

Sailing among the Galapagos Islands during the hours of darkness is made much easier if the yacht is equipped with radar. On GPS alone, considerable latitude for the accuracy of the chart must be given. On the other hand, intelligently used GPS will help to solve the riddle of the currents, which are far from predictable. To many sailors the only solution is to motor in (from a position well offshore), and out of Academy Bay in daylight. For those who persevere, the marine and bird life to be seen while sailing quietly past the islands can be fascinating. Academy Bay itself is easily negotiated in daylight.

Radio

Channel 16 is monitored, but will only reply in Spanish.

One of the giant tortoises, measuring over 4ft in length, involved in the breeding programme at the Darwin Research Station. Photo Andrew Hogbin.

Anchorage and moorings

Yachts anchor off the town and land at steps on the stone quay. The anchorage is subject to some swell and generally little wind, and a stern anchor is essential when it becomes crowded. The bottom is hard in places, and anchors need to be set with care.

Formalities

At Academy Bay, the port captain has an office close to the main dock and dinghy landing. Skippers must present themselves at his office and pay the port fees. A second call has to be made at the Police for Immigration formalities. The port captain has ultimate authority over the anchorage and represents the Ecuadorian Navy, who maintain patrols throughout the islands and may arrest any yachts undertaking illegal passages or anchoring without permission.

Facilities

Engineering and technical facilities are extremely limited. None the less, it is possible to obtain *ad hoc* support in the event of both mechanical and electrical problems. Fuel can be obtained from the local garage (a taxi ride) or via a local agent, who will 'guarantee' good quality. Gas is not available. Water can be bought ashore or delivered through an agent direct to the boat. However, it may be of poor quality and should be kept separate from the rest of the yacht's supply. Very limited chandlery items are available. Provisioning is also fairly basic, from the mini market, or the few small shops and a very small local fresh produce market. Practically everything has to be brought in from the mainland from a supply vessel and prices are not the cheapest. It is best to stock up with major non-perishable items in Panama.

It is difficult to receive spares without the help of a local yacht agent. In 2001, a reliable agent was Ricardo

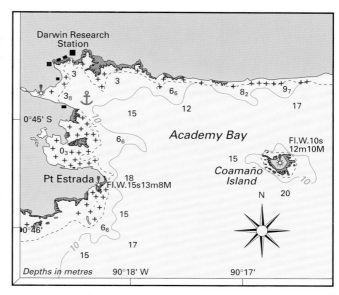

Plan 36 *Academy Bay, Galapagos.*

Arenas of 'Servigalapagos', e-mail: pelicanb@pa.ga.pro.ec, website: www.servigalapagos.com.ec. If required, he would also help with arranging for fuel and water, and for local tourism.

Communications

Phone calls can be made from Puerto Ayora and there is an internet café. Flights go to and from the mainland each day. Puerto Ayora is served by a bus service to the airport at Baltra. From here, flights go to Guayaquil and Quito for international connections. Crew changing is, therefore, relatively easy. Mail drops are not recommended, unless very urgent. 'Servigalapagos' may be a possibility. Courier and spares delivery can be unreliable, with delays in Quito. Even when using an agent, patience is required!

12

Atuona, Hiva Oa, Marquesas, French Polynesia

09°48'S 139°02'W UT-9¹/₂

Springs: 1.1m	Flag: France	
Neaps: 0.8m	Currency: Pacific francs (CFP)	
Charts	Admiralty	US
General	4607	83020
Approach	1640	83218
Harbour	1640	83218

General

Atuona is the nearest port of entry when arriving from the Galapagos Islands and is, at the same time, almost at the windward extremity of the Marquesan group of islands. Only little Fatu Hiva is further upwind. As an entry port, it is therefore well situated. It is not, however, an ideal bay for a long period of rest as there is a constant risk of an uncomfortable swell sweeping in. If

you have arrived from Panama or Mexico, the relatively laid-back attitude of the *Gendarme* in charge will be a very welcome contrast to the bureaucracy that you have left behind. Water is not in short supply, and fruit should be available – although it may be a trifle difficult to find except via the generosity of a local landowner. Paul Gauguin's final resting place is beneath a frangipani tree in the small graveyard above the anchorage; Jacques Brel is buried close by. A visit to the museum, which includes Gauguin's original 'House of Pleasure', is recommended.

Approach and entry

Atuona lies on the south side of the island of Hiva Oa. There is no particular difficulty either finding or entering the anchorage, which is in the northern corner of the Taaoa Bay. There is a breakwater on the starboard hand and a small commercial quay beyond it. If arriving from a foreign port there is no need to go alongside; anchor opposite the quay and seek clearance at the *Gendarmerie* in the village, three-quarters of a mile around the bay.

Radio

There has not been any requirement to call on the radio on arrival in the past, and it is unlikely that even channel 16 is being monitored unless a ship is expected.

Anchorage and moorings

Yachts generally anchor across the bay from the quay, behind the transit formed by the yellow and black posts on the east side of the bay. They usually lay their main anchor to seaward and a kedge out aft to hold the bows to the swell. In moderate swell conditions this will make for quite acceptable comfort, but if the swell becomes more severe then you might as well go out to windward and visit Baie Hanamoenoa on Tahuata. It is possible to land at a pier on the east side of the bay where a water tap and beach shower will also be found. The use of a stern anchor for the dinghy is strongly recommended. Alternatively one can land at the head of the breakwater that forms the commercial harbour.

Formalities

EU passport holders will be granted a three-month visa for French Polynesia which can be extended to six months on request; no bond is required. At present, non-EU passport holders are only granted a one-month visa which will only be extended under special conditions. A

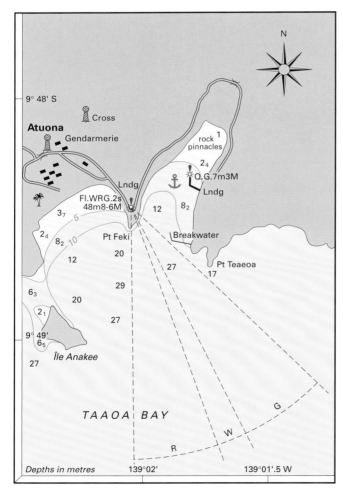

Plan 37 *Atuona, Marquesas.*

The approach to Atuona. Photo Andrew Hogbin.

bond *is* required, equivalent to the price of an air ticket to the country on one's passport.

Facilities

The town of Atuona is the administrative centre for the Southern Marquesas. It boasts a population of 1500 and has a radio station, post office, hospital, hotels and restaurants. The supermarket in the middle of the town sells a limited range of products, with fresh produce sometimes available from a van that parks opposite. The fuel garage in the harbour also has limited provisions. This is the best place in the Marquesas to fill up with fuel and water, using jerry cans. In 2002 diesel prices were approximately US\$1/litre. Duty-free fuel is available with clearance papers from French Polynesia. Gas must be obtained from Nuku Hiva or Papeete.

Communications

There are small inter-island aircraft and flights to Papeete, where connections can be made with international routes. Telephone and fax are available in the village, but it is not possible to make transfer charge calls to a number of countries, including the UK.

13

Taiohae Bay, Nuku Hiva, Marquesas, French Polynesia

08°56'S 140°05'W UT-9½

Springs: 1.1m	Flag: France	
Neaps: 0.8m	Currency: Pacific francs (CFP)	
Charts	Admiralty	US
General	4607	83020
Approach	1640	83207
Harbour	1640	83207

General

Taiohae Bay is often simply known by the island name Nuku Hiva, which is the most important administrative centre in the Marquesas Islands. The bay is big and well sheltered from the prevailing winds and also, in most ordinary conditions, reasonably free from swell. It is, undoubtedly, the most popular gathering place for passing yachts in the whole group. If entering in Nuku Hiva you are unfortunately at the leeward end of the chain, so this is not a good starting point for exploring the rest of the group. There are, however, a number of other attractive bays around the island that are well worth visiting. A visit to Rose Corser's museum and gallery on the west side of the harbour is recommended. Those who have read Herman Melville's *Typee* will certainly want to anchor in Baie du Controlleur and hike up the valley looking for the tikis. The bay is three fingered and you should choose the middle one, Anse Hangaa Haa. It is best to seek directions from a local if you wish to find the tikis in order to avoid walking a lot further than necessary. The cathedral, which houses carvings that were commissioned from the best carver from each island in 1975, is well worth a visit.

Approach and entry

Taiohae Bay is in the middle of the south coast of Nuku Hiva; the entrance is open and clear and presents no problems. There is a sectored directional light at the head of the bay. The white sector leads into the bay. How easily this light is identifiable against the lights of the village is difficult to say.

Taiohae Bay on Nuku Hiva is one of the main gathering places for yachts in the Marquesas Islands. Photo Michael Pocock.

Radio

Shore radio has not normally been manned.

Anchorage and moorings

It is possible to go alongside the quay for short periods if there is no commercial vessel expected, but for anything over an hour the only option is to anchor in the bay. Anywhere to the west of the town clear of the quay approach (and about 200m off the beach) is suitable, and visiting yachts become quite widely spread.

Formalities

All administration in connection with arriving yachts is dealt with by the *Gendarmerie* opposite the post office up the hill to the right, a very short distance from the quay. See Atuona on page 126 for details.

Facilities

Taiohae is the economic and administrative centre for the Marquesas, with a population of 1800. It has a bank, post office, hospital, hotels and restaurants. The three supermarkets along the waterfront sell similar products, but Maurice Store also has a range of fresh produce. Fresh produce can also be purchased at the Saturday market, which starts at 0430 – it pays to get there on time! Water is available at the public quay on the east side of the harbour, but should not be used as drinking water as it is contaminated. Clean drinking water can be obtained from Baie de Taioa (Daniel's Bay). Daniel and his wife were recently moved out of the bay, and his house and restaurant flattened to make way for a television programme. The bay is now occupied by Jean Louis, a relation. Fuel is available from the commercial dock on the east side of the bay. Gas refills are available from the hardware store up the hill. A laundry service and internet facilities are available from Stephanie at Yacht Services on the public quay. She stands by on VHF channel 67.

Communications

There are small inter-island aircraft and flights to Papeete, where connections can be made with interna-

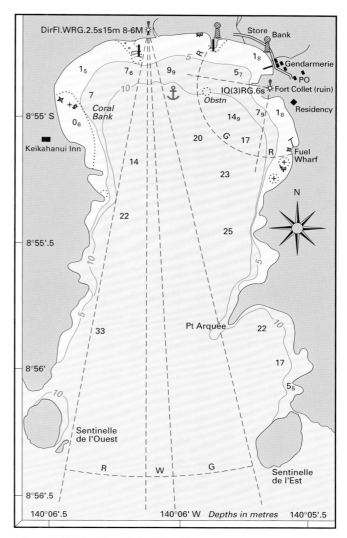

Plan 38 *Taiohae Bay, Nuku Hiva, Marquesas.*

tional routes. Telephone and fax are available in the village, but it is not possible to make transfer charge calls to a number of countries, including the UK. It is worth noting that in all French islands mail that has been held for 14 days is automatically returned to the sender. The best alternative is to have it sent c/o Keikahanui Inn, run by Rose Corser, which is once more a popular meeting place for yacht crews.

14

Papeete, Tahiti, Society Islands, French Polynesia

17°32'S 149°34'W UT-10

Springs: 0.2m	Flag: France	
Neaps: 0.1m	Currency: Pacific francs (CFP)	
Charts	Admiralty	US
General	4657	83021
Approach	1382	83382
Harbour	1436	83385

General

Papeete is the bustling, vibrant, noisy, administrative capital of French Polynesia. By Pacific standards it is a humming metropolis. This is a fascinating city, and for a short time can be very entertaining. Papeete is a major stopover for trans-Pacific air routes, particularly for Air France. This gives the city a very important status in the mid-Pacific and makes it the focal point for the whole of French Polynesia. Most needs can be met, but inevitably at a price.

Approach and entry

Papeete is a busy commercial port and visiting yachts must be alert to the movement of ships. Port control should be called on VHF channel 12 before entering the Passe de Papeete. As you pass the commercial docks the city waterfront will open up on the port bow. The Paofai Temple, a conspicuous Protestant church, is almost

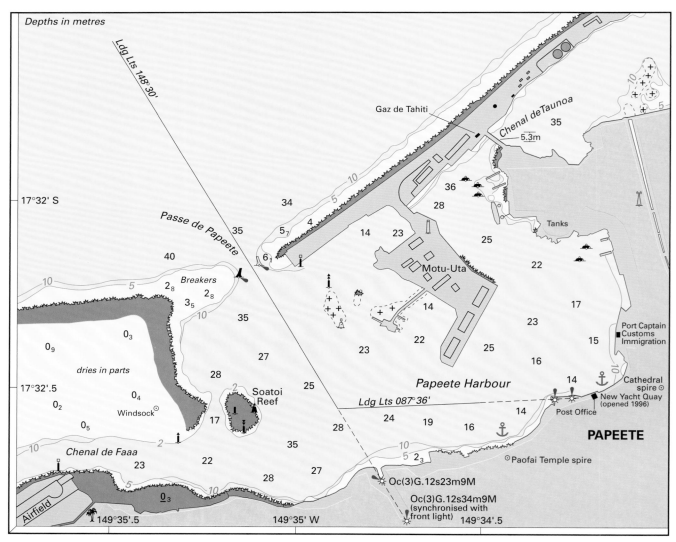

Plan 39 *Papeete, Tahiti, Society Islands.*

Weekend racing off the shores of Papeete is keenly contested in these outrigger canoes. Photo Michael Pocock.

opposite the pass, and marks the centre of the 'low rent district' for anchoring with a long stern line to the beach. The alternative, with permission from harbour control, is to go to the well-appointed Quai des Yachts (opened in 1996) closer to the centre of town, where for a higher charge you can moor Mediterranean-style. The Quai is usually very busy.

Radio

As stated above, port control operate on VHF channel 12. Mahina Coast Radio Station monitors channel 16.

Anchorage and moorings

Within the main harbour, the two alternatives mentioned above are the only options. It is as well to lay out your anchor or anchors with some care as there may be quite strong cross-winds blowing along the shore that can cause havoc, particularly off the Paofai Temple. It is possible to anchor near the Beachcomber Hotel, or use Marina Taina, the small marina close to Maeva Beach, which is situated to the east and south beyond the air-port. Space may be tight here. Remember to ask for clearance on channel 12 before crossing the ends of the runway. 'Le truck' provides a novel way of travelling into Papeete. The Yacht Club de Tahiti is a pleasant club with excellent berths, and if space is available this is a most secure facility. To reach the club it is necessary to leave the port by the Passe de Papeete and re-enter the lagoon about 2 miles westward. All the necessary information about the port of Tahiti is contained in their excellent 'Guide for Yachtsmen', which is given out on arrival.

Formalities

As mentioned in the 'Formalities' section for Atuona, page 126, EU citizens no longer have to pay the bond. However, non-EU passport holders do still have to pay it. In this case, if you have arrived in Papeete from the Marquesas or the Tuamotus and have not yet paid the bond, then crunch time has now come. The bond, or *caution*, must be paid – equivalent to the price of an air fare to the country of origin listed in your passport. The bond must be paid into a bank, which will incidentally make a charge for looking after it, and it will be returned at the port of departure in whatever currency it was deposited. If it is intended to clear out in Bora Bora, then it is recommended that the bond is paid at the Westpac Bank (near the cathedral), which will handle the transaction in US$ without converting to Pacific francs. Enquiries or requests for visa extensions (currently three months for EU citizens and one month for non-EU citizens) should be addressed to:

Direction de la Reglementation et du Controle de la
  Legalité
Avenue Bruat,
BP 115
Papeete 98713
Tahiti
Polynesie Française

Traditional Tahitian dancing events, complete with spectacular costumes, are not to be missed. Photo Ros Hogbin.

Facilities

Haul-out facilities are available at Fare Ute in the industrial area and services include rigging, sailmaking, refrigeration, engine and electrical repairs. Only limited chandlery items are held in stock, but with such good air connections (Air New Zealand, Air France and local airlines to adjacent island groups) Papeete is a good place to receive parts from your home base. Water and electricity are available on the quay, and there is water on the beach for those anchored stern-to, further out from the town. However, experience has shown that after periods of heavy rain the water can be suspect and care should be taken when choosing a time to fill the tanks. Propane (and, for once, butane) can be obtained at Gaz de Tahiti. By far the easiest answer is to take smaller bottles in the dinghy. The depot is close to the low bridge that crosses the lagoon to the outer docks. Fuel can be bought at Marina Taina, where credit cards are accepted. It will be supplied duty free, if you collect it on leaving Papeete port and have obtained your paperwork from the Customs Office first. For large quantities of diesel fuel, contact Mobil, Total or Shell. If leaving Papeete, you can then exit by way of Taapuna Pass providing there is not a heavy swell running. Provisioning is excellent but expensive. There are two large supermarkets, and a very good market for fresh produce. Croissants and baguettes are available only a short walk from the Quai des Yachts! There are good telecoms facilities in Papeete and internet cafés are available. DHL, TNT and Fedex couriers are represented at the airport.

Communications

Papeete is an ideal crew changing port with very good air connections, but it must be remembered than anyone flying in on a one-way ticket will have to be covered by an additional bond; conversely, those leaving can show their tickets as an alternative. Rather than the post office, mail can be sent to the port captain:

c/o La Capitainerie
Quai des Yachts
Papeete
Tahiti
Polynesie Française

Port captain
Tel: 50 54 62
Fax: 42 19 50
This system allows yachtsmen to search through the mail for themselves, and anything that arrives after you have left can be picked up and brought on by a friend, always assuming that they will eventually catch up! An alternative is the yacht club:

c/o Yacht Club de Tahiti
BP1456,
Papeete
Tahiti
Polynesie Française

15 Opunohu/Cook's Bay, Moorea, Society Islands, French Polynesia

17°32'S 149°50'W UT-10

Springs: 0.2m	Flag: France	
Neaps: 0.1m	Currency: Pacific francs (CFP)	
Charts	Admiralty	US
General	4657	83021
Approach	1382	83382
Harbour	1436	83383

General

The island of Moorea is an exotic paradise, but can hardly be described as undiscovered. Literally on the doorstep of Tahiti, Moorea is a travel agent's dream. For all that, the invasion does not inflict itself that much on the anchorages and there is much to be enjoyed while conveniently placed just a short sail, or easy ferry ride, from Papeete. For many, Moorea provides the first island on their passage across the Pacific that has high dramatic scenery and a fringing reef. In the lagoons, particularly on the east side, there is crystal-clear water for snorkelling among the exotic fish. In the two great bays, favourites of Captain Cook, there are sheltered, secure anchorages. There is a fine walk from either Opunohu Bay or Cook's Bay up to the Belvedere viewpoint in the hills behind. You can walk up from one bay and down to the other and close the triangle along the shore.

Approach and entry

The two great bays are both on the north coast and have leading marks. Cook's Bay is lit with a sectored light, whereas Opunohu Bay is not. The outside of the reef is steep to and the bottom can generally be seen, even in 35m (116ft). The passes on the south-east and south-west sides of the island, which are little used by visiting yachts, are not particularly difficult, given an accurate chart and a good pair of eyes in the bows reading the colour of the water. It is possible to thread your way along inside the reef from Passe Vaiare to Point Tipae and again to enter Passe Matauvau and creep through a passage, deep enough for 2.2m (7ft) draught all the way to Baie Vaiaoahe. These are relatively unfrequented waters with marvellous swimming and a cooling breeze blowing in over the protecting reef. In certain winds the passes may become more exciting to enter, although they are not thought to become impassable except in extreme conditions. The north-west tip is rather dominated by the Club Méditerranée and is probably best avoided. For the gregarious, Opunohu Bay and Cook's Bay are the gathering places, easy to enter and very sheltered.

View from the mountains of Moorea, showing a pass through the coral reef and Tahiti in the distance. Photo Andrew Hogbin.

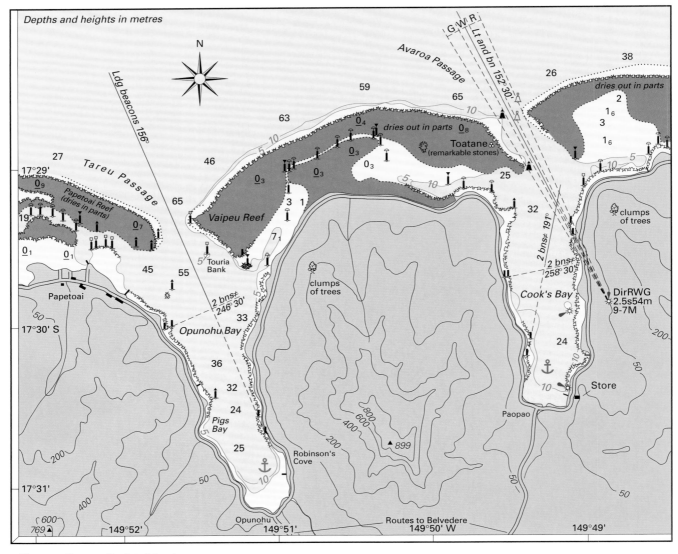

Plan 40 *Moorea, Society Islands.*

Radio

There is no separate radio coverage for Moorea.

Anchorage and moorings

In the reef lagoons it is possible to anchor almost wherever there is a convenient patch of sand. On the windward side, although the yacht may lie in flat water, the exposure to the tradewinds places a premium on holding power and it is as well to set the anchor carefully. In the two great bays the choice of position is dictated by depth. In both cases the soundings do not drop below 20m (66ft) until the head of the bay, and once below 10m (33ft) they shoal very rapidly. Pigs Bay and Robinson's Cove in Opunohu Bay are attractive, if there is space, but in each case the front is fairly steep and a stern line to the shore is a wise arrangement. There is a small marina at Vaiare, but berthing is limited. There are also a few moorings close to the Bali Hai Club in Cook's Bay.

Formalities

In theory, a yacht arriving from within the Society Islands should report to the *Gendarmerie*. In practice, this no longer happens.

Facilities

Water, showers and laundry are all served by a water tap on the beach in Cook's Bay close to the store at the head of the bay. There are small shops serving the tourist trade and limited stores are available. Fuel can be purchased for carrying in cans from the fuel pontoon at the Bali Hai Club in Cook's Bay. For anything of any consequence it is best to go to Papeete. There are telephones in both bays.

Communications

There are flights (taking 15 minutes!) and ferries to Tahiti. Rental cars are available for a circuit of the island. It has also been found that hitchhiking is not difficult.

Fare, Huahine, Society Islands, French Polynesia   *16°43'S 151°02'W UT-10*

Springs: 1.0m	**Flag: France**	
Neaps: 1.0m	**Currency: Pacific francs (CFP)**	
Charts	**Admiralty**	**US**
General	4657	83021
Approach	1060	83397
Harbour	1107	

General

Huahine is the next island down the chain from Tahiti or Moorea, and is the most relaxed and least touristy of the Society Islands. In order to make an arrival in daylight it is usual to make the passage of 100 miles an overnight affair. The principal village, and the most used anchorage, is at Fare on the western lee side of the island. There are lagoons to be explored south from Fare and on the eastern windward side. The latter is very much for those who want to get away from their fellow sailors and is generally fairly deserted. The small village at Fare is friendly and, being more isolated than Moorea, stocks a much wider choice. The ancient Maraes and fish traps are fascinating, and can be found using hired bicycles without too much effort. Try not to miss the sacred eels!

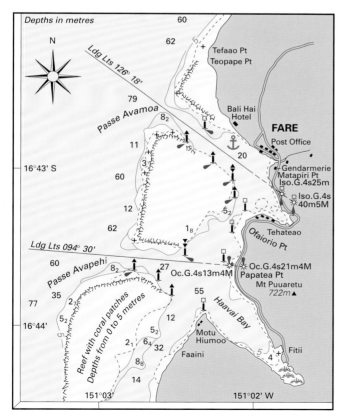

Plan 41 *Fare, Huahine, Society Islands.*

Approach and entry

Passe Avamoa, which leads into the anchorage off Fare, is marked and lit by leading marks. However, in good light these are hardly necessary once the pass has been identified. There is an outflow in this pass that is variously described as anything from fearsome, which is a translation of its name, to a modest 1 knot, as described in the Admiralty Pilot. No doubt it would be a problem if beating in under sail, but this is not a common sight at Fare! On the east coast, Passe Farerea leads into Baie de Maroe in the centre of the east coast, in the cleft between the two high land masses when seen from offshore. The long white line of sand which is Motu Muri Mahora to the south is an excellent pointer. The pass itself is a cable wide with small motus on each side.

Radio

There is no regular radio coverage for Huahine.

Anchorage and moorings

There is usually a certain amount of difficulty finding adequate swinging room in the limited area of shallow enough water off the village at Fare. A concentration of yachts builds in the area just off the beach below the Bali Hai Hotel, where the soundings are less than 12m (40ft). When this area is full there is nothing for it but to resign oneself to a depth of 20m (66ft) or so – and, beware, the wind can occasionally become quite fierce when blowing straight down the channel. Away from the village there are much easier spots in Port Bouray or Baie d'Avea for instance, but these places are relatively remote and totally without facilities. On the east coast, the best spot is tucked in behind Motu Muri Mahora in only 3–4m (10–13ft).

Formalities

The *Gendarmerie* is within easy walking distance of the landing at Fare so report to them on arrival.

Facilities

Fare village has a small supermarket, a bank and a post office. There is a fruit and vegetable truck that circles the island daily. There is a choice of restaurants and bars at Fare and several hotels on the island.

Communications

There is an airstrip with flights to Tahiti, and also a ferry service.

17 Uturoa, Raiatea, Society Islands, French Polynesia

16°44'S 151°26'W UT-10

Springs: 1.0m	Flag: France	
Neaps: 1.0m	Currency: Pacific francs (CFP)	
Charts	Admiralty	US
General	1060	83021
Approach	1103	83397
Harbour	1107	

General

Raiatea and Tahaa are separate islands surrounded by a single encircling reef and a common lagoon. Raiatea is second only in size to Tahiti within the Society Islands, and supports a significant population. Once inside the lagoon it is possible to cruise almost the whole way round both islands with a wide variety of anchorages. Only on the west coast of Raiatea is there a distance of about 6 miles between Toamaro Pass and Rautoanui Pass where the coral nearly dries out, and you must go to sea to get round. There are at least two major charter companies operating bare-boat fleets on Raiatea, so it is not quite so easy to get away from it all as you might expect. On the other hand, their presence on the island has meant the introduction of facilities that would never have existed otherwise. The islands are high (but not as high as Tahiti), with some good walking. The administrative centre is at Uturoa on the north-east shore. Anchorages close by are uncomfortably deep, but it is often possible to lay alongside in the small boat harbour long enough to do some shopping.

Approach and entry

Arriving from the east, the most used approach is by way of the Passe Teavapiti, which is about 1 mile to the south-east of Uturoa. Île Taoru lies in the middle of the pass with clear water either side. A course of 269° towards leading marks on the further shore leads in, but identifying them is not vital – providing the sun is high in the sky and the shoal water easily seen.

Church attendance is a major feature of life for the Polynesian islanders. The unaccompanied singing is generally quite superb. This church on the shores of Tahaa is a prominent landmark. Photo Bill Perkes.

Radio

There is no regular radio coverage for Raiatea or Tahaa.

Anchorage and moorings

Anchoring off Uturoa is not easy, and the main centre for visiting yachts is at Apooiti Marina, just west of the airport runway and about 3 miles from Uturoa. It is always possible to ride in a 'truck' or hire a bicycle to spare your feet. Apooiti Marina is the base for the Moorings Charter operations, with reserved berths for their yachts. There are moorings available for visitors 1 mile further west off the boatyard. Away from the centre, there are a number of reef and bay anchorages that are relatively peaceful. Baie Haamene on the west coast of Tahaa is very secure, with excellent holding in a mud bottom.

Formalities

The *Gendarmerie* is on the road into Uturoa from the north-west, close to the post office and the hospital. It is advisable to report to them on arrival.

Facilities

Raiatea is well provided with facilities, both for shopping in Uturoa, and for services in connection with the yacht. There are full yard facilities 1 mile west of the marina, with a travel lift and dry land storage. Some owners have laid up here for the cyclone season. The presence of at least two sizeable charter operations based on Raiatea ensures a higher than usual degree of expertise for repair work.

Communications

There is an airstrip with flights to Tahiti, and also a ferry service. A good mailing address is:

The Moorings Marina
Apooiti
BP 165
Uturoa
Raiatea
Society Islands

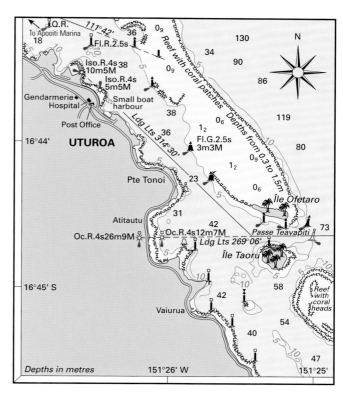

Plan 42 *Raiatea, Society Islands.*

Springs: 0.3m	Flag: France	
Neaps: 0.3m	Currency: Pacific francs (CFP)	
Charts	Admiralty	US
General	4657	83021
Approach	1060	83397
Harbour	1107	

General

Bora Bora is the most stunning, most exotic and dramatic of all the Society Islands. As you might expect, it is fully exploited for its tourism potential and, being within reach of the charter bases on Raiatea, frequented by a fair number of yachts. However, for the enterprising, the reef anchorages on the east coast are very rewarding and relatively unvisited. The passes that you must thread your way through are tortuous, to say the least, but not too difficult with a well-trained eye in the bows. The snorkelling is superb, and even quite close to the yacht club it is possible to swim alongside the most beautiful spotted and manta rays. Do not be put off by the hype, but enjoy Bora Bora. If you are there at the time of the 14 July celebrations, the competitive dancing by all the local village teams is a sight worth seeing.

Approach and entry

There is a beacon standing on the coral at the extreme south-west tip of the encircling reef at Pte Te Turi Roa and Pass Te Ava Nui is 4 miles north up the west side. It is broad and clear with port and starboard beacons. There is a sectored light that leads in on 112°T, but a night entry would be inadvisable for a stranger. Once in and well clear of the second port-hand marker, a turn to port will lead to the moorings off the yacht club. Otherwise, keep going on the entry bearing and fetch up off the village of Vaitape, but be prepared for some deep-water anchoring.

Radio

There is no regular radio coverage for Bora Bora.

The highest peak on Bora Bora. Photo Andrew Hogbin.

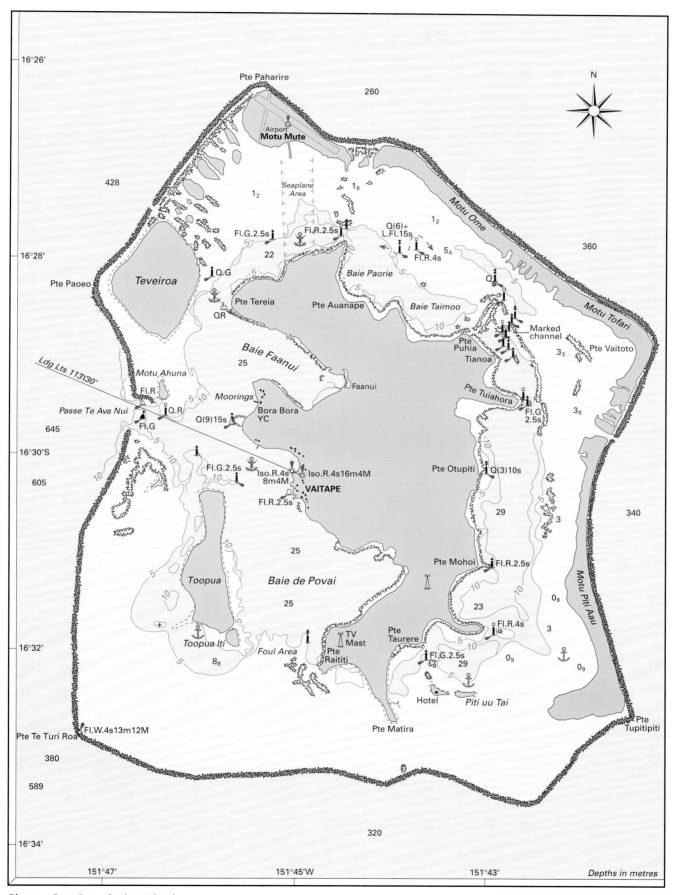

Plan 43 *Bora Bora, Society Islands.*

Anchorage and moorings

In the past, the moorings off the club (which is really only a restaurant) were free, but now free moorings are limited to restaurant patrons. The obvious areas to anchor within reach of the village are all fairly deep, but the more remote reef anchorages are much easier. By far the most delightful is at the south end of the east lagoon close to Piti uu Tai, but negotiating the channel through the reefs off Pte Puhia needs a practised eye and a steady nerve!

Formalities

Most visiting yachts will want to clear out of French Polynesia at Bora Bora, and this is quite acceptable even though you may wish to visit Maupiti and Mopelia on the way downwind. Part of the pleasure of clearing out for non-EU citizens is the recovery of your bond from the bank. Having been deprived of your valuable funds in French Polynesia, there is a feeling of relative affluence as you approach the Cooks or Tonga – with a consequent benefit to their economy! There will also be a few who will be coming the other way and entering French Polynesia. All of this is dealt with very helpfully at the *Gendarmerie* at Vaitape, but those going on to the east will have to check in more fully in Papeete.

Facilities

Water is available at the club if you eat there, but may not be obtainable from the town wharf. There are two supermarkets in Vaitape and a roving fruit and vegetable van. There is also a small shop ashore near Pte Taurere for fresh french bread, when anchored in the south-west corner of the lagoon, but no obvious public landing. There is a fuel dock just north of the leading lights at Vaitape jetty. Even with the relevant paperwork from Papeete, 100 litres (26 gallons) must be purchased to obtain duty-free rates. It is possible to come alongside or pull stern-to. Any serious service that is required for the yacht will have to be sought back upwind in Raiatea. There is a small internet café on the island.

Communications

There is an airstrip across the lagoon on Motu Mute, with internal flights within the Society Islands. A ferry shuttle service operates to connect with the main island. Mail can be addressed to:

The Bora Bora Yacht Club
BP 17
Vaitape
Bora Bora

Springs: 0.3m	Flag: France	
Neaps: 0.2m	Currency: Pacific francs (CFP)	
Charts	**Admiralty**	**French**
General	4657	
Approach		6207
Harbour		6207

General

The Austral Islands are well off the beaten track for the present-day multitude of yachts that are making east-to-west passages across the Pacific. They do, however, make an attractive, if little known, stopover for those taking the southerly option from New Zealand back across. The enthusiasm for Raivavae as a place for a pleasant interlude for rest and recovery before pressing on north towards Tahiti is prevalent among the few that have stopped there.

There is a good anchorage which has moderate depth, an enthusiastic welcome, particularly from the expatriate French members of the community and, despite warnings to the contrary in the Admiralty Pilot, there is clear water for navigation, and enjoyable (but demanding) diving. Onshore, there are a number of interesting artefacts, including tikis still standing in their original positions.

Approach and entry

The entrance to the lagoon is well described in the pilot, but with the warning that the marks are not well maintained and can be difficult to identify. A first glance at the chart, particularly at the scale of our plan, suggests that depths may be limited. At the largest scale, the soundings indicate a least depth of 4.5m (15ft), which, unless there is a heavy ground swell, should cause little problem. It was reported in 1995 that the pass was well marked with port and starboard piles in addition to the leading marks. If in any doubt, it would seem that standing on and off will soon encourage a local boat to come out and see you in. It goes without saying that you should not even think of approaching the island during the hours of darkness.

Radio

There is a possibility that someone may listen on channel 16 if a yacht has been sighted approaching, but this is not to be relied upon.

Anchorage and moorings

The anchorage off the village is well spoken of, with good holding in 10m (33ft) and a mud bottom. It is possible to anchor around the lagoon by the motus. One may go alongside the small wharf temporarily to pick up water.

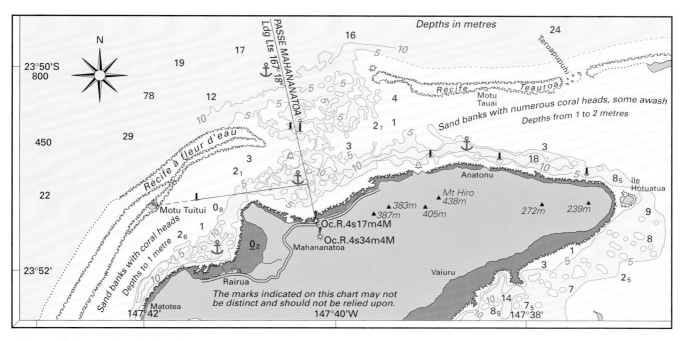

Plan 44 *Raivavae, Austral Islands.*

Formalities

Check in with the resident *Gendarme*.

Facilities

There are two general stores and a bakery, which accepts orders and produces pain-au-chocolat twice a week. There may be some fruit, but little in the way of vegetables. Water is available on the dock, but avoid collecting it after rain. There is a post office with a fax facility. There is also a medical centre with a doctor and two nurses. Fuel is not normally available for visitors.

Communications

An airport should be open in the near future.

Springs: 0.76m	Flag: Cook Islands	
Neaps: 0.43m	Currency: NZ dollar	
Charts	Admiralty	US
General	4657	
Approach	NZ 9558	83425
Harbour	NZ 9558	83425

General

Rarotonga is the largest of the 15 Cook Islands, and is the seat of government. It is 32km (19 miles) around, and has a fringing reef with a shallow lagoon, not navigable by yachts. It is a very friendly island much visited by tourists from New Zealand and Australia. There is a strong New Zealand influence, with the NZ dollar as the currency, although some of the coins are not transferable. The small harbour at Avatiu just to the west of the capital Avarua is limited with regard to space. The harbourmaster likes yachts to give him as much advance warning of their arrival as possible so that he can make the best use of the space available. It is very much cheaper than French Polynesia, so many people take advantage of the opportunities to hire mopeds, bicycles and cars to explore the island. There is also good walking along the inland road through attractive farmland. Particularly recommended is the cross-island walk, which takes about five hours with stops for lunch and a swim in the waterfall. The local dancing is reputed to be the best in Polynesia. They are also very proud of their navigation and their ocean-going canoes, several of which were sailed to Mururoa to support the protest against the 1995 atomic testing. The Cook Islanders are strongly religious and they welcome visitors at their services in the Cook Islands Christian Church and in the Catholic cathedral at Avarua. Most places close on Sunday, which is the traditional family day. The relaxed atmosphere and ease of visiting an English-speaking country are much appreciated. Visitors seem to spend longer in Rarotonga than they planned, which must be a good sign.

Approach and entry

Avatiu Harbour has a fairly narrow entrance through the reef, but the leading marks are clear, although it was reported in 2001 that only one fixed green was lit. Much better to arrive in daylight, because the harbour is a web of mooring lines and anchor chains that would be a menace to negotiate in the dark. Yachts are asked to go alongside the quay and to await Immigration and Health officials before moving to permanent moorings.

Radio

Call Rarotonga Radio on channel 16.

The Cook Islanders extend a warm welcome to visitors at their church services on Rarotonga. Photo Ros Hogbin.

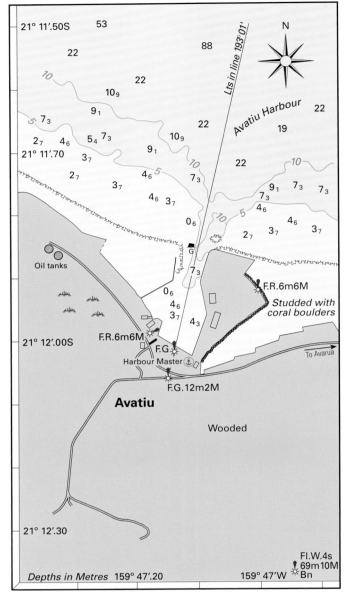

Plan 45 *Rarotonga, Cook Islands.*

Anchorage and moorings

Lying alongside, you are against large black tyres, and the prevailing wind blows grit off the quay on to the decks. As soon as clearance has been given, anchor in the harbour with stern lines to the quay. There is room for a couple of yachts off the north side of the navy wharf, but there is a shallow patch (approximately 1.5m (5ft)) immediately off the north end. The depth then drops to 4m (13ft) up to the south wall. If mooring to the south wall, it is best to drop the anchor south of the seaward wall of the green-roofed warehouse on the east quay. Lines need to be adjusted fairly frequently because of other boats arriving and leaving, and because of changes in wind direction. The harbour is very uncomfortable in northerly winds – the south-east corner of the north wall seems to be the worst affected. In extreme circumstances, yachts may be asked to leave.

Formalities

Immigration and Health officials come to the boat. The Customs House is five minutes' walk towards Avarua. The Health official will spray the cabin for bugs. There are overtime charges made for inward or outward clearance outside of 0800–1500 Monday to Friday, and a departure tax of NZ$25 to be paid. The NZ High Commission is open 1030–1430 Monday to Friday for visas. Tourist visas last for six months, with extensions allowed up to a maximum of six months. A permit must be obtained before leaving if it is intended to visit any of the other Cook Islands.

Facilities

There are no facilities specifically for yachts, but there are several hardware stores. Some help may be available in an emergency from the small boatyard next to the Navy pier. The harbourmaster's new office has toilets and showers. The Snow Bird laundry across the road at the head of the harbour operates a 'leave and collect' service. The port authority offices have washing machines and dryers in the shower block below, and faxes can be received. Outward faxes and international calls can be made 24 hours a day and seven days a week from the Telecom office in the town. There are branches of West Pac and ANZ banks (with an ATM) in town and at the airport. Bikes, scooters and cars can be rented from several places, at comparable prices. There is an hourly bus service, clockwise and anticlockwise round the island, which runs until 1700 on weekdays and for a shorter time on Sundays. There are several internet outlets, and Pacific Computers will allow laptop connections. There is a DHL office in the shopping centre on Cooks Corner.

Shops are open 0800–1600 (1200 on Saturday), and all shops are closed on Sundays. There are various supermarkets. Fresh vegetables are available in the market on most days, but there is an excellent Saturday market 0630–1200, which includes organic herbs and crafts. The cheapest black pearls are found at the perfume factory. Duty-free diesel (in 200-litre (52-gallon) drums) can be delivered to the wharf; for smaller quantities, go to the petrol station in the town. Gas and kerosene are available. There is drinking water on the wharf, although it is an untreated supply and should not be collected after heavy rain. Duty-free drink is available at a good price from the Bond store. The local FM radio station (103.3) gives Pacific news from New Zealand, followed by a local weather forecast. Weatherfax is available from Hawaii.

Communications

There are internal flights to Aitutaki and other Cook Islands, and international flights to New Zealand, Honolulu, Australia, Los Angeles, Fiji and Tahiti. The best mailing address is general delivery at the post office, but by all accounts the sorting is not ideal and you should check against all possible names.

21 **Aratunga,** Aitutaki, Cook Islands
18°54'S 159°47'W UT-10

Springs: 0.42m	Flag: Cook Islands	
Neaps: 0.27m	Currency: NZ dollar	
Charts	Admiralty	US
General	4657	
Approach		83425
Harbour		83425

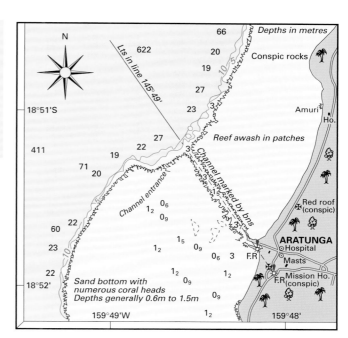

Plan 46 *Aitutaki, Cook Islands.*

General

Aitutaki is an inhabited island within an atoll, and its appeal to visiting yachtsmen will depend entirely on whether their yacht has sufficiently small draught to reach the lagoon anchorage. Even 1.8m (6ft) is deep enough to make grounding in the approach a distinct possibility. The persistence or otherwise of the trades will make a difference. In times of strong trades, the swell breaks over the windward end of the reef and there is always an outflow even on the flood, thereby supporting a good level. If the swell dies there may be less depth, and a certain amount of ploughing of furrows in the sand may occur. Aratunga, the principal village, is on the shore close to the anchorage. There is a wharf with a supposed depth alongside of 1.7m (6ft), where an infrequent supply vessel offloads. Sunday is very much a day of rest, and the unaccompanied hymn singing, in the large 1828 church, is quite spectacular.

Approach and entry

Unless you have a lifting keel, the pass will have to be negotiated with extreme care, aided by the colour of the water. There is nearly always an outflow and it is said that the north-east side should be favoured. It may be necessary to anchor outside and await an improvement in the tide.

Radio

Calling another yacht on channel 16 is probably the most likely way of making contact.

Anchorage and moorings

Anchoring in the lagoon is very limited for fixed-keel yachts. With care, six or seven may sit in pools while tightly anchored fore-and-aft. The stream runs quite strongly, and more than usual care is necessary when manoeuvring in limited space. A third anchor has been found useful to limit lateral movement and avoid snagging the coral heads.

Formalities

Aratunga is a port of entry, and Immigration and Health officials come to the boat. There are overtime charges made for inward or outward clearance outside of 0800–1500 Monday to Friday, and a NZ$25 per person departure tax to be paid.

Facilities

There are no facilities specifically for yachts. There is a fresh fruit and vegetable market, a baker – who provides fresh English-style bread – and a grocery store with basic tinned goods and durable vegetables. The fuel station also sells some vegetables. There is a post office and two banks, one inside the post office that is open on Mondays and Wednesdays, and a smaller one outside the village that will change cash or give an ATM in advance. On the waterfront is the Fishing Club, which is open on specific evenings, and the Blue Nun Restaurant, which is open for meals and drinks all day. Scooters can be rented in several locations. There is one big holiday resort on the island and plenty of small-scale accommodation, as well as a golf course.

Communications

There are regular flights to and from Rarotonga.

22 Pago Pago, Tutuila, American Samoa

14°18'S 170°40'W UT-11

Springs: 0.8m	Flag: USA	
Neaps: 0.6m	Currency: US dollar	
Charts	Admiralty	US
General	4631	83026
Approach	1729	83484
Harbour	1729	83484

General

The island of Tutuila is more commonly referred to by the name of its sole town, Pago Pago (pronounced 'pango pango'). This small island has gained a deservedly bad name as noisy, dirty and smelly, and offering little of appeal other than its low prices and the benefit of US territory for US residents. It is a recognised hurricane hole, and many yachts take advantage

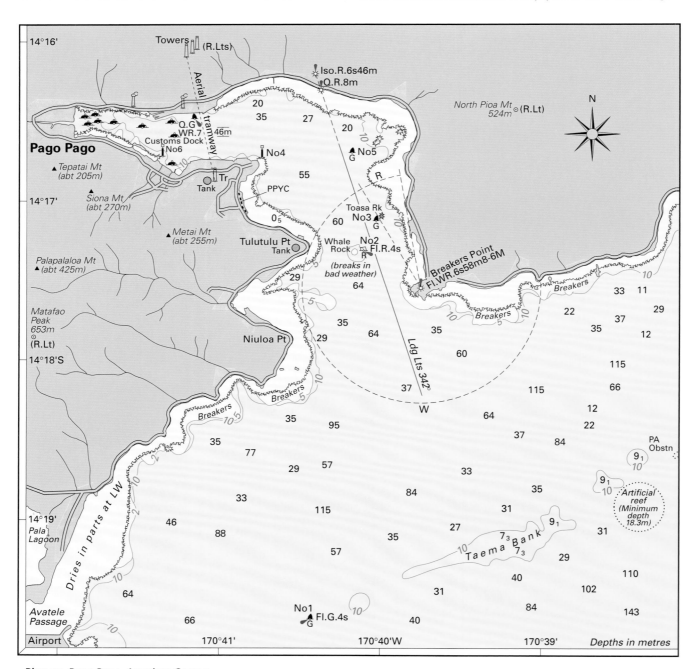

Plan 47 Pago Pago, American Samoa.

of this. Most yachts on a westward voyage take the more southern route, calling at the Cooks, then Tonga, and on to Fiji. It is a useful stop on a returning voyage eastwards en route to Hawaii. Winds tend to be light, and the best route to Hawaii requires extensive easting before heading north. Therefore the ability to load up with cheap, good fuel is a definite plus. There are twice-weekly airline flights to and from Hawaii.

The big advantage of using Pago Pago is to stock up with US produce and supplies. The island is US territory and is heavily subsidised by the USA. Fuel, groceries and nearly all supplies are much cheaper than anywhere else in the South Pacific, and even cheaper than in the USA. Because it is US territory, goods ordered from the mainland come in without hassle or duty. There is not much to see or do, other than to notice the aroma and 24-hour workings of the tuna processing plants on the north shore of the anchorage. The locals play cricket, although their version of the game is unique, with a raucous liveliness that would seem out of place on an English cricket field. There are some unremarkable restaurants and bars and the daily market is so-so.

Approach and entry

Wide open and easy to enter from the south, the bay is well marked with buoys and beacons, and the lights are well maintained. Once inside, the harbour turns to port, and the Customs dock and yacht anchorage is well lit.

Radio

Channel 16.

Anchorage and moorings

The harbour is deep, with 44m (145ft) in the centre, and shoals gently to the west. There are a few private mooring buoys occasionally available. The harbour floor is reportedly littered with junk, and this can cause anchoring problems. The bottom is mud, and the water is at all times murky. The local people have little compunction when it comes to washing anything unwanted into the bay. This is not your dream anchorage. Arriving and departing yachts can tie up at the Customs dock, and there is a shower and small yacht-hauling facilities nearby. The dock can also be used to take on fuel and supplies. At times the anchorage can get quite crowded, and a fair breeze can funnel westwards through the bay.

Formalities

Pago Pago is the sole port of entry for American Samoa and US immigration procedures are followed. Nevertheless, this is a South Pacific island, and the pace and procedure are rather less rigidly defined. Yachts continuing on to Hawaii or to the US mainland will need to re-enter.

Facilities

The waterfront is mainly geared towards the fishing fleet; nevertheless, the chandlers and hardware stores have a good range of basic supplies, and marine services are available. Because US residents have no restriction on length of stay or working, there are numerous 'cottage industries' for sail repair, divers, engineers, etc.

Communications

Air services to the USA count as internal flights. There are also international services to Auckland, Sydney and Papeete, making Pago Pago an ideal port for crew changes.

Apia, Upolu Island, Western Samoa
13°49'S 171°4'W UT-11

Springs: 0.97m	Flag: Western Samoa	
Neaps: 0.54m	Currency: Tala and sene	
Charts	Admiralty	US
General	NZ 86	83026
Approach	NZ 865	83473
Harbour	NZ 8655	83476

General

Western Samoa has been called the birthplace of Polynesia, since it is thought to be from the island of Savaii that the original Polynesians set out to settle in Hawaii, the Cook Islands, Easter Island and New Zealand. Western Samoa was originally a German colony, but after the First World War the country became a British colony administered by New Zealand. It is now an independent nation. The port of Apia on Upolu Island is the centre of government. Before 1990, tourism was actively discouraged, but it is now encouraged and Western Samoa has its own very rich culture. Robert Louis Stevenson, called by the Samoans 'Tusitala', Teller of Tales, built a house at Valima. He died in 1894, and his tomb can be found by climbing Mount Vaea, but preferably not in the heat of the day! His house has been beautifully restored and can be visited by taxi.

Approach and entry

If you are approaching from the north or west, the approach is obvious. Coming from the south, one should sail between the two islands of Savaii to the west and Upolu to the east. There is a small island and a reef to the west of Upolu, which must be cleared before turning east and beating towards Apia. The entrance to Apia Harbour appears very straightforward on the chart. The twin towers of the Roman Catholic cathedral will be the first landmarks to be identified from seaward, before the leading marks will appear just west of the towers. Entrance is best made in daylight, as the leading lights are not easy to see. The entrance is through a pass in the reef which is only marked by the leading marks.

Radio

Contact port control on VHF channel 16 during working hours.

In Apia, the raising of the colours at 0800 every morning is a serious moment and visitors are expected to stand still as a mark of respect. Photo Bill Perkes.

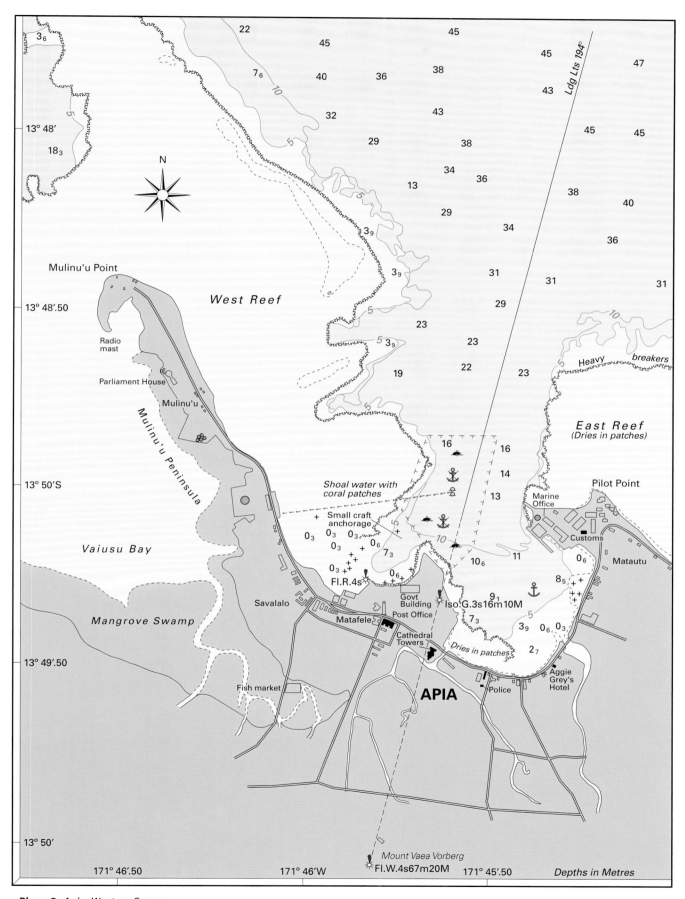

Plan 48 *Apia, Western Samoa.*

Anchorage and moorings

Anchor in 8m (26ft) off the three dinghy landings by Aggie Grey's well-known hotel.

Formalities

Go alongside the Customs wharf and do not leave the yacht until you have been cleared. Port control will advise Customs of your arrival. Clearance is for Apia only, and permission from the Office of Foreign Affairs, in the Prime Minister's Department, must be obtained for any cruising in Western Samoa. The Immigration office can be found in the big new government complex by the bus station. A visa is not required.

Harbourmaster
Tel: 685 23 700
Fax: 685 21 990

Facilities

Only minimal repairs can be effected here, and there is no way of hauling out a yacht. In the event of serious damage, the only option would be to have the yacht lifted on to the deck of a visiting ship and transported to New Zealand. Fuel is available from road tankers (contact Mobil, tel: 21 771 or BP, tel: 21 581), and bottles can be filled with butane at Samoa Industrial Gases at Vaitele about 5km (3 miles) west of Apia. Water is available by arrangement with the marine office on the main wharf, but they recommend treatment or boiling before drinking. There are several telecoms sites within Apia.

Communications

There are daily flights to Pago Pago and quite good connections with Fiji. The recommended mailing address is:

General Delivery
Apia
Western Samoa

24 Neiafu, Vava'u Group, Tonga

18°44'S 174°00'W UT+13

Springs: 1.19m	Flag: Tonga	
Neaps: 0.82m	Currency: Pa'anga	
Charts	Admiralty	US
General	4631	83560
Approach	NZ 8234	83555
Harbour	NZ 8235	

General

The Vava'u group of islands is at the northern, windward end of the Kingdom of Tonga, and Neiafu is the principal centre for the group. Tonga, very wisely, has opted to be technically, if not geographically, west of the dateline. This is in order to be on the same day as all their immediate neighbours, such as Fiji and New Zealand, with whom they have a close relationship. On arrival from the east you immediately skip a day – too bad if it's your birthday! After the relative affluence of the French islands, there is an immediate realisation that you really have reached the Third World. The Tongans, who are traditionally large people, are happy friendly souls who welcome their visitors warmly; after all,

Captain James Cook called them the Friendly Islands when he visited in 1773 and 1777. There are those within the islands who will tell visitors that the friendliness of the islanders was all a ruse to lull Cook into a false sense of security before they attacked and ate him. The story goes that they could not agree whether to attack by day or night, and he sailed away again before a decision was made! The Vava'u group is much influenced by a Moorings charter base. They are actually helpful to passing yachts; their in-house guide and chart are the best available for exploring the many anchorages. Moorings have given all the anchorages numbers, which has robbed them of some of their romance; but from a purely practical point of view, it is entirely sensible as nobody except a Tongan can cope with the pronunciation. Before leaving Neiafu to cruise among the islands, do enquire about the location of the next traditional Tongan feast. The feast is an enjoyable experience, but opinions vary on the merits of the traditional dancing that goes with it! Everyone enjoys Swallows Cave, but only the brave go to Mariner's Cave! The Tongans are strict Wesleyan Christians, modest and conservative in dress. The men wear shirts in public and women cover their shoulders. A visit to a nearby church to hear the local singing can be a wonderful experience.

Sundowners on a beach in the Vava' u group. Photo Bill Perkes.

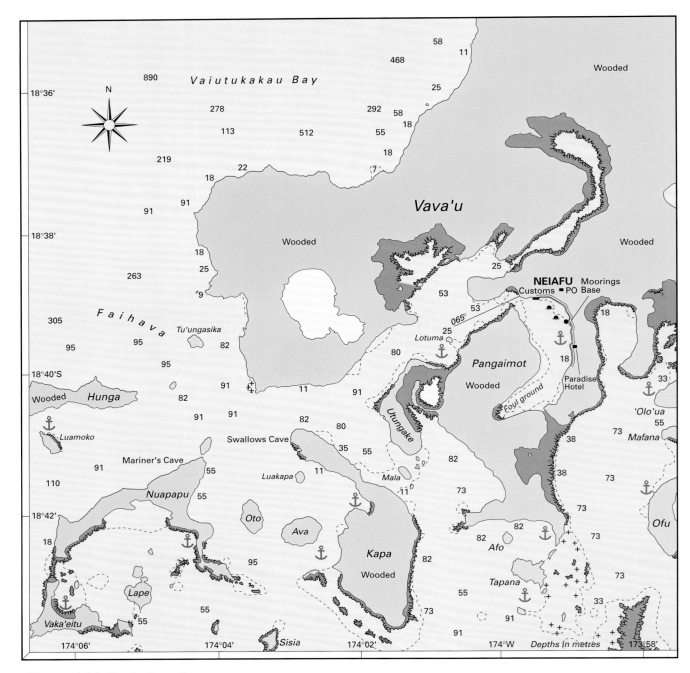

Plan 49 *Neiafu, Vava' u Group, Tonga.*

Approach and entry

Neiafu Harbour is approached through an easy channel that leads in a north-easterly direction from the main entrance between Hunga and the south-west point of Vava'u Island. There are leading beacons (065°T) that lead past the narrower part of the channel that has a spit extending on the starboard hand just before the harbour itself opens up on that side. New arrivals should come alongside at the main wharf to await clearance before moving further up the harbour to find a space to anchor.

Radio

There is no regular radio watch.

Anchorage and moorings

Within Neiafu Harbour, the best anchoring and the least depth is close along the north shore. There are occasionally some moorings available from the Moorings charter base. The area in front of the Paradise Hotel is generally very popular.

The traditional dug-out canoes are still in everyday use in Tonga. Photo Bill Perkes.

Formalities

Inward clearance covers all movement in the Vava'u group, but further clearance is necessary if going on to the Ha'apai group or to Nuku'alofa. Customs, Immigration and Agriculture officials will come aboard – maybe all at once! Be prepared to have your fruit and vegetables taken away.

Facilities

General stores and a flourishing fruit and vegetable market can all be found in the village, but the choice of goods is a great deal simpler than in the French islands. There is a fresh fish market in Neiafu, but get there early for the best fish. There is a chandlery with more items than one might expect. Coleman Marine in town will help, but spares may need to be flown in from New Zealand or Australia. Fuel can be obtained on the town quay or by arrangement with the Paradise Hotel quay.

A laundry service is available via the tourist office. General telecoms facilities are available. Radio Nuku'alofa broadcasts local weather on 1020 KHz at 0800, 1300 and 2000 local time. Tongan carvings and tapa work are very attractive, and considerably less expensive than the equivalent goods farther east.

Communications

There is an airstrip with flights to Nuku'alofa (and occasionally direct to American Samoa). Air New Zealand operates from Nuku'alofa. Mail can be addressed to:

General Delivery
Neiafu
Vava'u Group
Kingdom of Tonga

25

Nuku'alofa, Tongatapu, Tonga

21°08'S 175°12'W UT+13

Springs: 1.22m	Flag: Tonga	
Neaps: 0.85m	Currency: Pa'anga	
Charts	Admiralty	US
General	4631	83560
Approach	NZ 8275	83567
Harbour	NZ 8275	

General

Nuku'alofa, on the island of Tongatapu, is the capital of the Kingdom of Tonga and the seat of government, as well as being the location of the Royal Palace. While its political standing and cultural importance is paramount, its attractions as a centre for inter-island cruising bear no comparison with Neiafu and the Vava'u group of islands. As the capital of the Kingdom, Nuku'alofa naturally has more to offer within the town, which is dominated by several large cathedrals. It should be appreciated that the Tongans feel very strongly on the subject of Sunday observance; all work is forbidden and,

The Royal Palace is a useful mark when crossing the lagoon to reach the harbour at Nuku' alofa. Photo Michael Pocock.

in sympathy, visitors should be discreet with their own activities. Take a day off from varnishing on deck for the sake of keeping up good relations.

Approach and entry

The approach is not unduly difficult in daylight, but is best avoided in the dark if possible. There have been some unhappy experiences in the past, not unrelated to alleged adjustments to the lit marks at short notice. The main hazards are the reefs that must be cleared on the starboard hand when approaching from the north or west. Once clear of the Hakau Mama'o Reef, a course can be made more or less directly towards the Royal Palace just to the west of the town. Due regard should be paid to the Telemachus Reef before heading for the pierheads of the artificial harbour, passing Ualanga Lalu to port and Ualanga Uta and Monu to starboard. The Queen Salote Wharf stands out as a prominent feature, and the new harbour is immediately to the west. The Piha Passage, which provides an approach from the east, is much more restricted and should not be attempted without first-class information, which it is beyond the scope of this publication to provide. The Admiralty Pilot makes the point that the beacons and buoys in the Narrows cannot be relied upon.

Radio

The port authority keeps a watch on VHF channel 16 and likes to hear from yachts in the approach.

Anchorage and moorings

Yachts do anchor outside the harbour, either opposite Yellow Pier, protected by Monu reef, or on the west side of Pangaimotu, off the resort. As their numbers increase, the port authority sometimes makes them move. Harbour dues are the same wherever you anchor. There was work-in-progress in 2001 to increase the capacity of the inner harbour, which may provide more room for yachts. The official preferred form of mooring within the basin is stern-to on the north side of the harbour, Tahiti-style. Depending on anticipated traffic, it may be permitted to lay alongside on the commercial wharf and also to lie stern-to adjacent to the slipway directly opposite the entrance. This latter position is the closest to the town, which is described as only a short walk away. In the heat of the day, some would say that it is not short enough! When the harbour was new, the holding was sometimes quite suspect. It may be that with age the effects of fresh dredging will have disappeared as the bottom consolidates.

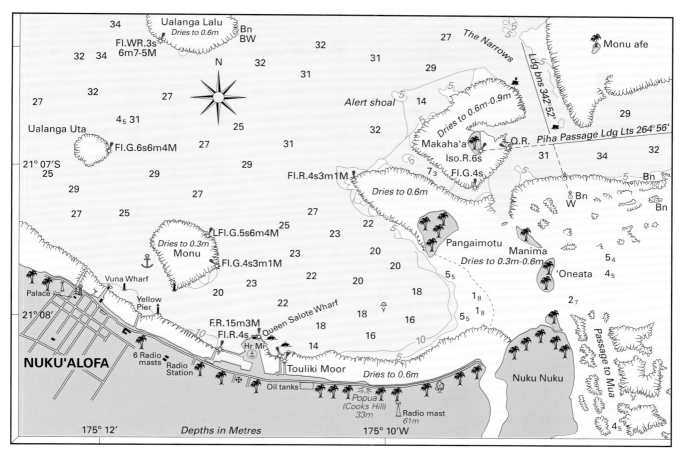

Plan 50 *Nuku' alofa, Tonga.*

Formalities

Inward clearance is necessary whether the yacht is arriving from abroad or from the Ha'apai or Vava'u groups. If from abroad, Customs and Quarantine will come aboard and they will request that they do so alongside at the Queen Salote Wharf. If coming from within Tonga, it is probable that you will be permitted to take up a berth and take your papers to the authorities. The Immigration offices are in the town. Officially, there is no clearance available outside of office hours, which are 0830–1230 and 1330–1630, Monday to Friday only.

Ministry of Marine and Ports
Tel: 23 168; 23 166 or 22 555
Fax: 23 733

Facilities

Within the harbour there is a slipway with up to 100 tonnes capacity, and a boat lift for 10 tonnes. Such labour as is available will need fairly close supervision. Fuel can be organised by bowser if the required quantity is sufficient, otherwise it can be obtained from the fishermen's dock (take your outward clearance certificate for duty free). Water is available at the fishermen's dock, Queen Salote Wharf. The town has a market and shops, banks and a post office. Experience has shown that the Poste Restante service is haphazard to a degree, and should not be relied upon.

There is a visitors' office on the seafront, west of the Dateline Hotel. Laundry can be dropped off at Savoy Dry Cleaners, a ten-minute walk from the market, heading south. There is an ANZ bank with ATM on the south-west corner opposite the covered market. There is a DHL agent situated at Vital Travel, Lonis Building, Wellington Road, Nuku'alofa. Internet, fax and mail drop facilities are found at:

Cyber Central
TCF Building
Wellington Road
Nuku'alofa

Communications

There are regular flights to Samoa, Fiji and New Zealand.

Springs: 1.3m	Flag: Fiji	
Neaps: 0.9m	Currency: Fijian dollar	
Charts	Admiralty	US
General	4632	83570
Approach	1673/1674	83572
Harbour	1660	

General

Suva is the capital of Fiji and is the largest and busiest centre for thousands of miles around. The mixture of ethnic origins between the indigenous Fijians and the imported Indian population, which has now become a major partner in the administration of the country, form a colourful and fascinating scene. Shopping in Suva – whether in the unique market, or in the streets – is a new experience, and one that can be very rewarding. The Royal Suva Yacht Club provides a meeting place in a very relaxed atmosphere that has no parallel in the Pacific. Yachts tend to congregate in Suva and stay for long periods, or come and go between here and the islands. Cruising among the islands and meeting the warm and friendly Fijian islanders is not to be missed. Suva is an ideal place to stock up, reduce the jobs list, and complete the formalities that are essential before the necessary permit for inter-island cruising is issued.

Approach and entry

The entry to Suva Harbour is easy in daylight, and not particularly demanding at night, once the leading lights are identified. Once through the pass, new arrivals should turn to starboard and head for King's Wharf where all the officials are based. At night it is not easy to find your way around in the upper parts of the harbour, and it would be better to find a space clear of any ship movements and put down an anchor. Port control will be watching on radar, so if in doubt speak to them on channel 16.

Radio

Port control monitors channel 16 VHF.

Anchorage and moorings

The Royal Suva Yacht Club has a small marina with stern-to berths, but space will always be limited. The majority of the fleet anchor off the club on a good mud bottom and enjoy the security of the club dinghy landing. There is a temporary membership fee for each yacht, half price for singlehanders and, considering the benefits, few people complain about the charge. There is no other landing facility with any degree of security in Suva. There is also the Tradewinds Marina in the Bay of Islands, north-west of Suva, but it is well beyond walking distance from the town.

Royal Suva Yacht Club
Tel: 679 312921
Fax: 679 304433

Formalities

Inward clearance can test your patience, particularly if you have not succeeded in adjusting to the Pacific tempo of life. Quarantine, Health, Customs, Immigration, port control and Security either come aboard or have to be coped with on shore (the Royal Suva Yacht Club has information on opening hours). With the right approach and a modicum of luck, experience has shown that it can all be completed in no more than two hours. On the other hand, it has been known to take as many days! Dress well, keep smiling, shake their hands, and develop a skill for filling out innumerable forms at lightning speed and you stand a chance of success. Above all else, do not be tempted to put down an anchor on the way to Suva prior to obtaining clearance; if, as well may happen, the authorities get to hear, they will be very angry indeed. Before a cruising permit is issued for visiting the outer islands, it is necessary to apply at the Ministry of Native Affairs where you will be lectured on the correct dress and behaviour to be adopted when arriving at a native village. There are many people who baulk at this emphasis on ritual when first introduced to the subject. There are, however, very few who, having been to the island villages, are not prepared to admit to the merits of the system.

Port Authority
Tel: 679 312 700
Fax: 679 300 064

Facilities

There is a slipway in a shipyard on the waterfront and the yacht club has a scrubbing berth for shoal-draught boats. Labour can be employed, but in recent years there has not been an established yacht yard known for good service. There is a fuel and water pontoon at the club, accessible at high water. Fiji Gas, very close to the club, will fill cylinders. Certain items of yacht equipment, particularly electronics, solar panels and outboard motors, are available at duty-free prices. Try

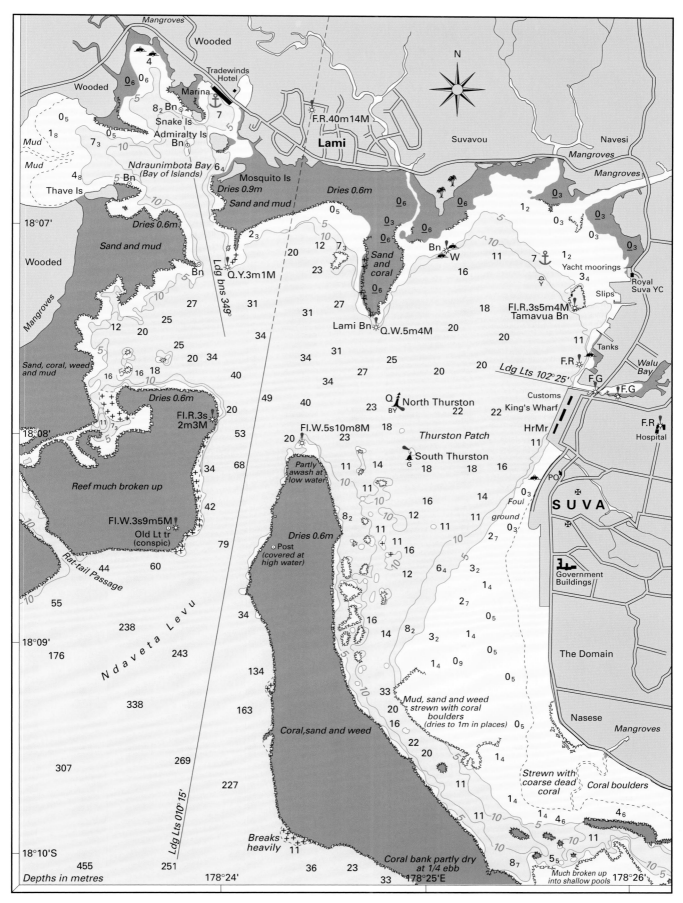

Plan 51 *Suva, Fiji.*

View from Suva Yacht Club along the pontoon and out into the anchorage. Photo Jane Russell.

AWA, not far from the club. The Yacht Shop in Lami – a taxi ride away on the industrial estate – has some local chandlery items. Other items may be obtained from Vuda Point Marina on the other side of the island. Shoes and simple clothing are well priced and there are supermarkets and shops galore. The fruit and vegetable market is magnificent and a delight to visit.

Communications

The international airport at Nadi is 144km (90 miles) away and much closer to Lautoka, but there are local air and coach connections. The bus service into town is cheap, cheerful and frequent. There are e-mail facilities in town. The yacht club provides an efficient and helpful mail and fax service. The address is:

c/o Royal Suva Yacht Club
GPO Box 335
Suva
Fiji

Springs: 1.5m	Flag: Fiji	
Neaps: 0.9m	Currency: Fiji dollar	
Charts	Admiralty	US
General	4632	83570
Approach	1670	83574
Harbour	1670	

General

Lautoka is the second largest centre on the island of Viti Levu and is conveniently close to the international airport at Nadi. Lautoka is the sugar capital of Fiji, and the town is dominated by the Indian element of the population who operate the sugar industry – and most other businesses as well. Fiji's tourist industry is concentrated in the vicinity of Nadi. This is very apparent if cruising in the extremely beautiful Yasawa group. There is, in this group, a tendency towards tourist fatigue that is not apparent in the rest of the Pacific, and that is in complete contrast to the remainder of the Fijian islands. Lautoka itself is a useful re-supply point and port of entry/departure, but has few pleasures to offer. Visitors should be warned of the frequent smutty fall-out that is an unavoidable by-product of the sugar industry.

Approach and entry

From whichever direction you approach Lautoka, you need to keep your wits about you. The easiest approach is from the south-west, as would be the case when having come clockwise round the island from Suva. The Malolo Passage and the Nadi waters are a regularly used ship channel and the marks are well maintained. Coming across Bligh Water from the east or directly south from the northern part of the Yasawas entails a good deal more reef dodging, and the existence of a mark on the chart may not be borne out in reality.

Radio

Port control monitors channel 16 VHF.

Anchorage and moorings

Call port control for instructions. A temporary berth may be offered, but it is probably best to anchor away from the busy wharf areas.

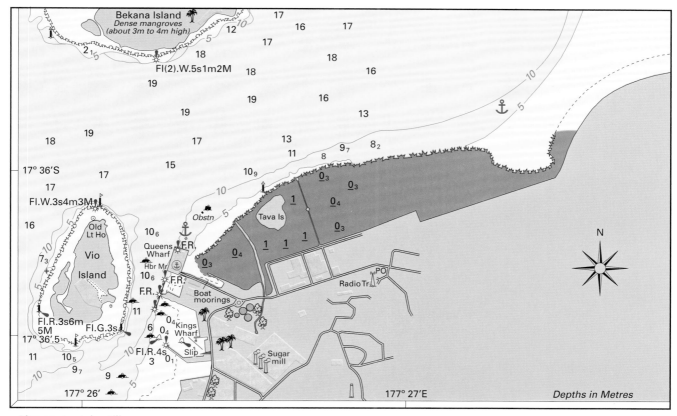

Plan 52 *Lautoka, Fiji.*

Formalities

Clearance at Lautoka has never been quite as long-winded as at Suva. The officials are based on the Queens Wharf, which entails some hot walking to and fro. More yachts probably clear out here than clear in, and the system seems to work reasonably well. New arrivals from abroad should call port control on channel 16 for directions. It may be necessary to go alongside at the Queens Wharf for quarantine clearance before moving on to the marina.

Facilities

Lautoka has a good market and provisioning within walking distance. Fuel and water are available, but the port does not focus very much on yachts. Phone, fax and internet facilities are available in the town. Weather information is available from Nadi international airport and the harbourmaster. A small amount of mechanical/electrical support may be available, but it would be best to go to Vuda Point Marina, just 2–3 miles from Lautoka, which has good repair and haul-out facilities, as well as a supermarket, chandlery, dive shop, brokerage and sailmaker. The marina has a beachfront bar, restaurant and accommodation. Contact details:

Tel: 679 668 214
Fax: 679 668 215

Communications

The international airport at Nadi is only a taxi ride away and is a trans-Pacific staging post for several major airlines. Lautoka is therefore an excellent crew-changing location. The main couriers are represented in Fiji. Vuda Point Marina would be the best mail drop:

Vuda Point Marina
PO Box 5717
Lautoka
Fiji

28

Opua, Bay of Islands, North Island, New Zealand

35°19'S 174°09'E UT+12*

Springs: 1.9m	Flag: New Zealand	
Neaps: 1.3m	Currency: NZ dollar	
Charts	Admiralty	US
General	NZ 42	76040
Approach	NZ 5125	76041
Harbour		76041

General

Opua, in the beautiful Bay of Islands, is the most popular port of entry for the majority of yachts arriving from the Pacific islands. There is a great feeling of returning once more to civilisation. The charts are of a high standard, the lights are likely to be lit, and on shore all those specialised items that it was impossible to obtain for the last six months are suddenly once more available. Many visiting sailors find that with a probable six-month stay in the country, it is worth their while acquiring a second-hand car and, having done so, they make Opua or Russell their base and do the rest of their New Zealand cruising on wheels. There are those who would say that by doing so they miss some really good cruising, but each to his own. The Bay of Islands, although very small, has very many delightful anchorages and is only really crowded over the Christmas holiday period. It is possible to go walking on most of the islands, with splendid views to be enjoyed from the higher ground.

Approach and entry

Making an approach from Fiji or Tonga, the entrance to the Bay of Islands is about 15 miles south of the Cavalli islands and 8 miles west of Cape Brett. The bay is wide and clear until you have passed Fraser Rock on your port hand and entered the well-marked Veronica Channel which, after about 4 miles, brings you to Opua on the starboard hand. New arrivals will be directed, on VHF, to the new marina.

Radio

For Opua Marina, call initially on channel 12.

Anchorage and moorings

Once clearance has taken place, Opua Marina offers two free nights berthage, space permitting (during the months of October–mid-December). The marina has 30 swing moorings available outside the breakwater for long- or short-term rental. It is quite possible to anchor, though holding is not always reliable.

Formalities

Opua is a port of entry where the officials are well used to yachts coming in for clearance. It is strongly recommended that an ETA is radioed to Russell Radio on VHF channel 16 as soon as it is possible to do so. All clearances will be carried out in the marina – Ministry of Food and Agriculture (MAF), Customs and Immigration. These officials are available seven days a week, even though they travel up from Whangarei. There is no longer any fee payable for checking in. No visas are required for Commonwealth nationals; others should obtain visas before arriving. A six-month visitor's permit, which can be extended to 12 months, will be issued on arrival. There are heavy penalties for any stops prior to official clearance at a recognised entry port.

Facilities

Opua Marina, which opened in February 2000, has 240 berths and a full range of facilities. There are two yacht yards of varying capacity, one of which can haul yachts of up to 15m (50ft). Cater Marine operate a chandlery within one of the boatyards. There are sailmakers, rigging and engineering outfits that can undertake repairs. Opua has one shop – a general store that has a fuel berth. The post office has an e-mail facility. There are more shops, including several banks in Paihia, a ten-minute drive away. There are toilets, showers and laundry facilities beside the Opua Cruising Club. Drinking water is available at the cruising club pontoon. There is a good local hospital. The Opua Cruising Club is very welcoming to yacht crews, and for a small payment you may use the premises. The club encourages visitors to enter their own yachts in the Wednesday and Friday evening races during the summer months.

Communications

The Opua Post Centre has long been known as an excellent mail drop. Letters can be held for 2–3 months, or longer, if the postmistress is contacted.

c/o Opua Post Centre
1 Beechy Street
Opua 0290
Bay of Islands
New Zealand
Fax: 00 64 9 40 274008

There is an excellent Northliner Express coach service to Auckland, which can be booked through the Opua Post Centre and will stop at Opua. The nearest airport is at Keri Keri, which runs daily flights to Auckland. Auckland international airport is a 3½-hour drive from Opua. There are several couriers to choose from.

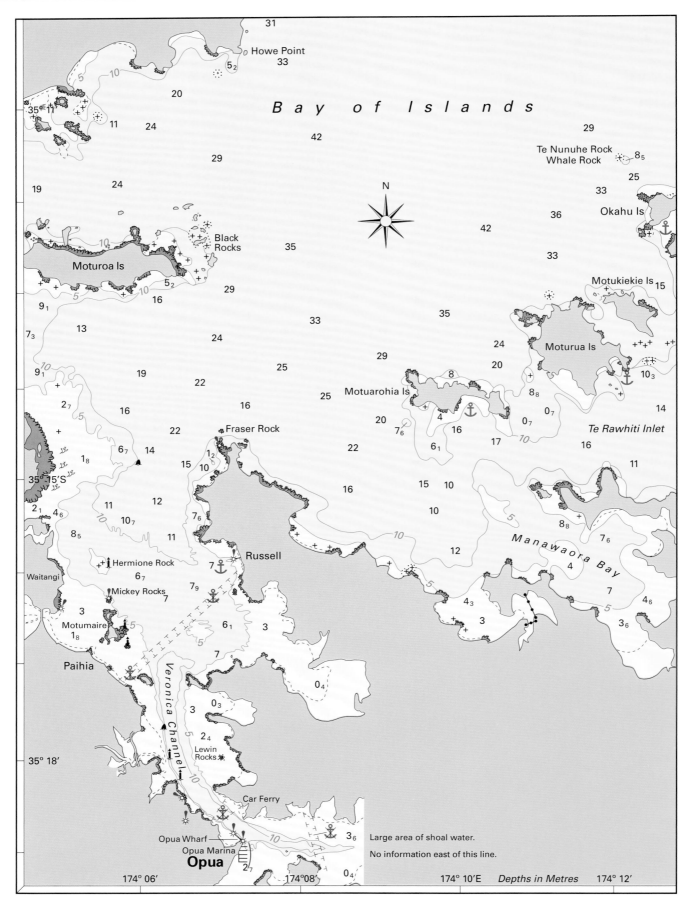

Plan 53 *Opua, New Zealand.*

29

Whangarei, North Island, New Zealand
35°42'S   174°21'E   UT+12

Springs: 2.3m	Flag: New Zealand	
Neaps: 1.7m	Currency: NZ dollar	
Charts	Admiralty	US
General	NZ 52	76050
Approach	NZ 521	76056
Harbour	NZ 5213	76056

General

Whangarei (pronounced 'fongeray') is not such a convenient port of entry as either Opua or Auckland, because it lies 24km (15 miles) up a winding river and the authorities are not forgiving to new arrivals who pause in any of the attractive anchorages for a rest on the way up. Whangarei's chief attraction to the visiting overseas sailor is that it is the ideal place to go for a serious session of refitting, particularly for those who want to carry out as much of their own work as possible. Over the years, the town has recognised the economic value of attracting visitors who want a secure inexpensive place to moor, with a variety of competitive specialist firms within walking distance. The result is that from November till the following May there is a great, and incidentally very congenial, gathering of overseas yachts taking advantage of these facilities.

Approach and entry

The entrance to Whangarei Harbour lies in the extreme north-west corner of Bream Bay between Bream Head and Marsden Point. Given the proper chart, NZ 5213, the channel marks are easily identified. It is prudent to have advance knowledge of the state of the tide as the

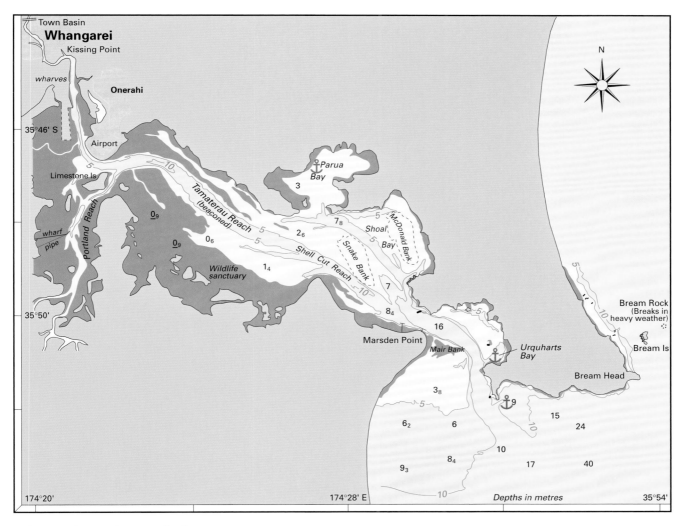

Plan 54 *Whangarei, New Zealand.*

The Town Basin at Whangarei is the favourite place for visiting yachts to gather and refit after the long crossing. Photo Andrew Hogbin.

streams run hard and little headway will be made against the full force of a spring ebb. Urquharts Bay, immediately on the starboard hand, is a very convenient and sheltered anchorage in which to wait for the best time to carry the flood upriver, always supposing that clearance has been obtained at another port. If entering at Whangarei, remain underway rather than risk the wrath of the Quarantine officials. There is plenty of depth in the channel until the approach to Kissing Point, beyond the limit of commercial traffic. Deeper-draught yachts should be careful to choose high water for the upper reaches. At the top of the tide it is possible to carry 2.1m (7ft) all the way, but local advice is to keep close to the port-hand markers and proceed with caution.

Radio

The commercial port authority can be contacted on channel 16, but the marina manager of the Whangarei Town Basin in the centre of town can be contacted on channel 64.

Anchorage and moorings

The basin immediately downstream of the road bridge has been dredged and piled to provide 108 fore-and-aft moorings, as well as 50 floating berths and 15 shoreside berths, both with power and water. Alternatively, there is a small marina, Riverside Marina, operated by Ray Roberts about 400m downstream from the town basin on the north side. It is generally fairly full, and it may well be advisable to try to book in advance.

Formalities

Those requiring entry clearance should stop at a marked wharf in the commercial area south of Kissing Point. All procedures are the same as at Opua, except

that there is no charge for the time spent alongside or the use of the incinerator. There are plans to carry out clearances at Marsden Point, at the harbour entrance.

Facilities

Austral Yachts/Dockland 5 and Riverside Marina are both well-equipped yards. They have haul-out facilities and dry storage facilities. There are independent riggers, sailmakers and cover makers. However, the main strength of Whangarei is the easy access to small specialist firms who will fabricate in stainless steel, galvanise chain, repair alternators, and do any number of other things promptly and at prices that will be a delight to anyone used to European rates. The town has a population of over 30 000, so medical or dental services are easily found, and the Pak'N Save Supermarket is only a short walk from the dock and ideal for stocking up before departure. There are a wide variety of stores all within walking distance of the Town Basin Marina. Diesel is available at Riverside Marina; petrol must be obtained from nearby service stations. Gas bottles can be delivered and picked up from the Town Basin Marina. Laundry, shower and toilet facilities are available in the Town Basin Marina. There are also two laundrettes in town. Weather information is available from Taupo Maritime Radio on channel 16, Russell Radio on channel 63, and Whangarei on channel 64. Daily weatherfaxes are posted at the Town Basin Marina.

Communications

There is an excellent bus service to Auckland. Cable Action Communications offer an e-mail facility: cable-actioncommunications@usa.net.

The post office in the town operates an efficient Poste Restante service. Alternatively, mail can be addressed to the following:

c/o Town Basin Marina
37 Quayside
Town Basin
Whangarei
New Zealand
Tel/Fax: 00 64 9 438 2033

Riverside Marina
PO Box 1709
Whangarei
New Zealand
Tel: 00 64 9 438 2248
Fax: 00 64 9 438 9581

Springs: 2.9m	Flag: New Zealand	
Neaps: 2.0m	Currency: NZ dollar	
Charts	Admiralty	US
General	NZ 53	76050
Approach	NZ 532	76052
Harbour	NZ 5322	76052

General

Auckland, known as the 'City of Sails', rivals the capital of Wellington for prominence in every visitor's mind. It is certainly the capital of yachting and, as a recent venue for the America's Cup, has gained in stature. The Waitemata Harbour has a magnificent setting against the backdrop of the city and the bridge.

Approach and entry

The entry to Waitemata Harbour from the Hauraki Gulf is broad and clear, and presents little difficulty by day or night.

Radio

The commercial port authority can be contacted on channel 16.

Anchorage and moorings

Unless you are lucky enough to borrow a vacant mooring, the choice is limited to a number of marinas – most of which are a little way out of town. Westhaven Marina is the closest physically to the city. It cannot be missed on the port hand immediately below the bridge. Call the office for a berth on channel 13. There may be the option of lying four square between piles at a very modest charge, but the dinghy facilities are not ideal. During the 2000 America's Cup events, liveaboards were restricted, but Westhaven was again open for liveaboards in 2001. Orams Yard, close to the centre of town, has a small marina and directly across the harbour is Bayswater Marina. It requires a 20-minute car or bus ride to the centre of Auckland, but there is a regular ferry from the marina, which takes about 10 minutes. Bayswater Marina welcomes liveaboards. Just to the north of Auckland, on the south side of the Whangaparaoa peninsula, is the very popular Gulf Harbour Marina, much used by visiting yachts. Although it is further from the city, it has excellent haul-out facilities, long-term hardstand storage, a chandlery and liveaboard berths.There is a daily ferry service from Gulf Harbour to downtown Auckland. Travel by car or bus can take an hour or more. These three marinas are the most often used by Pacific crossers, but there are several others listed in the Auckland area. Further information is available by obtaining a free copy of *The Boaties Book* published by the Auckland Yacht and Boating Association (www.ayba.org.nz).

Westhaven Marina Office
Tel: 00 64 9 309 1352
Fax: 00 64 9 367 5477
www.westhaven.co.nz

Bayswater Marina
Tel: 64 9 446 1600
Fax: 64 9 446 1605
www.bayswater.co.nz

Gulf Harbour Marina
Tel: 64 9 424 6200
Fax: 64 9 424 0703
www.gulf-harbour.co.nz

Formalities

Clearance for yachts entering New Zealand will be given promptly on arrival. A call on channel 16 to the harbour authority will give directions to an alongside berth on the city waterfront. Quarantine, Immigration and Customs officials will all come aboard. It is worth bearing in mind that there are severe penalties for any stops made prior to clearance, and that the Quarantine authority will confiscate any fresh foodstuffs, most tinned meat, and certainly any honey. New Zealand officials are very polite, friendly and thorough. Be prepared to have fridges and cupboards searched for items that may jeopardise local industries.

Facilities

There is probably no other place in the southern hemisphere where such a wide choice of facilities and expertise is available to the visiting yachtsman. Having said that, unless you place your business in the hands of a yard, you will find that the specialists you deal with are fairly widely dispersed – the loan of a car is to be valued very highly! Inexpensive used cars may be purchased with a 'buy back' option, through used-car dealers, or at auction. For marine gear of all types, the area around Beaumont Street has three chandleries within easy reach of each other and a wide variety of brand-name service centres and retailers.

Communications

This major city has an international airport and all the communications facilities that anyone could wish for.

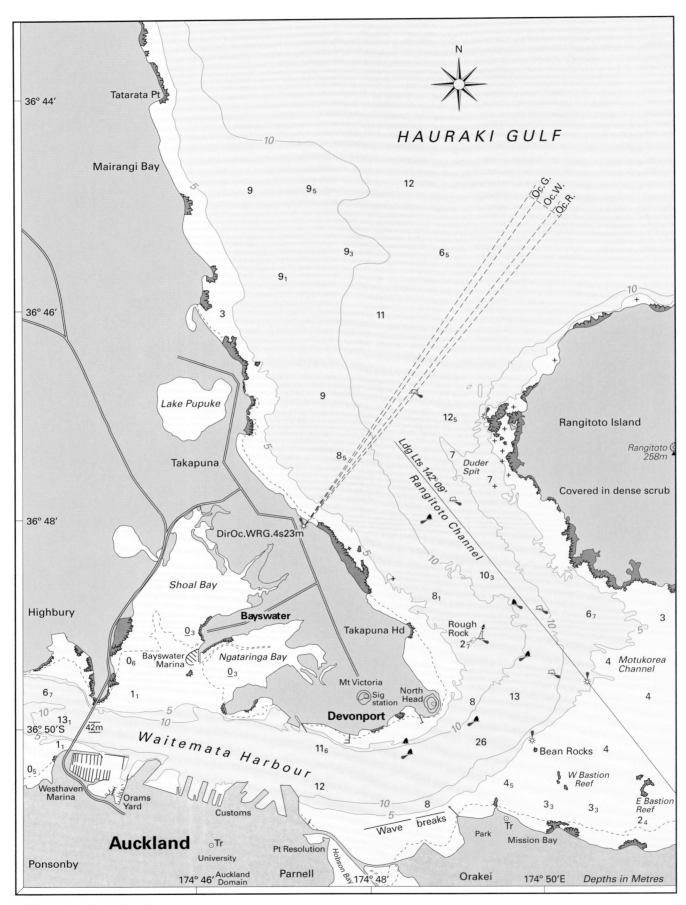

Plan 55 *Auckland, New Zealand.*

Springs: 1.1m	Flag: Vanuatu	
Neaps: 0.2m	Currency: Vatu	
Charts	Admiralty	US
General	4604	82025
Approach	1494	820560
Harbour	1494	82571

General

Port Vila, the main entry port for Vanuatu, makes a delightful stopover between Fiji and New Caledonia. With the Vanuatu Tourist Board promoting these islands as 'the untouched paradise', who but the hardest-hearted sailor could fail to be seduced by that title. Do go and see the Vanuatu Show held once a week at the Chief's Nakamal. The Wan Smallbag theatre group, by song, dance and sketch, tell the story of their country and customs. Other spectacles include the Land Divers of Pentecost in April/May and Tanna Island Dance in August. For more information, visit the Vanuatu Visitors' Bureau website (www.vanuatu.net.vu) and the 'Yachting World' website (www.yachtingworld.net).

Approach and entry

Arriving from the east, pass Pango Point marked by a light (which experience has shown to be less than 100 per cent reliable), and pick up the leading marks (078°) that lead into Mélé Bay. Continue on the transit between Arbel Point, which has a radio mast on it, and Ifira Island, going between the red and green buoys, and the Quarantine buoy will be found close to port when approaching the shoreline.

Radio

Channel 16 on VHF for the authorities.

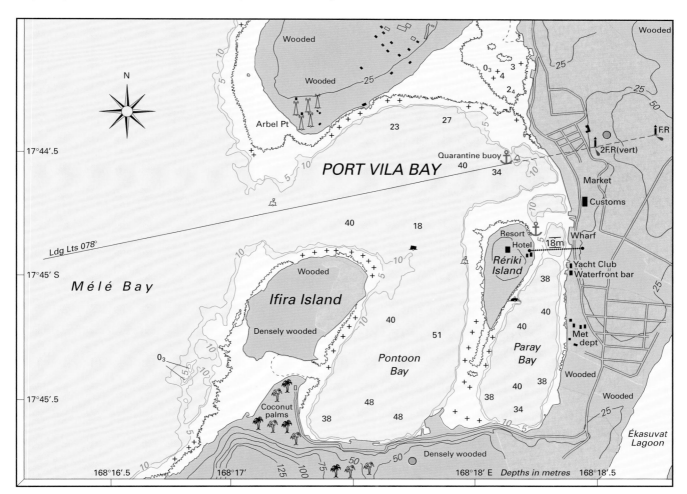

Plan 56 *Port Vila, Vanuatu.*

The local women of Port Vila on market day. Photo Ros Hogbin.

Anchorage and moorings

No marinas, but it is possible to moor stern-to by the Waterfront Bar and Grill or pick up a mooring, belonging to 'Yachting World'; contact them on channel 16. Anchorage is on the north-east side of Rériki Island on a sandy patch between the coral reefs. If going between Rériki Island and the mainland, perhaps to re-fuel, do beware of the overhead power cable that had a clearance of only 18m (59ft); however, there are reports that it has now been raised. There are many moorings for visitors in Paray Bay.

Waterfront Bar
Tel: 00 6 78 23273

Formalities

Anchor in the designated Quarantine area or tie up to the Quarantine buoy. Announce your arrival by calling 'Yachting World' on VHF channel 16, and be patient. Customs and Agriculture control will visit the yacht; do not go ashore first. There are strict quarantine regulations for fresh fruit and vegetables, and also fresh meat. Once cleared, proceed to Immigration ashore for an entry permit. A one-month visa is issued initially. A cruising permit will be required for sailing among the many islands within Vanuatu. Officials do not work on Sundays.

Facilities

No haul-out, but minor repairs are possible. Use 'Yachting World' for all main services. Radio equipment can be acquired, duty free, quite reasonably. The people who run the Waterfront Bar and Grill, which has a great reputation for good food at low prices, are the main source of information on where to find whatever is wanted. There is very limited chandlery. Fuel and drinking water can be obtained at the 'Yachting World' dock, next to the Waterfront Bar. Propane gas is available nearby and petrol can be obtained at the Shell Garage across the road. There are banks and reasonable shops, including two laundrettes, supermarkets and a market in the town. The local meteorological office and the yacht club post information daily on their notice board. The Waterfront Bar or the post office can be used for telephone and fax services. There is an internet café called Cortex Cyber E Space, located on Main Street.

Yachting World
PO Box 1507
Port Vila
Efate Island
Vanuatu
Tel/Fax: 00 6 78 23273

Communications

There are flights to New Caledonia, Australia, New Zealand and Fiji. There are also local flights to Tanna to see the volcano. Mail can be addressed to the Post Office, Poste Restante, or alternatively to:

c/o VCYC
PO Box 1252
Port Vila
Efate Island
Vanuatu

32 Nouméa, New Caledonia
22°17'S 166°26'E UT+11

Springs: 1.1m	Flag: French	
Neaps: 0.5m	Currency: CFP	
Charts	Admiralty	US
General	936	82030
Approach	2907	
Harbour	480	

General

New Caledonia makes a useful stopover between Vanuatu and wherever you are going in Australia. Nouméa, the capital, lies towards the southern end and on the lee side of the largest island of La Grande Terre. Many of the inhabitants are Europeans concerned with mining enterprises on the island. Various mineral deposits have been found, including nickel, chrome and iron ore, thus there is extensive mining, leaving large bare areas of red earth, contrasting with the green of the vegetation. French is spoken in Nouméa, and the shops are certainly up to Papeete standards, offering a tempting but expensive array of French fashions and food. The best cruising grounds are in the Loyalty Islands and in the well-known Isles of Pines; in both places the water is incredibly blue and clear. However, if it becomes necessary to sell your yacht, Nouméa is one of the best places in the Pacific to do this. Many a deal is struck in Port Moselle Marina.

Approach and entry

When arriving from Vanuatu and after negotiating one of the passes between the Loyalty Islands, head for the Havannah Channel (see plan no 16), providing there is sufficient daylight. Once in the lagoon, yachts continue first west and then north-west inside the reef. After rounding Îlot Brun, Nouméa Harbour can be seen. Coming in from the east or south, the Amédée Light, which lies close to the Passe de Boulari, makes a splendid mark for entering the lagoon.

Radio

Channel 16 to contact Nouméa Radio and channel 67 for Port Moselle Marina.

Anchorage and moorings

It is possible to anchor in the Petite Rade or the Baie de l'Orphelinat within Nouméa Harbour. There is the Port Moselle Marina (where the first night is free) and also the Club Nautique de Caledonien, but that is some way out of town.

Harbourmaster
Tel: 00 6 87 27 59 66
Fax: 00 6 87 27 54 90

Formalities

Nouméa is the only port of entry in New Caledonia. Contact Port Moselle on channel 67. Customs and Immigration will board on arrival at the marina, but their offices in town will have to be found for outward clearance. No visa is required for a stay of less than 30 days.

Facilities

A larger than usual locally based fleet of yachts inevitably supports a reasonable number of facilities. There is at least one yard with a travel lift, and a big well-stocked chandlery in town. However, depending on the current rate of exchange, visitors may find Nouméa

The Amédée Light stands close to the Passe de Boulari when entering the lagoon from the west and is the tallest metal lighthouse in the world. Photo Michael Pocock.

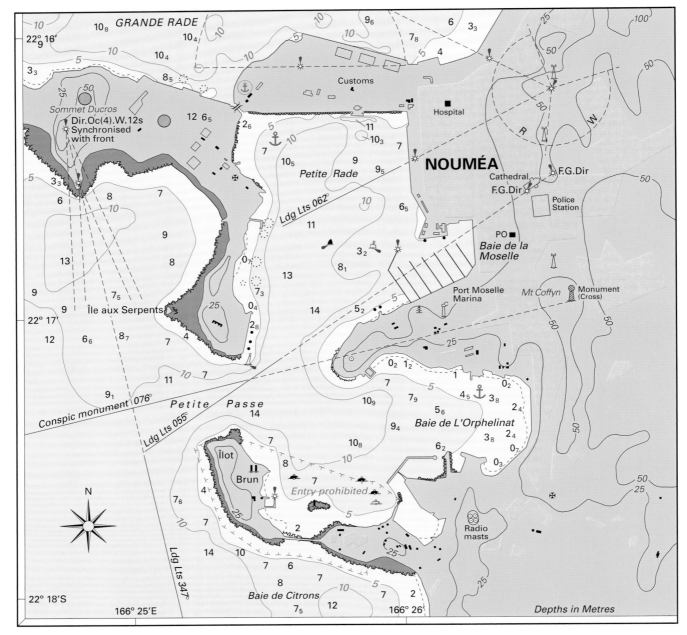

Plan 57 *Nouméa, New Caledonia.*

expensive, particularly if the purchases can in fact be delayed until either New Zealand or Australia. Laundry can be picked up and delivered at the marina. There is a good market next to Port Moselle and supermarkets on the waterfront. The marina has a range of services, including duty-free diesel and petrol available after clearing out.

Communications

There is an international airport with flights to Singapore, New Zealand, Australia and Vanuatu, and also domestic flights to the Loyalty Islands and Isles of Pines. Nouméa is a sophisticated city with all modern means of communication. Port Moselle Marina will hold mail:

Port Moselle Marina
BP 2960-98846
Nouméa
New Caledonia
Tel: 00 6 87 277197
Fax: 00 6 87 277129

33 Sydney, New South Wales, Australia

33°50'S 151°17'E UT+10

Springs: 1.3m	Flag: Australia	
Neaps: 0.9m	Currency: Australian dollar	
Charts	Admiralty	US
General	AUS 423	74000
Approach	AUS 361	74151
Harbour	AUS 200	75264

General

Sydney Harbour must rank as one of the finest natural harbours in the world. It is, if anything, enhanced by the growth of civilisation, with the combined features of the bridge, the Opera House and the high rise of the city itself all creating a grandeur that is undoubtedly impressive. Sydney is Australia's most prominent maritime city and is host to more major yachting spectacles than any other. All the main attractions of the city are concentrated centrally and, no matter where the visitor is berthed, the efficient public transport system will always provide a swift and easy route to the principal places of interest.

Approach and entry

There is no problem entering Sydney Harbour. Sail in between the North and South Heads, and then turn south or north of Middle Head depending on whether you are heading for Middle Harbour or Sydney Harbour. There is only the one isolated shoal patch just to the west of South Head, called, delightfully, the Sow and Pigs. There are now flashing lights that mark the edge of this shallow patch, but with the aid of a large-scale chart this is easy to pass on either side. There is a bar across the entrance to Middle Harbour with a least depth believed to be 2.7m (9ft). If arriving from overseas, you are required to give 3 hours' notice of your ETA by radio, and in return you will be advised to proceed for clearance to the Customs/AQIS boarding station, on the eastern side of the Pilot Station jetty, unless you have animals on board, when you will be directed to the Customs buoy in Watsons Bay.

The Harbour Bridge, completed in 1934, was a masterpiece of engineering in its day. Photo Michael Pocock.

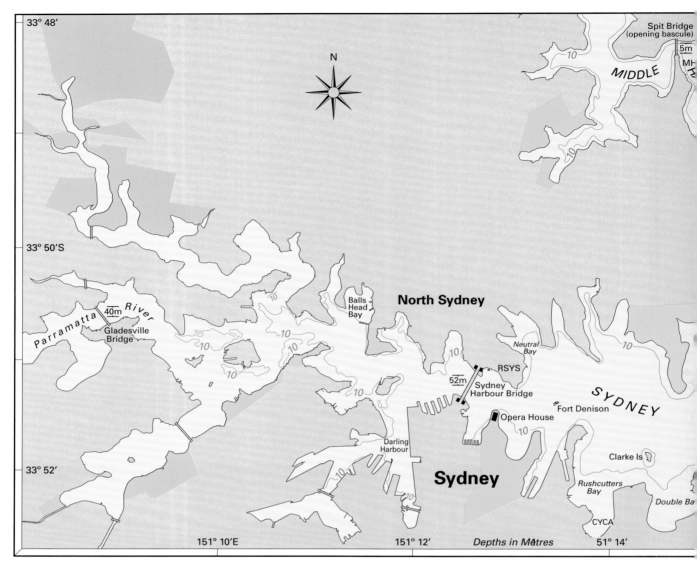

Plan 58 *Sydney (Port Jackson), Australia.*

Radio

Port radio monitors channel 16. For giving notice of arrival, call any Telstra coastal radio station on channel 16 or SSB 2182, 4125. Callers will be directed to a working channel.

Anchorage and moorings

The official international anchorage is Balls Head Bay on the starboard hand above the bridge. Most of the berths in Sydney are allocated. However, the Cruising Yacht Club of Australia in Rushcutters Bay may be able to offer a berth. The club is the organising centre for many major racing events including the annual Sydney to Hobart classic which starts on Boxing Day. The club marina has 180 berths and 30 moorings with provision for some visitors. There is also a commercial marina in Rushcutters Bay which may be a useful overflow. The Royal Sydney Yacht Squadron across the water from the Opera House has a marina with 90 berths and an

associated repair facility with an area of hardstanding. The Middle Harbour Yacht Club, on the port hand about 1½ miles from Middle Head, may have space in their marina. This is an extremely friendly and active club that has a relatively low-key atmosphere and a busy programme throughout the week. There are a variety of commercial marinas up the Parramatta river above the bridge.

Telephone
Royal Sydney Yacht Squadron 02 9955 7171
Cruising Yacht Club of Australia 02 9363 9731
Middle Harbour Yacht Club 02 9969 2711

Formalities

Australia is a bureaucratic nation and the formalities for visiting yachts have a history of being anything but user friendly! For those entering from overseas there is one major pitfall that is worth avoiding. It is essential to obtain an entry visa in advance. Arrival without one

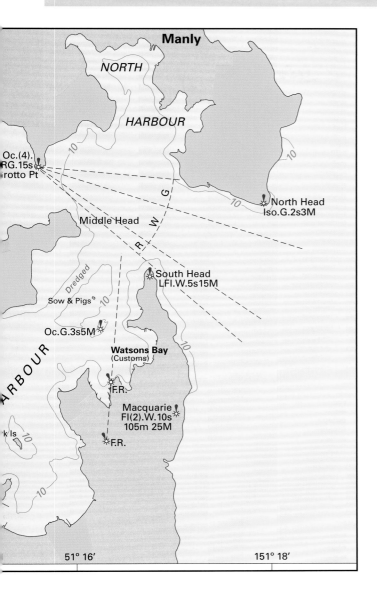

plete. Once entered, an overseas yacht is required to report on arrival at each Customs port visited.

Facilities

This is a major yachting centre with a wide choice of facilities and supporting services, albeit quite widely spread. Very good haul-out opportunities exist at the Royal Sydney Yacht Squadron, the Cruising Yacht Club of Australia and at the Royal Prince Alfred Yacht Club. The last of these is on the Pittwater, a branch of Broken Bay just north of Sydney Harbour. Above the bridge in the upper reaches of the Parramatta there are various commercial facilities to choose from. The *Sydney Region Boating Directory*, a free booklet published annually by Marine Directories, tel (02) 9810 5990, e-mail mardir@bigpond.net.au, provides very useful lists of contact details for all major nautical services.

Communications

Sydney is a major city with all the communications facilities that are needed.

will result in a fine and, most probably, a limited stay. Before arrival at a port of entry, 24 hours' notice should be given by radio to any coastal station, asking them to inform Quarantine and Customs. Alternatively, you can contact the Australian Customs Service on 02 9317 7482 or harbour control on 02 9296 4001. Clearance must be obtained from Quarantine, Customs and Immigration before anyone from the yacht goes ashore. There is a flat rate per vessel charge for quarantine clearance between 0800 and 1700 on weekdays. Make sure you arrive in office hours and not at the weekend, or you will be charged substantial overtime rates. All dairy and egg products, fresh meat and meat products, seeds, nuts, fresh fruit and vegetables and live plants, honey and some tinned meats will be confiscated. Before a cruising permit is issued (valid for 12 months or the length of the captain's visa, whichever is shorter), a detailed itinerary must be submitted, listing all the places you intend to visit in the course of your time in Australia. This is a pretty tall order on the day of arrival, and is necessarily going to be far from com-

Coffs Harbour, New South Wales, Australia

*30°18'S 153°09'E UT+10**

Springs: 1.3m	*Flag: Australia*	
Neaps: 0.7m	*Currency: Australian dollar*	
Charts	*Admiralty*	*US*
General	AUS 424	74000
Approach	AUS 363	74162
Harbour		

General

Coffs Harbour is the only port of entry between Brisbane and Newcastle, and has long been popular with visiting yachts arriving from the east. It is about

230 miles north of Sydney and is a breakwater harbour with good comfortable berths in the inner basin.

Approach and entry

The yacht facilities are in the eastern corner of the inner harbour, but those arriving from a foreign port should not enter further than the outer harbour until they have been boarded or received radio clearance to proceed.

Radio

Channel 16 VHF or repeater channels 81 and 82. Weather bulletins are broadcast by Sydney Radio at

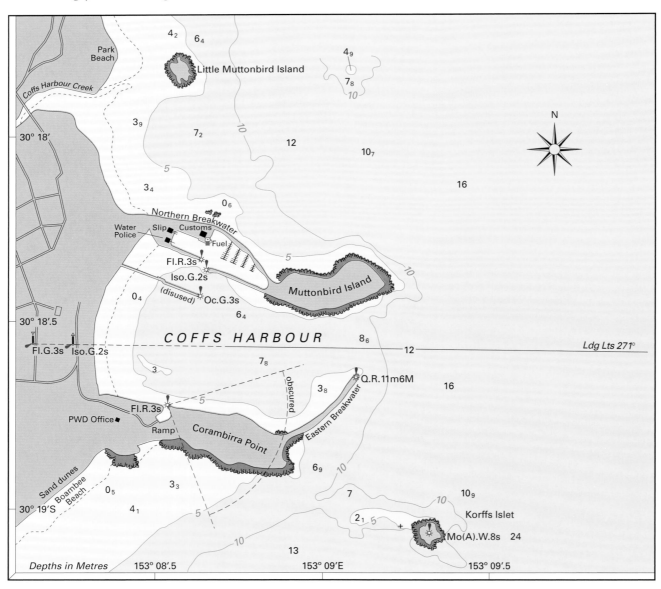

Plan 59 *Coffs Harbour, Australia.*

0803, 1203 and 1703 on channel 67 and 2201, 4426, 6507 and 8176 kHz.

Anchorage and mooring

It is possible to anchor anywhere in the outer harbour, but it is better to stay well clear of the beach. Swell is a problem and this can cause a yacht to drag. There is no anchoring permitted in the inner harbour and one must take a berth. Look for one marked with a V (for visitor). The marina is run by the Public Works Department from offices on Coffs Harbour Jetty. Showers, toilets and laundry are provided, and the key should be available from the office of the Public Works Department located at the marina. Water and power are connected at the marina berths. The marina charges are much more reasonable than in Sydney.

Formalities

The formalities for entering are tiresome, but no more so than anywhere else in Australia, and the reader should refer to either Sydney Harbour (no 33) or Brisbane harbour (no 35) for full details. When clearing for New Zealand, Customs may open on a Saturday at no charge.

Facilities

The slipway between the yacht club and the water police can handle vessels up to 70 tons. Water is obtainable at the marina; fuel is only obtainable by arrangement at the fishermans fuelling berth (see plan). Showers are also available at the club, along with bar meals and snacks. There are good shops, banks and a laundry, and a post office in the town.

Communications

There is a local airport with internal flights connecting with the major cities. There are also daily bus and train services. Australia has a first-class telephone system, including credit phones that take credit cards such as Visa and American Express. Coffs Harbour is a holiday resort, with all the associated facilities that you would expect of such a place.

35 Brisbane, Queensland, Australia

27°30'S 153°00'E UT+10*

Springs: 2.1m	Flag: Australia	
Neaps: 1.3m	Currency: Australian dollar	
Charts	Admiralty	US
General	AUS 424	74181
Approach	AUS 236	74182
Harbour	AUS 237 and 238	74186

General

Brisbane is a fine modern city on the banks of the Brisbane river, some few miles above the wide expanse of Moreton Bay. It is a good port of entry, particularly now that formalities are carried out in Scarborough Marina, at the south end of Deception Bay, rather than halfway up the river on the way to the city. In October the blue of the jacaranda trees is an unforgettable feature of the city. It is conveniently situated for yachts arriving from the South Pacific to sit out the cyclone season. It is also a good place from which to begin a cruise north to the Whitsundays and Great Barrier Reef and south to the Gold Coast.

Approach and entry

Approaching Moreton Bay, it is necessary to choose between the North West Channel, which opens close to Caloundra Head (and is recommended as the safest initial approach), or the North East Channel, which is much closer to Moreton Head. In either case, the navigator must have his wits about him and not relax until well into the bay. There is then a choice between finding the entrance beacons that mark the start of the dredged channel into the Brisbane river, or negotiating the relatively shallow channels that lead to Manly Harbour. The river is clearly marked and the only serious consideration is the stream that runs hard, particularly on the ebb. Clearance for arrivals from overseas is given at the Quarantine Yacht Berth in Scarborough Marina, Redcliffe. The entrance beacons to Scarborough Harbour include a yellow special mark.

Radio

Channel 16 or 73 VHF, or 2182, 4125 SSB. Single Sideband is in general use in Australian waters, and the operators are keen to establish contact with vessels – particularly after each weather forecast and traffic list.

Boats moored off the Botanical Gardens in the heart of Brisbane. Photo Michael Pocock.

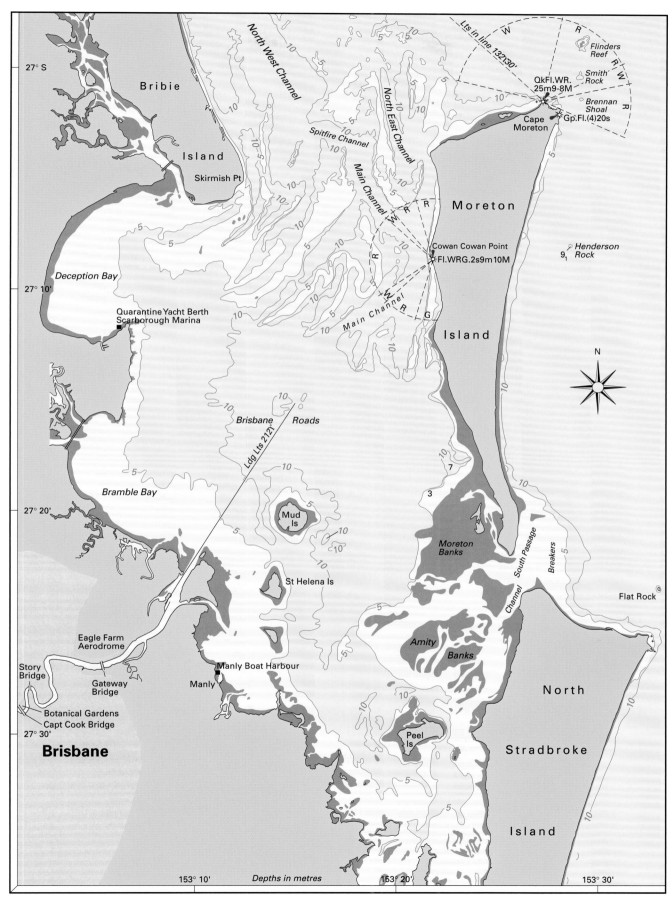

Plan 60 *Brisbane, Australia.*

Anchorage and mooring

In Brisbane itself, visiting yachts lie between piles off the Botanical Gardens just above the Story Bridge right in the heart of the city. These moorings are available from the Port of Brisbane Authority. There is a dinghy dock, and showers and washing machines nearby. Another attractive alternative is to lie in Manly Harbour. There are marina berths available either commercially or within the facilities of the Royal Queensland Yacht Squadron. Manly is a 30-minute train or bus ride from the city.

Formalities

Yachts arriving from overseas should go first to the Quarantine berth in Scarborough Boat Harbour. It is marked by code flags L and Q and a Quarantine sign, illuminated after dark. There is 2.0m depth at chart datum within the harbour. Contact Quarantine, Customs or Scarborough Marina in advance by VHF or SSB. It is essential to obtain an entry visa in advance. Arrival without one will result in a fine and, most probably, a limited stay. There is a flat rate per vessel charge for Quarantine clearance between 0800 and 1700 on weekdays. Make sure you arrive in office hours and not at the weekend, or you will be charged substantial overtime rates. All dairy and egg products, fresh meat and meat products, seeds, nuts, fresh fruit and vegetables and live plants, honey and some tinned meats will be confiscated. Before a cruising permit is issued (valid for 12 months or the length of the captain's visa, whichever is shorter), a detailed itinerary must be submitted, listing all the places you intend to visit in the course of your time in Australia. This is a pretty tall order on your very first day of arrival, and is necessarily going to be far from complete. Once entered, an overseas yacht is required to report on arrival at each Customs port visited.

Facilities

If facilities are needed for servicing the yacht, then Manly will probably be a better location than the city centre of Brisbane. Manly is the principal centre for local sailing activity, and all needs can be met. Most yacht clubs offer hauling and slipping facilities. There is a fast train service from Manly to the city. Marine weather forecasts are given out on VHF channel 67 by Brisbane Radio at 0833 and 1803 daily. These forecasts cover coastal areas and Moreton Bay.

Communications

There are first-class local bus and train services to and from Brisbane City and good air connections to all other states and overseas. The main post office has a reliable Poste Restante mail service:

Poste Restante
GPO
Brisbane 4000
Australia

36 Bundaberg, Queensland, Australia

24°52'S 152°20'E UT+10*

Springs: 2.0m	Flag: Australia	
Neaps: 1.1m	Currency: Australian dollar	
Charts	Admiralty	US
General	AUS 426	74190
Approach	AUS 365 or 366	74191
Harbour	AUS 243	74191

General

Bundaberg, known locally as Bundy, is in the heart of the Queensland sugar growing country; it is well known for Bundaberg rum, a very stimulating local product. It is a popular port of entry for those approaching from New Caledonia. The town itself lies a few miles upstream on the Burnett river, where the first road bridge forms the limit of navigation for a masted vessel. As an initial introduction to a small Australian town it is a worthy representative, with quite good facilities for both medical and nautical requirements. Surprisingly, there is an astonishing variety of urban birdlife to be seen just by sitting on deck on a mooring. Bundaberg Port Marina brochure gives a list of local attractions, which include turtle hatching and whale watching.

Approach and entry

The entrance channel to the river has been dredged and is well marked by beacons. The streams run hard and must be respected, particularly in the lower reaches. If clearance is required, then it is necessary to enter the small basin on the south side of the channel at Burnett Heads, close to the mouth of the river.

Radio

Contact Bundaberg Air Sea Rescue on VHF channel 16 or 81.

Anchorage and moorings

Below the bridge in Bundaberg there is a marina and some associated moorings on the port hand, and harbour authority moorings to starboard. There are a number of advantages gained by using the marina or the marina moorings. The excellent showers and laundry facilities are very welcome after a sea passage. Those on the moorings can take their dinghies to the marina, thus enjoying a secure landing on the more convenient side for getting to the shops, while also enjoying the same facilities as the berth holders.

Formalities

As already stated, clearance for yachts coming in from overseas is given at the Quarantine yacht berth in Bundaberg Port Marina, near the mouth of the Burnett river. The formalities are tiresome, but no more so than elsewhere in Australia, and the reader should refer to either Sydney Harbour (no 33) or Brisbane Harbour (no 35) for full details.

Facilities

There are slipways and service facilities available should you arrive in need of immediate attention. There is also a good chandlery within the marina.

Communications

There is a local airport with internal flights connecting the major cities. There are also daily bus and train services south to Brisbane or north to Cairns.

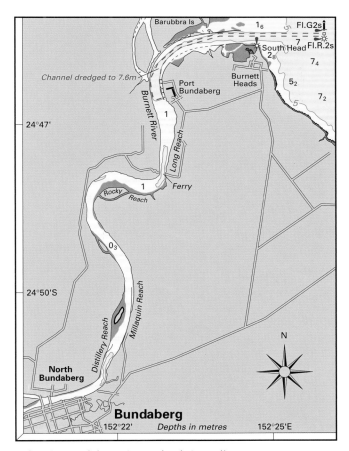

Plan 61 *Bundaberg, Queensland, Australia.*

37

Cairns, Queensland, Australia

16°55'S 145°47'E UT+10*

Springs: 1.8m	Flag: Australia	
Neaps: 0.9m	Currency: Australian dollar	
Charts	Admiralty	US
General	AUS 373	74253
Approach	AUS 830	74253
Harbour	AUS 262	74252

General

Cairns is a popular entry port for those heading towards Cape York and the Torres Strait, having come from Papua New Guinea, the Solomon Islands or Vanuatu. Cairns is both a major tourist centre for the north-east and a commercial port. There is a large prawn fishing fleet which operates as far afield as the Gulf of Carpentaria, and a prosperous shipbuilding industry. There are rain forests and sugar cane areas to be seen and, as a result of the tropical climate, the streets are lined with attractive flowering shrubs: hibiscus, frangipani and bougainvillaea.

Approach and entry

Arriving direct from the Pacific islands, a vessel should enter through Grafton Passage, leaving Euston Reef Light to port and then steering for the lead light on Fitzroy Island, which has a range of 22 miles. Grafton Passage is 5 miles wide, but care must be taken to allow for strong currents setting across the passage. The entrance to Cairns is easy by day or night, with port and starboard beacons all the way into the river.

Radio

Channel 16 VHF for Cairns Port Radio, or call Townsville Radio on 2182, 4125, 6125 kHz (working frequencies 2201, 4426 and 6507 kHz). Coastal forecasts are on these frequencies at 0603 and 1603 daily (local time) and Seaphone channel 27 with forecasts at 0633 and 1633 daily.

Anchorage and mooring

There are marine berths available from two marinas in Cairns and one a few miles north, as well as pile berths opposite the city on the eastern side of the estuary. Anchorage is possible at the entrance to the estuary, but holding ground is not secure during wind against tide conditions. Yachts that anchor on the eastern side of the river across from the town take their dinghies over and leave them on the yacht club beach.

Formalities

The formalities for entering are tiresome, but no more so than anywhere else in Australia, and the reader should refer to either Sydney Harbour (no 33) or Brisbane Harbour (no 35) for full details. Yachts requiring inward clearance should call Townsville Radio on 4125 kHz to give an initial ETA, and call again on channel 16 to update the ETA with Cairns port control. Yachts are generally directed to no 1 berth just inside the river to await clearance.

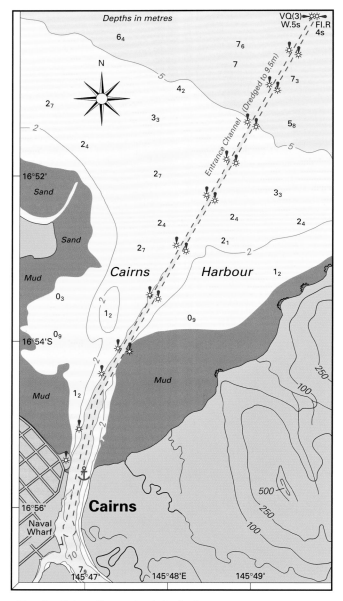

Plan 62 *Cairns, Queensland, Australia.*

View from the anchorage in Cairns towards the marina and Yacht Club on the north side of the river. Photo David Russell.

Facilities

There are several slipways, two travel lifts (40 and 160 tons), two yachts clubs, and all repairs are available. Fresh water and fuel are obtainable at the marina pontoon. Propane can be got from the Allgas depot close to the river. Good shopping, and all the major banks are within easy distance.

Communications

There are regular bus and train services to all destinations and an international airport. The recommended mailing address is:

Poste Restante
GPO
Cairns
Queensland 4870
Australia

38

Honiara, Guadalcanal, Solomon Islands
9°25'S 159°58'E UT+11

Springs: 1.1m	Flag: Solomon Islands	
Neaps: 0.2m	Currency: Solomons dollar	
Charts	Admiralty	US
General	3997	82374
Approach	1713	82377
Harbour	1750	82377

General

Since the Second World War, Honiara has been the capital of the Solomon Islands. It is an entry port, but most visitors are likely to have cleared in to the country elsewhere as Honiara is situated roughly in the middle of the many islands that make up the country. Guadalcanal was the scene of some of the fiercest fighting between American and Japanese forces during the Second World War, and the remains of battle are now tourist attractions or sites of pilgrimage, depending on one's viewpoint. In recent years, the local economy and

civil issues have had an impact on the numbers of visitors to the islands, but there seems to be a will to overcome this.

Approach and entry

Yachts are expected to anchor in Bokana Bay. Entry to the bay is straightforward, provided the leading marks can be distinguished. The lower one is hard to pick out and it is advisable to avoid entering with the sun in your eyes. The reefs on either side of the entrance channel are not easy to locate as the water is not very clear. A night entry is not recommended, as the power and reliability of the lights cannot be confirmed. Dinghy landing is usually easy on the beach at the head of the bay.

Radio

It is sensible to assume that no radio watch is maintained by any shore-based organisation.

Anchorage and moorings

Yachts anchor off the breakwater at the south-eastern end of the bay and tie up stern-to at the breakwater. It is easy enough to secure a line, but chafe is a real problem. Bokana Bay is open to the north and west, and conditions can become uncomfortable or worse when the wind is from those directions. Squalls can spring up suddenly and yachts may have to beat a hasty retreat. Local lore states that if Savo Island is blotted out by cloud, expect wind from the north-west. Much more secure anchorage is available some 20 miles across Iron Bottom Sound in Tulaghi Harbour (BA 1766), the pre-war capital that was destroyed in the hostilities.

Formalities

The yacht club situated at the southern end of Bokana Bay will direct the skipper to Customs and Immigration should clearance, either in or out, be needed. All the necessary paperwork can be conducted ashore, but officials may visit the yacht.

Facilities

The yacht club extends free membership for a limited period to members of recognised yacht clubs and their crew. The clubhouse is a pleasant haven of shade and a source of cold drinks, filling snacks and information. It can arrange laundry services. There are a number of shops within easy walking distance of the club, and an excellent open-air market somewhat further away

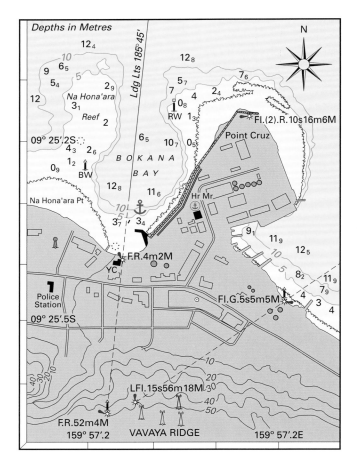

Plan 63 *Honiara, Guadalcanal, Solomon Islands.*

where fruit and vegetables, fish, and also local artefacts are sold. More food shops exist in Chinatown, about 1 mile to the east. There is a petrol station to the west of the yacht club from which small quantities of fuel can be bought; larger quantities can probably be arranged through the port captain. Unless the need for large quantities of fuel is pressing, it is probably easier to fuel at Gizo where Mobil has an alongside wharf. Chandlery is extremely limited. Some engineering and ship-repair facilities are available. For up-to-date information about local conditions in the Solomon Islands, contact a local dive operator – Kerrie Kennedy – who should be able to advise:

DiveGizo@welkam.solomon.com.sb
Tel: 677 60253
Fax: 677 60297

The British High Commission is also a useful source of information about local conditions in both the Solomon Islands and neighbouring countries. There is a Papua New Guinea consulate, from which visas to visit that country can be obtained.

Communications

International flights are available. International phone calls can be made from the post office.

Moongazer *anchored at Tavanipupu in the Marau Sound at the south-east end of Guadalcanal Island. Photo Marcia Pirie.*

39 **Tarawa,** Gilbert Islands, Kiribati

1°22'N 173°56'E UT+12

Springs: 1.7m	Flag: Kiribati	
Neaps: 0.5m	Currency: Australian dollar	
Charts	Admiralty	US
General	731	83005
Approach	700	83059
Harbour	3269	

General

Tarawa Atoll is not only the principal atoll of the Gilbert Island group, it is also the administrative centre for the whole of the Republic of Kiribati. It is the only port of entry for the group and, as such, is an essential first stop for any yacht calling in at the Gilberts. Tarawa is a large triangular atoll. There is a string of islands on the north-eastern side and another string

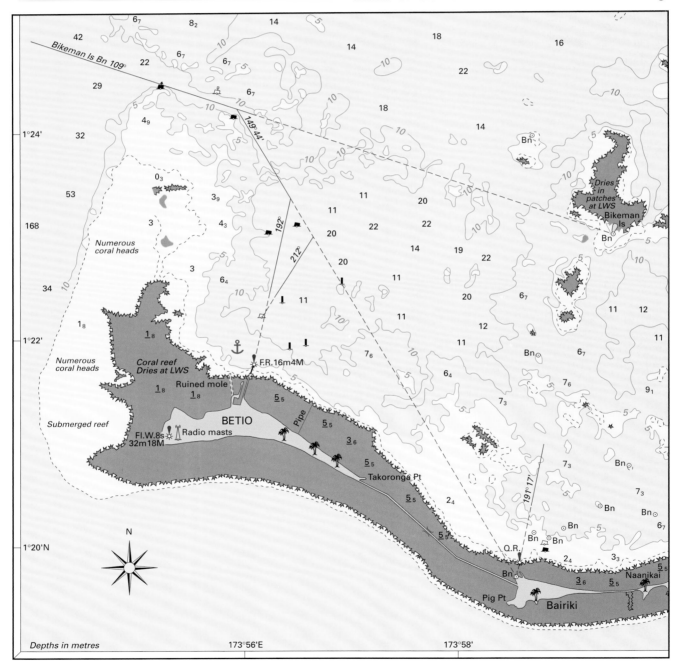

Plan 64 *Tarawa, Gilbert Islands, Kiribati.*

joined by a causeway forming the base or southern side of the triangle. The harbour and the administrative centre are at Betio and Bairiki, both on the southern side. Tarawa was occupied by the Japanese in the Second World War, and subsequently liberated in a major action by US forces. There are many rusting relics of the battle to be seen. The island of Abiang, just north of Tarawa, is a delightful place to visit, and the return to Tarawa is an easy daysail to clear out. Stamps from Kiribati are collectors' items and a Philatelic Office adjoins the post office. A ride to the airport is worthwhile to see the Taro pits and more rural villages.

Approach and entry

The approach to Tarawa must be made with extreme caution because the reef that forms the west side, through which the pass lies, is largely submerged. The entry to the lagoon is by way of a pass 4 miles north of Betio on a course leading towards Bikeman Island on 109°T. This isolated island well out in the lagoon has a tripod beacon towards its southern end, 11.6m (38ft) high, with a white triangular topmark. Bikeman Island itself is now little more than a sand cay and may yet disappear altogether. When no 3 float is abeam to port, then alter to 149°T for a course into the lagoon. Leave the rectangular topmarks to port and the triangular ones to starboard.

Radio

On arrival, call Tarawa Radio on channel 16.

Anchorage and moorings

Yachts can anchor inshore of commercial vessels in 6m (20ft) sand off Betio. There is, however, a considerable fetch across the lagoon, so that there is an uncomfortable exposure to winds from west through north to east. Any attempt to enter the small boat harbour should only be made at high water. Exploring the rest of the lagoon can be a way of finding a more comfortable berth, but the clarity of the water is not ideal for eyeball navigation. Be aware that there is a sunken ship in the middle of the area where the yachts anchor. A smoke-stack pipe can be seen above the water at low tide, but otherwise it is unmarked.

Formalities

Customs and Immigration will come aboard to give clearance, and will make a charge for overtime outside of normal working hours. It is best to start clearing procedures early in the day. You may now need to have a 'de-rat' certificate to clear in and, if you don't, obtaining one costs $50. Visa charges depend on the country of origin in your passport. Current information also suggests that bureaucrats in Kiribati were refusing to give people permission to stop at outer islands, eg Butaritari, without going back to check out of Tarawa.

Facilities

Facilities at Betio are distinctly limited. There are a number of stores, but not many items in them. There is a small store with imported goods just across the bridge on the way to Bairiki. There is a bakery, two banks and a post office and a few inexpensive restaurants. Fuel is obtainable by the barrel from Mobil, or in smaller quantities from the Betio Gas Station. The town water is not recommended, but rainwater can be obtained from the fisheries building at the end of the breakwater. Fresh vegetables are generally only available when the supply ship arrives. A delivery by air from New Zealand takes place from time to time, but demand and cost is high and the first there are the lucky ones. There is a central telephone centre in Bairiki. Internet access may by now be available.

Communications

There is a good bus service running between Betio, Bairiki and the airport 24km (15 miles) down the line of islands. There is a regular air service to the other islands of the Gilbert group, and a weekly flight to Honolulu and a shipping service to Australia. This is not a good place for a mail drop.

40 **Majuro,** Marshall Islands
7°07'N 171°10'E UT+12

Springs: 1.8m	Flag: Marshall Islands	
Neaps: 1.2m	Currency: US dollar	
Charts	Admiralty	US
General	761	81007
Approach	984	81782
Harbour	984	

General

Majuro can be a useful stopping place for practical pur-poses, but has little to attract the visitor. The capital con-sists of three villages strung along about 8km (5 miles) of linked atoll. The local culture is heavily overlaid by the trappings of Western life, sustained by a variety of hand-outs from the US government. Several of the outer islands are more interesting and agreeable. To visit them by boat, a cruising permit must be obtained in Majuro.

Approach and entry

The town and port are at the eastern end of the lagoon, which is entered by the Calalin Channel towards the north-west corner. The GPS position of the entrance is reported to be ¼ mile north of its charted position. The passage is well marked by three pairs of beacons, but note that since the latest charts were issued, the buoy-age has been changed to IALA System A and several of the beacons moved to new positions. Likewise, the markers on the banks in the lagoon have been renum-bered. The beacons are reputedly lit, but entrance in the dark is not recommended. Having cleared the passage, yachts should head for Uliga, 11 miles away and roughly in the centre of the eastern end of the lagoon.

Radio

The harbourmaster's office, situated at the entrance to the pier, does not appear to monitor the radio systemat-ically – and certainly not outside weekday working hours. The harbour authority claim to monitor 2724 and 5205 kHz full time.

Anchorage and moorings

The L-shaped pier in the middle of Uliga is reserved for commercial vessels. However, moorings are available off the north end of the pier, the Robert Reimers Enterprises Hotel, the Tide Table Restaurant, as well as to the south of the pier near the Mobil storage tanks. Anchoring is permitted off the Mobil tanks, but beware of the many sunken ships – which are visible due to the clarity of the water. Generally there is good holding in sand and mud. The anchorage offers excellent shelter from prevailing winds, but can be very uncomfortable when the infamous westerlies blow. Yachtsmen have been confined to their boats for days on end. Dinghies may be taken ashore near the anchorage; however, a favoured spot is against the stone wall adjacent to the fuel dock north of the pier. When securing a dinghy there, use a long painter and secure lock. Do not use a stern anchor as commercial boats frequently use the dock and shift the dinghies.

Formalities

The correct procedure for arriving yachts is for the skipper to visit the Customs and Immigration offices, both in the government building (Capitol) in Dalap, about 3km (1½ miles) away by road, during weekday working hours. It is best to take a taxi there. Taxis act as buses and pick people up along the way. They may also divert off the main road to deliver people to their homes. Long trousers and a long-sleeved shirt with a collar are needed for checking in at the government building. There is a charge of $25 per visa for each person arriving. It is no longer necessary to apply for a cruising permit or visas in advance of arrival. Permits for visiting the outer islands must be obtained from the Ministry of the Interior. On departure, the skipper should visit the same offices, having first obtained a clearance from the harbourmaster. It costs $80 irrespec-tive of the length of stay, made up of a $50 harbour charge and $30 light dues.

Facilities

There are no facilities specifically for yachts and there is no longer a yacht club. Early in 1996, an American was trying to establish a marina in an old boatyard near the anchorage, but only a rather encumbered dinghy dock was operative. It is possible to hire a mobile crane capa-ble of lifting the average yacht. Basic boat repair and mechanical maintenance are said to be available. There are no chandlers, although the extensive ACE Hard-ware store carries a few marine items. Goods ordered from West Marine or elsewhere on the US west coast normally arrive within a few days by air parcel post. Diesel has to be ferried in cans from the fuel dock, which is too shallow for most keel boats. Diesel can also be bought at about half price from the Mobil depot on the outskirts of town if you need enough to warrant hiring a pick-up truck and a 40-gallon drum. Low-cost diesel can also be obtained from the commercial wharf,

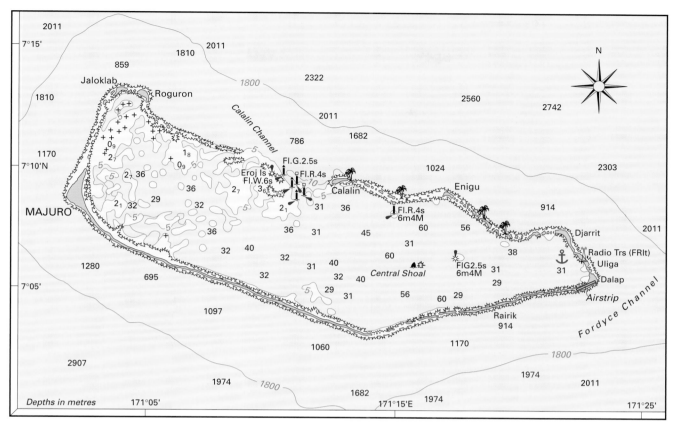

Plan 65 *Majuro, Marshall Islands.*

but arrangements must be made ahead, possibly purchasing for several boats at a time. Propane is available across the street from the commercial wharf. Propane is available from Mobil. There is an all too copious supply of rainwater and a catching system is essential.

There is a Johnson/Evinrude dealer across the street from the laundry, and a dry cleaners just south of the dinghy dock. The laundry service is good and only slightly more expensive than going to the laundromat (although some people have complained of missing items). There is a grocery/hardware store called Gibson's in Dalap, which carries outboards and some fishing and diving equipment. Gibson's also has a 'wholesale' store in the same complex and will deliver orders over $50.00 to the dinghy dock for free. For recreation there is a cinema, ten-pin bowling, pool halls and plenty of bars. The locals play volleyball and the youngsters play a version of baseball, using a crumpled coke can as a ball. The Tide Table Restaurant is a hang-out for yachties and local ex-patriots, as well as many government officials and 'royalty'. There is an ATM machine in the Robert Reimers Enterprises grocery store. Two banks will give cash advances against credit cards. The Outrigger Marshall Islands Resort is located south of the government building and Gibson's shopping centre in Dalap. It offers first-class accommodation, resort facilities and restaurant.

A moderately priced shared taxi service operates up and down the island. Several shops, including two small supermarkets, cater for all reasonable provisioning needs, although there is no local produce and fresh food supplies vary with the arrival of shipments. Marshallese handicrafts are renowned, and include reproductions of the famous 'stick charts' used by traditional navigators. There is a very small, but interesting, museum. A hospital with a dental clinic has some expatriate staff, but medical evacuation will be arranged to Hawaii for severe problems.

Communications

Continental Air Micronesia ('Air Mike') runs an island hopper service between Honolulu and Guam, which serves Majuro three days a week in each direction. Air Marshall Islands (AMI) fly an elegant Saab to Fiji via Tarawa and Funafuti, and to Honolulu. The post office is run as part of the US postal service and shipments and mail from the USA goes for domestic rates, although at times delivery can be very slow. They will hold mail for yachts at the main post office across from the Robert Reimers Enterprises Hotel and ACE Hardware. It is a very secure place to receive mail. The National Telecommunications Authority, which offers a 24-hour phone and fax service, is just north of the government centre and can be identified by the large satellite dish in front of the building. FEDEX is available at Gibson's shopping complex.

41 **Pohnpei,** Caroline Islands, Federated States of Micronesia

6°58'N 158°12'E UT+11

Springs: 1.0m	Flag: FSM	
Neaps: 0.2m	Currency: US dollar	
Charts	Admiralty	US
General	761 or 762	81016 or 81019
Approach	981	81435
Harbour	981	81453

General

Pohnpei, the seat of the capital of the Federated States of Micronesia, is an obvious stopping point for yachts making their way from the south or east towards the north-west Pacific or to the Philippines. A green, high, volcanic island, it offers a pleasant, sheltered anchorage with reasonable shore facilities and some tourist attractions, including the important ruins of the medieval city of Nan Madol.

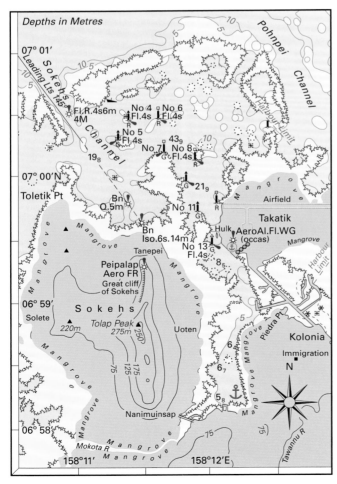

Plan 66 *Pohnpei, Caroline Islands.*

Approach and entry

Approach from the north-west and enter the winding but well-marked Sokehs (also spelt Jokaj) channel, ignoring the Pohnpei (also Ponape) channel 1½ miles to the north-east. Sokehs ridge (276m (911ft)) provides a conspicuous starboard-hand mark. The channel leads to the fishing/commercial dock at Takatik on the north side, where check-in procedures are carried out.

Radio

Apart from local radio, the four-times daily bulletins from the US Coast Guard station in Guam include an 'island/atoll' summary, which covers Pohnpei. It is usually perfunctory, but would presumably give warning of trouble. Pohnpei is not normally affected by typhoons.

Anchorage and moorings

After clearance (see below), yachts should continue up the bay for just over 1 mile and anchor in 6–7m (20–23ft) off Rumor's Bar and Marina on the east side of the bay, where a fuel jetty with a large Mobil sign is clearly visible. The channel to the anchorage is buoyed but fringed with reef, and local guidance is worth taking if available.

Formalities

Yachts entering the Federal States of Micronesia are required to obtain a cruising permit in advance. This may be done from a convenient previous port of call by exchanges of fax with the Office of the Attorney General in Palikir (00 691 320 3243). Ask for an application form and then return the completed form by fax. The permit you then receive is valid for 3 months and is said not to be extendable. As you approach the harbour, the local authorities may or may not respond to a VHF call. If they don't, find a place on the quay at Takatik and go to the harbour office, a small upstairs cabin in the middle of the quay. The office will call the Customs and Immigration officials who should arrive within an hour or so (unless detained by a flight at the airport). On departure, visit or telephone the Customs and Immigration offices in Kolonia and arrange a rendezvous for check-out at the same quay.

Facilities

The marina at Rumors accommodates only powerboats and the fuel dock has insufficient depth for keel boats, but there is a good dinghy dock. Propane is available in town. Diesel is usually available from a pump on the dock – and also soft drinks, beer, liquor and ice, although all of these are cheaper in town. There are showers and a laundrette, and an agreeable waterside bar which on some evenings serves food. The centre of Kolonia is about 1 mile from Rumors. Taxis can be called from the marina, or you can catch a lift on the road. There are two very adequate supermarkets, with a heavy emphasis on US produce, and several pleasant restaurants, including a superior one in the village hotel, 10km (6 miles) out of town by taxi.

There are no facilities for yachts as such, apart from selective outboard motor servicing; but large branches of ACE Hardware, True Value and NAPA offer many boat-usable items. There is a US-run machine shop. Cars and pick-ups can be hired at reasonable prices and the excursion to Nan Madol is a must. Take the inflatable with outboard. It is not easy to find, so get good instructions. The Kapingamarangi village in Kolonia has several shops offering distinctive handicrafts of high quality, mainly in wood, shell and woven materials.

Communications

Continental Air Micronesia (Air Mike) runs an island hopper service between Honolulu and Guam, which serves Pohnpei three days a week in each direction. A 24-hour fax and overseas telephone service operates in central Kolonia.

42 Apra, Guam, Mariana Islands

13°27'N 144°45'E UT+10

Springs: 0.6m	Flag: USA	
Neaps: 0.2m	Currency: US dollar	
Charts	Admiralty	US
General	1101	81048
Approach	1109	81054
Harbour	1109	81060

General

As Guam lies in the north-east trades belt, it is unlikely that yachts will approach it from the west, but it is a very useful stepping stone on the way to the north-west Pacific from the south, or for those bound farther west to the Philippines and beyond. Typhoons *do* occur in the area, and are particularly prevalent during the second half of the year. The island is home to a major US naval base in the south and air base in the north. About 1½ million tourists (mostly Japanese) visit the island annually.

Approach and entry

Guam is a large, high island, and therefore visible a considerable distance off. Generally the island is steep-to with a narrow fringing reef, except at the south-west corner where Cocos Lagoon reef extends nearly 3 miles offshore. Apra Harbour is the only port of entry and is situated on the western side of the island, north of the Orote Peninsula. The entrance to the harbour is easy to find between the sheer face of Orote Peninsula to the south and Glass Breakwater to the north. Fixed green leading lights (difficult to identify in daylight) on a heading of 083°T lead to the commercial port at Cabras Island. At the entrance, the current usually sets to the south-west and can run at up to 3 knots.

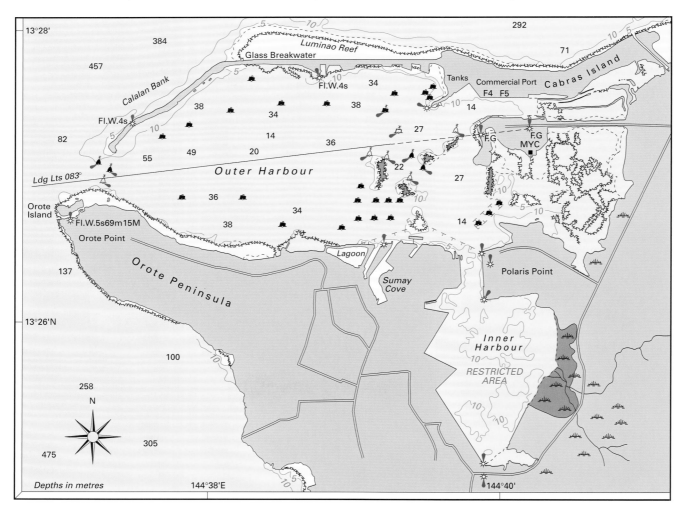

Plan 67 *Apra, Guam, Mariana Islands.*

Radio

Vessels arriving in Guam who are entering the outer harbour, shifting berth or departing are technically required to give 24 hours' notice to the harbourmaster. In practice, Guam harbour control likes to be called on VHF channel 16, 13 or 12 with an ETA, as soon as you are within range, which may be up to 50 miles.

Anchorage and moorings

Having completed formalities, yachts should make their way to the Marianas Yacht Club moorings. Depth around the anchorages ranges 4–16m (13–53ft). There is no room to anchor among the club moorings, but these are free to visitors for the first two weeks. Take a vacant mooring and then go ashore to the yacht club. In the past, berths have sometimes been available in Sumay Cove. There is a modern marina at Agat, but available slips are few – and most are for yachts of 9m (30ft) or less. The boat basin at Agana is not recommended for yachts.

Marianas Yacht Club
Bob Bullock, Commodore
PO Box 1262
Agana
GU 96932
USA
Tel: 671 477 3533

Formalities

Yachts are usually directed to the commercial port at Cabras Island, berth F-4 or F-5, where they are met by Guam Customs (who act for Agriculture and Health) and US Immigration. There is a nominal port fee and overtime is charged outside normal working hours. While you are at the commercial wharf, note that Piti Channel to the east leads to the typhoon 'Harbour of Refuge'.

Facilities

The capital and commercial centre is Agana, 11–19km (7–12 miles) from the yacht club. Public transport exists, but services are infrequent and taxis are expensive. The preferred option is for yachts to join forces and rent a car. The United Seamen's Services on the road to town has useful tourist information and faxes can be sent and received there. LPG and almost US-standard shopping are available in town. Goods mailed from the USA take 5–10 days to arrive. Overnight delivery is possible using one of the special delivery companies. Most repairs can be achieved in Guam. The Guam Shipyard can arrange to haul out yachts of any nationality. Fuel and water are conveniently available at the marina at Agat.

The United Seamen's Services
Tel: 671 472 2369
Fax: 671 472 9790

Communications

As an outpost of the USA, Guam is well served by all modern means of communications, and flights to many international destinations are available from Guam International Airport located less than 10km (6 miles) from the yacht club. Mail can be sent to the Marianas Yacht Club (address given above).

43 Fukuoka (Hakata), Kyushu, Japan

33°37'N 130°23'E UT+9

Springs: 2.2m	Flag: Japan	
Neaps: 0.3m	Currency: Yen	
Charts	Admiralty	US
General	3480	97425
Approach		97421
Harbour		97423

General

Fukuoka is the political, economic and cultural centre of Kyushu and is a large city of some 3 million inhabitants. The port is called Hakata. Numerous national and international flights are available from Fukuoka Airport.

Approach and entry

All significant hazards are well marked and lit, so approach and entry at any time is straightforward. Both the Fukuoka City Yacht Club marina and the more recently developed Marinoa Marina have port and starboard lights at their entrances.

Radio

Yachts in Japan are not allowed to use VHF. Calling up the Hakata port control would probably elicit response, but would be unexpected.

Anchorage and moorings

The Fukuoka City Yacht Club makes no charge to foreign visitors for the use of its marina for the first 2 weeks, and its charges thereafter are comparable with British south coast marina tariffs. The Marinoa Marina is more expensive and does not operate a policy of initial free berthing. However, its berths are more secure and are fitted with water and electricity. At the Fukuoka City Yacht Club, water is supplied at fairly frequently placed taps along the boardwalks.

Formalities

Fukuoka is a port of entry. Both the Fukuoka City Yacht Club and the Marinoa Marina will notify the appropriate officials of the arrival of a foreign yacht, and the officials will come to the yacht to clear her. Foreign

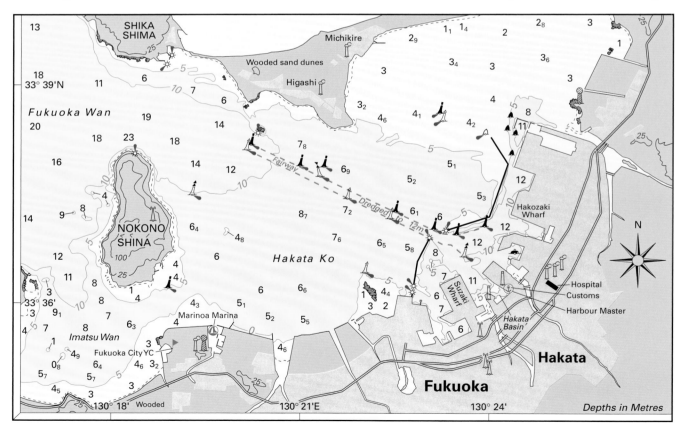

Plan 68 *Fukuoka (Hakata), Kyushu, Japan.*

vessels have to clear in and out of every port in Japan, so whether the visitor has already entered Japan elsewhere or not, clearance at Fukuoka is necessary.

Facilities

As might be expected of a huge city, virtually everything is available but often at a distance. The public underground transport system is extremely efficient and fairly user-friendly for the non-Japanese speaker. Car hire is easy to arrange, but an international driver's licence is essential if you are to avoid considerable hassle securing a translation of a foreign licence – without which car hire is impossible. There are numerous shops within a taxi ride of both marinas, and there is a small marine store with limited chandlery at the Marinoa Marina. Both marinas have haul-out facilities and engineering workshops. The Marinoa has a fuel berth; at the Fukuoka City Yacht Club, fuel is brought by tanker to the dock and this can be arranged through the club's office. Faxes can be sent and received through the offices of both marinas. Although there are numerous public phone boxes throughout Japan, international calls can only be made from public phone boxes marked for the purpose, and these are fairly rare. All phone boxes take coins or phone cards. The phone cards can be bought from machines that are sited close to most phone boxes.

44 **Honolulu,** Oahu, Hawaii, USA

21°17'N 157°51'W UT-10

Springs: 0.6m	Flag: USA	
Neaps: 0.2m	Currency: US dollar	
Charts	**Admiralty**	**US**
General	1510	19004
Approach	1378	19357
Harbour	1368	19364

General

Honolulu, on the island of Oahu, is the usual arrival port for any yacht that has sailed out from the western seaboard of the USA or Canada. The harbour is on the lee side of the island, with a relatively sheltered approach. It is one of the great crossroads of the Pacific, both for those under sail and also the masses of air-borne holidaymakers who flock to the Hawaiian Islands in huge numbers. It is by far the largest centre of commerce and tourism within the islands. As a staging

The Hawaii Yacht Club in the Ala Wai Marina has always been welcoming to visiting overseas yachts. Photo Marcia Pirie.

post for those going on to Alaska or British Columbia, it is ideal; it has good yacht services and a wide choice of more general supplies.

Approach and entry

The harbour approach is a little over 10 miles from Makapuu Point at the east end of Oahu, past Diamond Head, the finishing point of the Transpac and other races. The Ala Wai small boat harbour is immediately beyond the massive wall of high-rise hotels that is the famous Waikiki Beach resort. It is said that the amber leading lights are difficult to distinguish against the multitude of shore lights. However, the level of lighting is so great that it is probably not too difficult to find your way in somehow.

Radio

Call on channel 16. The port authority keep a 24-hour watch, and will probably request a shift to channel 12 as a working channel.

Anchorage and moorings

The choice in broad terms is between the Ala Wai Basin, which is entirely operated on a marina basis, or the Keehi Lagoon, administered by the Hawaii Division of Boating and Ocean Recreation, where you may be allowed to anchor, but more likely required to take a mooring. A new private marina is under construction. The Ala Wai is far the most pleasant and convenient, but is inevitably the more expensive; and, due to pressure on the space available, a stay will probably be limited. Part of the facilities are run by the Hawaii Yacht Club whose pontoon is the second on the starboard hand as you head up the entrance channel. They have a reputation for being very welcoming to visiting yachtsmen, and will offer berths at a reasonable rate if space permits. The disadvantages of the Keehi Lagoon are the distance from the centre and the proximity of the main runways of both Honolulu Airport and the military airbase. The constant noise and the pollution of jet fuel sprayed over the anchorage are more than many people can bear.

Formalities

If arriving from outside the Hawaiian Islands, clearance is required. Arrival must be reported within 1 hour. This is most easily accomplished by telephoning from the Aloha Marine fuel dock just before the yacht club. Arrangements will be made for officials to visit the yacht

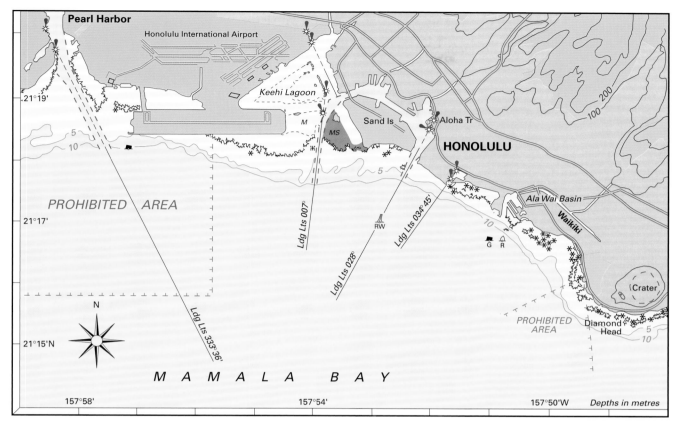

Plan 69 *Honolulu, Oahu, Hawaii.*

from Customs, Immigration, Health and Agriculture. Foreign-flag yachts will be issued with a 6 months' cruising permit. It is important to have a valid visitor's visa for all non-US citizens if arriving by yacht, and these must be obtained before entering the country, to avoid incurring a penalty.

Facilities

Yachting facilities in Honolulu are exceptionally good, but not (as one might expect) the cheapest. There are haul-out and chandlery possibilities both at Ala Wai and at Keehi Lagoon. Honolulu is a big city by Pacific standards and there are suppliers for nearly every need. Specialist items can be flown out from mainland USA very easily. Car rental is not expensive, and there is a good bus service.

Communications

It is worth knowing that mail addressed 'General Delivery' is handled at the international airport, which is well out of town. A better mail drop would be either American Express or:

Hawaii Yacht Club
1739-C Ala Moana Blvd
Honolulu
HI 96815

There are flights in all directions going out all day long, so Honolulu could not be better as a crew changeover spot.

45 Hilo, Hawaii, USA

19°44'N   155°4'W   UT-10

Springs: 0.7m	Flag: USA	
Neaps: 0.2 m	Currency: US dollar	
Charts	Admiralty	US
General	1510	19004
Approach	1309	19320
Harbour	1490	19324

General

Hilo is the principal port for the island of Hawaii, which is in turn the 'big island' of the Hawaiian group of islands. It is a natural arrival port for yachts arriving from the south or east: Panama, Galapagos or French Polynesia. Hawaii is a high volcanic island lying in the path of the north-east trades, so rainfall can be quite dramatic, particularly on the windward side; 100mm in 24 hours is not unusual. After a long passage, all the facilities of civilisation are at last available. Car rental is very reasonable on Hawaii, and exploring by road is well worthwhile. You do not need to be a keen vulcanologist to appreciate a trip up to the Hawaii Volcanoes National Park. It is a unique day out.

Approach and entry

From the navigational point of view, there is nothing particularly difficult about finding Hilo and entering the port. The weather, on the other hand, is occasionally *very* windy, the more so if coming from the west. The trade winds are accelerated by the effects of the high islands, and the Alenuihaha Channel between Hawaii and Maui has a justifiably evil reputation. Entering Hilo at night there is a sectored light at Coconut Point that guides you into the bay, and leading lights (097° 30'T) that give a safe line all the way into the port.

Radio

Call on channel 16; the port authority keep a 24-hour watch.

Anchorage and moorings

Yachts lie in Radio Bay, which is directly beyond Pier No 1 on which the forward of the leading lights is mounted. The entry to the basin is around the north end of the pier, and visiting yachts generally lie with an anchor out ahead and their sterns to the south wall of the basin. In strong northerlies it is a somewhat precarious position, so lay out your best anchor on a long scope.

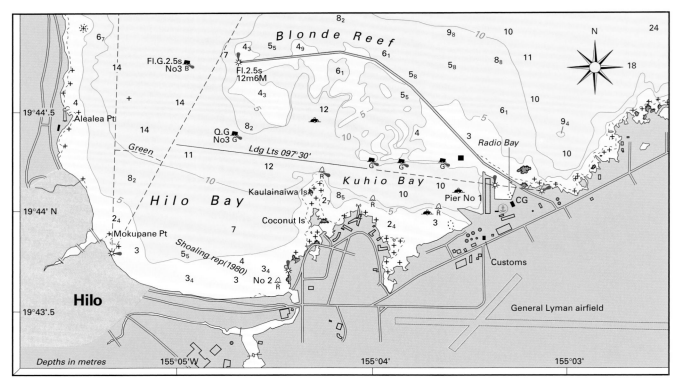

Plan 70 *Hilo, Hawaii.*

A Hawaiian canoe in Hilo. Photo Noël Marshall.

Formalities

If arriving from outside the Hawaiian Islands, clearance is required. Arrival must be reported within 1 hour. Customs and Immigration will be dealt with ashore, but a health inspector will want to come aboard and will confiscate any fresh meat, fruit or vegetables. Foreign-flag yachts will be issued with a 6 months' cruising permit. It is important to have a valid visitor's visa for all non-US citizens if arriving by yacht, and these must be obtained before entering the country, to avoid incurring a penalty.

Facilities

Hilo is a much smaller city than Honolulu, so that for non-urgent requirements it may well be sensible to delay any purchases in expectation of much greater choice later. Water is available in unlimited quantity, but fuel has to be carried, unless a large enough amount is needed to warrant a bowser.

Communications

It is worth knowing that mail addressed 'General Delivery' is handled at the international airport, which is a fair distance (or a taxi ride) from the yachts.

Appendix A

When All Else Has Failed

A crash course in astro-navigation

The batteries are flat, the GPS is defunct, and all of a sudden the sextant and almanac have become vital pieces of equipment. Here is a crash course in astro-navigation.

The overriding principle of sun sights – or, for that matter, sights of any other celestial body – is that there is on the surface of the earth, at all times, a position called ground zero (GZ), at which the sun is directly overhead and this position is utterly predictable. If at noon (local mean time) you happen to be in exactly the same latitude as the current declination of the sun, then it must be directly overhead, at an altitude of 90°, and you are at ground zero. The almanac enables you to establish the GZ position of the sun for any second of the day.

At the same time you, the navigator, have a position that you are trying to establish and it is necessary to start with an estimated position (EP). The process of working a sight enables you to determine the degree of inaccuracy of that EP. The end result of your calculations will be an Azimuth, or bearing of the sun from the EP, and an Intercept, which is a measurement in sea miles between your estimated position (EP) and your actual position.

The limitation of the process is that the Azimuth cannot be determined precisely owing to the distance of the sun, and so it is necessary to draw a line at right angles to the Azimuth through the intercept position and realise that the yacht's true position lies somewhere on that line. It is known as the Position Line.

This fundamental fact must be accepted: that each individual sight taken will only produce a line. A confirmed position can only be resolved by the crossing of two lines, preferably at a significant crossing angle. As the Azimuth takes all day to change from easterly at dawn to westerly at sunset, it is essential to take your sights at well spaced intervals to achieve useful crossing angles.

What kit is needed?

Apart from the sextant, what other kit do you need? First, an accurate means of recording the time of each sight. A digital wristwatch checked against a time signal is ideal. Secondly, you need a current almanac, or at least one that is for the previous year, although this does complicate the workings. The best and easiest to use is *The Nautical Almanac* issued in London by HMSO, and in Washington by the US Naval Observatory. This is published every year and contains very abbreviated Sight Reduction Tables.

Life is a whole lot easier, however, if you use the *Sight Reduction Tables for Air Navigation* (as issued by the HSMO) or the US equivalent, which are called *Tables of Computed Altitude and Azimuth* (as issued by the United States Navy Department), and which are in separate volumes for each band of latitude. They can be bought through any chart agent or second-hand, and are a worthwhile investment. Otherwise, all you need is a notebook, a pencil and a protractor for plotting the answer.

Taking a sight

To take the sight, brace yourself in a good secure position on deck, as high as is safe, with a clear view of the sun and the horizon. Select strong enough sextant filters to enable you to see the sun and the horizon clearly and adjust the arc so that you are looking at the sun and the horizon at once. Then gently twirl the vernier until the image of the sun is just kissing the horizon at its lowest point. Learn to swing the sextant very slightly so that the sun is swinging like a pendulum just above the sea. This enables you to identify the true upright position at which the sight should be read. When you are quite certain that the sun is just kissing and not cutting the water at that upright position, stop twiddling and read the time instantly or call out 'now' for your mate to read the time for you. Write down the time, converted to UT(Universal Time), and the sextant reading, which is the Observed Altitude.

Corrections must now be made for this and that. The sextant may have an index error, which, if you do not know it, is most easily checked by setting the arc to zero and looking at the horizon. It will probably appear to have a very slight step, and this can be eliminated with the vernier wheel. When you are quite sure that you have an unbroken line, read off the error. If it is positive (on the scale) it must become a subtraction, and if negative (off the scale), it must become an addition. As this is a crash course we will blur the issue of semi-diameter and height of eye by recommending that you use what is known as a 'fisherman's dip', which is a constant figure of 12 minutes which is added to the sextant reading, together with the index error plus or minus, to convert the Observed Alt to the True Alt.

Now for the calculations; the first move is to establish the relative positions of the GZ of the sun and the EP of the yacht. The latter is easy, it is the lat/long of the dead reckoning positioning. Now for the sun, and this is where you must reach for the Almanac. Each double page spread covers three days of the year and from the right hand side it is possible to read off the GHA (Greenwich Hour Angle) and the declination of the sun for every hour of the day. Remember that the time is in UT. Write these down for the hour in which the sight was taken. Now by turning to the buff

TWO SAMPLE SUN SIGHT CALCULATIONS (morning and noon)

No 1 *Taken 2 days out of Palmerston Atoll. South of the equator east of the dateline. See Fig 3.*

1 August

Observed Altitude		36° 58'	Local time	1038/13	Log reading 1321
Index error	minus – 02'		Time difference	– 1000	
Fisherman's dip	plus + 12'				
True Altitude		**37° 08'**	UT	2038/13	

From the Almanac

Sun GHA for 2000	118° 25.5'	**Declination**	N 17° 59.4'
Sun GHA for 38/13 (minutes & seconds)	009° 33.3'		
Total GHA	**127° 58.8'**		
Assumed Longitude	166° 58.8'W		
Difference LHA	39°	**Assumed Latitude**	S 19°

From the Sight Reduction Tables Vol 2 (Latitudes 0°–40°) Page 119 (Latitude 19° Declination <u>contrary</u> name to latitude)

For 17° Declination and LHA = 39 Alt	37° 25'	Corr – 39	**AZIMUTH 131°**
Corr for 59.4' (table page 248) negative	– 39'		
Calculated Altitude	**36° 46'**		
True Altitude (from above)	**37° 08'**		
INTERCEPT	**22 MILES TOWARDS**		

NOON SIGHT

Observed Altitude		**53° 15'**		Log reading 1333
Index error	minus	– 02'		
Fisherman's dip	plus	+ 12'		
True Altitude		**53° 25'**		
Zenith Distance (subtract from 90°)		**36° 35'**	**Declination**	N 17° 58' (<u>contrary</u> name)
Subtract contrary declination		17° 58'		
NOON LATITUDE		**18° 37'**		

Fig 3 *No 1 sample sun sight plotted.*

Note that the EP is on the Assumed Latitude (19°S) and at the Assumed Longitude (166°58'.8 W). Being in the southern hemisphere the Azimuth is the angle between the bearing of the sun and the north-south axis, measured away from the pole (upwards from the south), and towards the east because it is a morning sight. By plotting the course steered and the distance run as an intersection of the Position Line and the Noon Latitude, a noon position of 18° 37'S, 167 ° 06'W is established.

No 2 *Taken on passage Fiji to New Zealand. South of the equator west of the dateline. See Fig 4.*

6 November

Observed Altitude		55° 59'	Local time	0946/31	Log reading 3828	
Index error	minus – 02'		Time difference +	1200		
Fisherman's dip	plus + 12'					
True Altitude		**56° 09'**	UT	2146/31		

From the Almanac

Sun GHA for 2100		139° 05.7'	Declination	S 15° 43.5'
Sun GHA for 46/31 (minutes & seconds)		011° 37.8'		
Total GHA		**150°.43.5'**		
		360°		
Assumed Longitude		175° 16.5' E		
Subtract from 360°		184° 43.5'		
Difference	**LHA**	34°	**Assumed Latitude S 28°**	

From the Sight Reduction Tables Vol 2 (Latitudes 0°–40°) Page 171 (Latitude 28° Declination <u>same</u> name as latitude)

For 15° Declination and LHA = 34	Alt	55°57'	Corr +28	**AZIMUTH 105°**
Corr for 43' (table page 248) positive		20'		
Calculated Altitude		**56° 17'**		
True Altitude (from above)		56°09'		
INTERCEPT		**8 MILES AWAY**		

NOON SIGHT

Observed Altitude		**77° 23'**		Log reading 3843
Index error	minus	**– 02'**		
Fisherman's dip	plus	+ 12'		
True Altitude		**77° 33'**		
Zenith Distance (subtract from 90°)		**12° 27'**	Declination	S 15° 48' (<u>same name</u>)
Add same name declination		15° 48'		
NOON LATITUDE		**28°15'S**		

Fig 4 *No 2 sample sun sight plotted.*

Note that the EP is on the Assumed Latitude (28°S) and at the Assumed Longitude (175°16'.5E). The Azimuth is again measured upwards from the south and to the east. The course steered and the distance run have again been plotted as an intersection of the Position Line and the Noon Latitude, to give a noon position of 28° 15'S, 174 ° 57'E.

coloured pages towards the end of the book you will find a page for each minute of the hour, and on it a column of corrections for each second of that minute. These are to be added to GHA to give you the precise angle for the exact time of your sight. The result is in fact the longitude of the GZ measured in a 360° notation. Write it down in your notebook together with the declination of the sun, which, as you know, is the latitude of the GZ for the hour of the sight.

We now have the lat/long of the GZ and of the EP. In order to enter the Reduction Tables we need to refine this information a little further. First we want the Local Hour Angle (LHA). This is essentially the difference in longitude between the GZ and the EP. However, for reasons of simplicity you need the answer in a whole number of degrees, so it is necessary to fudge the EP so that the result of subtracting the one from the other is a round figure. This is easy enough when the GZ and the EP are both still east of the date line. When the EP has an east longitude (having crossed the dateline), convert it into 360° notation by subtracting it from 360° and remember that this lesson is directly related to the Pacific and will not necessarily agree with other people's methods elsewhere in the world. Having both expressions of longitude in the same notation, it is a simple sum to subtract the smaller from the greater to arrive at an LHA and, believe it or not, we are not concerned with a negative or positive value. It is generally going to be well below 90° and reducing towards zero as local noon approaches, and increasing in the afternoon.

Before you can open the Reduction Tables there is one other fudge that is necessary and that is to adjust the EP once again so that the latitude is also a round figure. This is because the tables are only printed for whole degrees of latitude. You should not worry that the inaccuracy of your work is increasing. It is not, but the Intercept maybe. You now have all the data needed to enter the tables. They are an assumed latitude (of the EP), an LHA and a declination.

Now you can open the Reduction Tables. First you must find the pages for your Assumed Latitude and you will see that there are headings for either 'Declination Same Name as Latitude' or 'Declination Contrary Name to Latitude'; this effectively allows for all conditions of sun and ship. If you are south of the equator in the southern summer, the names will be the same; but, more likely, you will be south while the sun is in the north, in which case they are contrary.

The degrees of declination head the columns and you must find the page which includes the declination that you have found in the Almanac. LHA is in the marginal columns, and by cross reference a set of figures will be read off. The first item is the Calculated Altitude (Hc), the next is a correction value (d), and the last is the Azimuth (Z) in degrees reaching 180° when LHA is zero.

The column heading for declination will be to a whole degree, or in some cases to half a degree, and it is now time to turn to the end of the book to find the table for Corrections for Minutes of Declination that should be applied to the Calculated Altitude.

In your notebook you should now have a True Altitude and a Calculated Altitude. The difference between the two is the Intercept in minutes of a degree and, coincidentally, in sea miles. If the True Altitude is the greater, then the Intercept is measured towards the sun and vice versa. To transfer the results on to the chart, plot the EP, using the fudged values of course, and then with the protractor mark of the Azimuth. The angle given in the tables is measured down from north or up from the south depending on whether the EP is north or south of the equator. If the sight was taken before local noon the Azimuth will be towards the east, and in the afternoon it will be towards the west. Measure off the Intercept from the EP either towards or away from the sun depending on whether the True Altitude was greater or smaller than the Calculated Altitude. Mark the spot and draw a line at right angles to it; this is your Position Line.

Each time that you take a sight it is important to record the logged distance and the compass course, so that when you cross two Position Lines you can take into account the distance run in the interval. If, of course, the log has crashed along with the GPS, then you will need all your ingenuity to maintain a DR on estimated distances.

Almost inevitably, you will be operating on a small scale chart and plotting sights will be hopelessly miniature work that is quite impractical. There are two options, one is a pad of graph paper on which you can, with a little cunning, construct a grid to correspond with your patch of ocean at a usable scale. The second is to look through the drawer for a larger scale chart in the same latitude, rewrite the longitude markings to suit, and ignore all the features. When you have crossed two Position Lines and established an accepted position, lift the coordinates and return to the small scale passage chart.

It is generally believed that the noon sight is the easiest observation to take, but there are times when the yacht's latitude and the sun's declination are too close and then the altitude is too high for accuracy. For the rest of the time it is the ideal sight to cross with a morning or afternoon sight to obtain two crossing lines. Studying the almanac carefully will tell you roughly when to expect local noon. Take the sextant on deck some few minutes ahead of time and take a sight without recording the time. As noon approaches, the altitude should continue to increase. Turn the vernier only one way and wait for the sun to reach its zenith. The reading that you want is the highest for the day.

When you have it, write it down, correct it to a True Altitude as before, and subtract it from 90°. The answer is known as the Zenith Distance. Take the declination for noon from the Almanac and, if it is the same name as the Assumed Latitude, add it to the Zenith Distance to obtain your True Latitude. If the names are contrary, subtract.

One important piece of advice is that you should keep your notebook in the most orderly fashion possible. It is no good at all keeping your calculations higgledy-piggledy on scrap paper. One of the things that is constantly needed in the taking of sights is troubleshooting to find the errors. If there are two of you taking sights, then try to establish a common format so that each of you can rework the other's sums. Clearly, if a sight taken at 1100 works out farther from the destination than the one taken at 1000, even though you have been bowling along at 6 knots, one or other must be wrong. Reworking both sets of figures is the first move, and therefore they must be clear to read.

It must be emphasised that this is a crash course for the purpose of making a landfall when the GPS has failed. It is very basic and, with appropriate study, capable of considerable refinement. Given the time, there is a great deal that can be learned from the introductory pages of the Almanac or, if you have it on board, Mary Blewitt's super little book *Celestial Navigation for Yachtsmen*.

The foregoing has been an attempt to break down the operation into its simplest terms with particular reference to the Pacific. The involvement of spherical geometry has been avoided. Just remember that by the use of the tables you are resolving the elements of a triangle drawn on the surface of the earth. You have the meridian of the sun for one side, the latitude of the observer for another, and the third is the all important line from the observer at his EP to the sun at its GZ.

Remember always to use UT as the time and to change the sign (from adding to subtracting or vice versa) when the equinox occurs and the declination changes from S to N or N to S. The closer you come to land, the more sights you should take, and throw out the rogues until you get a reasonable cocked hat. Finally, remember that from the deck of a small yacht, and using the methods described, 5 miles will be a small error and you should allow for a good deal more with darkness approaching.

Appendix B Suggested Further Reading

Below is a list of useful titles both in current publication and out of print.

Preparations for Ocean Cruising
Cruising Under Sail, incorporating *Voyaging Under Sail,* Eric Hiscock, Adlard Coles Nautical
Ocean Cruising Countdown, Geoff Pack, David and Charles
Ocean Cruising on a Budget, Anne Hammick, Adlard Coles Nautical
Sell Up and Sail, Bill and Laurel Cooper, Adlard Coles Nautical
Living Afloat, Clare Allcard, Adlard Coles Nautical
The Care and Feeding of Sailing Crew, Lin and Larry Pardey, Norton
Boat Cuisine – The All-weather Cookbook, June Raper
Collins Gems: Guide to Flags, HarperCollins

Radio
Amateur Radio, Gordon Stokes and Peter Bubb, Lutterworth Press UK
Communications at Sea, Mike Harris, Adlard Coles Nautical
Marine SSB Operation, Michael Gale, Fernhurst

Weather
Weather for the Mariner, Kotsch (Rear Admiral US Navy Retd), Naval Institute Press, Annapolis, Md
Weather for New Zealand Sailors, Lt Cdr K E Brierley, Endeavour Press
Metservice Yacht Pack, Bob McDavitt, NZ
The Sailor's Guide to Wind, Waves and Tides, Capt Alex Simpson, Adlard Coles Nautical

Technical
Boatowner's Mechanical and Electrical Manual, Nigel Calder, Adlard Coles Nautical
Refrigeration for Pleasureboats, Nigel Calder, International Marine Publishing
The Marine Electrical and Electronics Bible, John Payne, Adlard Coles Nautical
Marine Diesel Engines, Nigel Calder, Adlard Coles Nautical
The 12-Volt Bible for Boats, Miner Brotherton, Adlard Coles Nautical
Understanding Rigs and Rigging, Richard Henderson, International Marine
The Voyager's Handbook, Beth Leonard, Adlard Coles Nautical
Handbook of Offshore Cruising, Jim Howard, Adlard Coles Nautical

Navigation
Celestial Navigation for Yachtsmen, Mary Blewitt, Adlard Coles Nautical

Medical
Your Offshore Doctor, Michael Beilan, Adlard Coles Nautical and Sheridan House
The Ship Captain's Medical Guide, HMSO

Accounts of Pacific Experiences (recent and historical)
On the Wind of a Dream, Cdr Victor Clark DSC RN, Hutchinson
The Kon-Tiki Expedition, Thor Heyerdahl, Allen and Unwin
Aku-Aku: the Secret of Easter Island, Thor Heyerdahl, Allen and Unwin
Captain James Cook: a Biography, Richard Hough, Hodder and Stoughton
The Explorations of Captain James Cook in the Pacific, Grenfell Price, Dover Publications NY
Endeavour – Captain Cook's First Epic Voyage, Peter Aughton
We The Navigators, David Lewis, University of Hawaii Press, Honolulu

Cruising and Travel Guides
World Cruising Routes, Jimmy Cornell, Adlard Coles Nautical
World Cruising Handbook, Jimmy Cornell, Adlard Coles Nautical
Landfalls of Paradise, Earl Hinz, University of Hawaii Press, Honolulu
Cruising Guide to Tahiti and the Society Islands, Marcia Davock, Westcott Cove, Ct USA
Migrant Cruising Notes: Micronesia, Phil Cregeen, Compass Marine Services, Whangarei NZ
A Yachtsman's Guide to Ha'apai, Phil Cregeen, Compass Marine Services, Whangarei NZ
South Pacific Anchorages, Warwick Clay, Imray Laurie Norie & Wilson
Cruising the Coral Coast, Alan Lucas, Imray Laurie Norie & Wilson
Fodor's Australia, New Zealand and the South Pacific, Hodder and Stoughton
South Pacific Handbook, David Stanley, Moon Publications Inc
A Yachtsman's Fiji, Michael Calder, Imray Laurie, Norie & Wilson
Charlie's Charts of Polynesia, Charles Wood
Charlie's Charts of the Hawaiian Islands, Charles Wood, Charlie's Charts
Royal Akarana Yacht Club Coastal Cruising Handbook, Royal Akarana YC, NZ
Cruising in New Caledonia, Nouméa Yacht Charters
Cruising Guide to the Kingdom of Tonga, Vava'u Group, Moorings/Kelvin Hughes
Cruising Guide to the Gulf Islands, Wolferstans

Relevant publications in the Lonely Planet Series
A Cruising Guide to Vanuatu, Port Vila Yachting World

Appendix C | British and US Sailing Directions

British Admiralty Sailing Directions

NP 7 South America, Pilot, Vol III (includes Panama and Galapagos)

NP 8 Pacific Coasts of Central America and the USA

NP14 Australia Pilot Vol II (Sydney, Tasmania and Bass Strait)

NP 15 Australia Pilot Vol III (E Coast just north of Sydney to Cape York)

NP 51 New Zealand Pilot

NP 60 Pacific Islands Pilot Vol I (Solomons, FSM and Marianas)

NP 61 Pacific Islands Pilot Vol II (Marshalls, Gilberts, Ellice Islands, Fiji, Tonga, Vanuatu and New Caledonia)

NP 62 Pacific Islands Pilot Vol III (Hawaiian Islands, Line Islands and French Polynesia)

US Defense Mapping Agency Sailing Directions

SD 122 South Pacific Ocean (Planning Guide)

SD 125 West Coast of South America (includes Galapagos)

SD 126 Pacific Islands (not Hawaii)

SD 127 East Coast of Australia and New Zealand

SD 152 North Pacific Ocean (Planning Guide)

SD 153 West Coast of Mexico and Central America (includes Panama)

Appendix D | Suppliers of Books and Charts

United Kingdom

Brown & Petting Ltd, Redwing House, 36–44 Tabernacle Street, London EC2A 4DT (Tel: 0171 253 4517; Fax: 0171 608 0570) (BA, US and Canadian chart agents)

Captain O M Watts, 7 Dover Street, London W1X 3PJ (Tel: 0171 493 4633; Fax: 0171 495 0755)

Force 4 Chandlery, 30 Bressingden Place, Buckingham Palace Road, London SW1E 5DB (Tel: 0171 828 3900/3382; Fax: 0171 828 3383)

Imray Laurie Norie & Wilson Ltd, Wych House, The Broadway, St Ives, Huntingdon, Cambridgeshire PE17 4BT (Tel: 0480 462114; Fax: 0480 496109)

Kelvin Hughes Ltd, Kilgraston House, Southampton Street, Southampton SO15 2ED (Tel: 023 8063 4911; Fax: 023 8033 0014; e-mail Southampton@ Kelvinhughes.co.uk)

James Telford & Co Ltd, 5–9 Donegal Quay, Belfast, Northern Ireland BT1 3EF (Tel: 0232 326763; Fax: 0232 234566) (BA chart agents)

USA/Canada

Armchair Sailor Bookstore, Lee's Wharf, Newport, RI 02840 (Tel: 800 292 4278; Fax: 401 847 1219) (BA, US and Canadian chart agents)

Blue Water Books & Charts, 1481 SE 17th Street, Fort Lauderdale, FL 33316 (Tel: 305 763 6533; Fax: 305 522 2278) (BA, US and Canadian chart agents)

Boat America, 884 So Pickett Street, Alexandria, VA 22304 (Tel: 703 370 4202; Fax: 703 461 2852)

Boxwells Chandlery, 68 Long Wharf, Boston, MA 02110 (Tel: 617 523 5678) (US and Canadian chart agents)

C Plath, 222 Severn Avenue, Annapolis, MD 21403-2569 (Tel: 301 263 6700; Fax: 301 268 8713) (US distributor for lmray publications)

Cruising Guide Publications, PO Box 13131, Sta 9, Clearwater, FL 34521, USA (Tel: 813 796 2469; Fax: 813 797 1243)

Fawcetts' Boat Supplies, 110 Compromise Street, Annapolis, MD 21404 (Tel: 301 267 8681, 800 456 9151)

International Marine Publishing Co, 21 Elm Street, Camden, ME 04843

Marine Press of Canada, 224 St Paul Street West, Montreal PQ H2Y 1Z9 (Tel: 514 845 8342; Fax: 514 845 8368) (BA, US and Canadian chart agents)

Maryland Nautical Sales Inc, 1143 Hull Street, Baltimore, MD 21230 (Tel: 301 234 0531; Fax: 301 685 5068) (BA, US and Canadian chart agents)

McGill Maritime Services Inc, 369 Place d'Youville, Montreal, PQ H2Y 2B7 (Tel: 514 849 1125; Fax: 514 849 5804) (BA, US and Canadian chart agents)

New York Nautical Instrument & Service Corp, 140 West Broadway, New York, NY 10013 (Tel: 212 962 4522/4523; Fax: 212 406 8420) (BA, US and Canadian chart agents)

Sheridan House Inc, Publishers, 145 Palisade Street, Dobbs Ferry, NY 10522

Tropic Isle Publishers Inc, PO Box 610935, North Miami, FL 33261-0935, USA

Wescott Cove Publishing Co, PO Box 130, Stamford, CT 6904

West Marine Catalog and Port Supply Chandlers, 500 Westridge Drive, Watsonville, CA 95076 (Tel: 408 728 2700, 800 538 0775)

Appendix E — Great Circle Distance Table

SELECTED GREAT CIRCLE DISTANCES BETWEEN PORTS IN NAUTICAL MILES	HONOLULU	FUKUOKA (Japan)	APRA	TARAWA	MAJURO	HONIARA	CAIRNS	BRISBANE	SYDNEY	NOUMÉA	PORT VILA	AUCKLAND	
KODIAK	2200	3326	3855	3739	3474	4648	5414	5798	6178	5223	4855	5912	58
VICTORIA	2317	4497	4872	4272	4111	5301	6187	6375	6709	5660	5325	6086	60
SAN FRANCISCO	2071	4892	5030	4105	4014	5160	6090	6142	6435	5378	5074	5664	56
PUERTO VALLARTA	2934	6250	6196	4856	4892	5865	6792	6564	6731	5774	5570	5681	56
PANAMA (Balbao)	4556	7734	7840	6364	6463	7277	8109	7627	7627	6928	6837	6467	65
ACADEMY BAY	4167	7782	7444	5747	5914	6559	7320	6787	6770	6118	6065	5610	56
NUKU HIVA	2094	5673	4673	2817	3070	3546	4340	3928	4040	3176	3069	2965	29
PAPEETE	2379	5502	4310	2437	2757	2976	3638	3212	3299	2490	2437	2209	22
FARE (Huahine)	2315	5405	4214	2340	2660	2890	3612	3152	3250	2421	2358	2176	21
BORA BORA	2295	5362	4169	2295	2616	2847	3571	3117	3219	2383	2316	2152	21
RAIVAVAE	2773	5801	4546	2698	3041	3110	3730	3182	3215	2521	2531	2076	20
RAROTONGA	2552	5168	3872	2052	2411	2426	3083	2593	2685	1880	1856	1624	16
PAGO PAGO	2265	4426	3128	1312	1679	1748	2517	2175	2371	1388	1245	1562	15
APIA	2245	4390	3094	1275	1642	1722	2499	2168	2370	1378	1226	1578	15
NEIAFU	2582	4469	3111	1400	1782	1612	2295	1889	2062	1119	1045	1238	11
NUKU'ALOFA	2741	4523	3142	1493	1876	1597	2222	1775	1929	1026	1002	1079	10
SUVA	2741	4147	2752	1199	1574	1198	1871	1515	1736	724	616	1143	10
OPUA	3751	4810	3369	2201	2552	1737	1873	1177	1131	880	1191	98	
AUCKLAND	3818	4903	3463	2294	2647	1833	1945	1236	1161	976	1289		
PORT VILA	3022	3683	2251	1116	1416	620	1273	1068	1384	371			
NOUMÉA	3347	3936	2495	1485	1786	857	1210	795	1058				
SYDNEY	4401	4215	2861	2468	2705	1541	1057	390					
BRISBANE	4086	3886	2503	2112	2329	1154	750						
CAIRNS	4030	3158	1823	1994	2085	942							
HONIARA	3093	3084	1644	1056	1197								
MAJURO	1986	2762	1604	383									
TARAWA	2037	3116	1878										
APRA	3304	1442											
FUKUOKA (Japan)	3819												

SUVA	NUKU'ALOFA	NEIAFU	APIA	PAGO PAGO	RAROTONGA	RAIVAVAE	BORA BORA	FARE (Huahine)	PAPEETE	NUKUH HIVA	ACADEMY BAY	PANAMA (Balboa)	PUERTO VALLARTA	SAN FRANCISCO	VICTORIA
75	4868	4713	4391	4416	4751	4903	4455	4469	4519	4047	4575	4407	3025	1672	1177
53	5011	4852	4513	4526	4611	4530	4180	4178	4198	3553	3413	3238	1881	638	
15	4613	4459	4124	4132	4114	3961	3649	3642	3651	2970	2924	2901	1369		
50	4806	4681	4396	4389	4066	3647	3533	3507	3472	2716	1555	1645			
39	5902	5818	5612	5593	5051	4445	4545	4507	4438	3769	861				
54	5098	5028	4851	4829	4239	3610	3751	3710	3635	3013					
72	2156	2057	1844	1824	1356	998	821	792	757						
22	1466	1394	1261	1232	619	394	141	97							
44	1395	1317	1172	1144	565	467	45								
03	1357	1277	1128	1100	534	497									
18	1529	1498	1453	1419	686										
40	862	815	782	747											
64	485	328	37												
54	499	340													
29	159														
00															

Appendix F

International and US Marine VHF Radio Frequencies

INTERNATIONAL			CHANNEL	USA		
	Operating frequency (MHz)				Operating frequency (MHz)	
	Receive	Transmit		Receive	Transmit	
(duplex)	160.650	156.050	01	156.050	156.050	(simplex)
(duplex)	160.700	156.100	02	–	–	
(duplex)	160.750	156.150	03	156.150	156.150	(simplex)
(duplex)	160.800	156.200	04	156.200	156.200	(simplex)
(duplex)	160.850	156.250	05	156.250	156.250	(simplex)
(simplex)	156.300	156.300	06	156.300	156.300	(simplex)
(duplex)	160.950	156.350	07	156.350	156.350	(simplex)
(simplex)	156.400	156.400	08	156.400	156.400	(simplex)
(simplex)	156.450	156.450	09	156.450	156.450	(simplex)
(simplex)	156.500	156.500	10	156.500	156.500	(simplex)
(simplex)	156.550	156.550	11	156.550	156.550	(simplex)
(simplex)	156.600	156.600	12	156.600	156.600	(simplex)
(simplex)	156.650	156.650	13	156.650	156.650	(simplex)
(simplex)	156.700	156.700	14	156.700	156.700	(simplex)
(simplex)	156.750	156.750	15	156.750	156.750	(simplex)
(simplex)	**156.800**	**156.800**	**16**	**156.800**	**156.800**	**(simplex)**
(simplex)	156.850	156.850	17	156.850	156.850	(simplex)
(duplex)	161.500	156.900	18	156.900	156.900	(simplex)
(duplex)	161.550	156.950	19	156.950	156.950	(simplex)
(duplex)	161.600	157.000	20	161.600	157.000	(duplex)
(duplex)	161.650	157.050	21	157.050	157.050	(simplex)
(duplex)	161.700	157.100	22	157.100	157.100	(simplex)
(duplex)	161.750	157.150	23	157.150	157.150	(simplex)
(duplex)	161.800	157.200	24	161.800	157.200	(duplex)
(duplex)	161.850	157.250	25	161.850	157.250	(duplex)
(duplex)	161.900	157.300	26	161.900	157.300	(duplex)
(duplex)	161.950	157.350	27	162.000	157.400	(duplex)
(duplex)	162.000	157.400	28	162.000	157.400	(duplex)
(simplex)	157.850	157.850	37	–	–	
(duplex)	160.625	156.025	60	–	–	
(duplex)	160.675	156.075	61	160.675	156.075	(duplex)
(duplex)	160.725	156.125	62	160.725	156.125	(duplex)
(duplex)	160.775	156.175	63	160.775	156.175	(duplex)
(duplex)	160.825	156.225	64	160.825	156.225	(duplex)
(duplex)	160.875	156.275	65	156.275	156.275	(simplex)
(duplex)	160.925	156.325	66	156.325	156.325	(simplex)
(simplex)	156.375	156.375	67	156.375	156.375	(simplex)
(simplex)	156.425	156.425	68	156.425	156.425	(simplex)
(simplex)	156.475	156.475	69	156.475	156.475	(simplex)
(simplex)	156.525	156.525	70	156.525	156.525	(simplex)
(simplex)	156.575	156.575	71	156.575	156.575	(simplex)
(simplex)	156.625	156.625	72	156.625	156.625	(simplex)
(simplex)	156.675	156.675	73	156.675	156.675	(simplex)
(simplex)	156.725	156.725	74	156.725	156.725	(simplex)
	(= International Ch 77)		75	156.875	156.875	(simplex)
	–	–	76	–	–	
(simplex)	156.875	156.875	77	(= USA Ch 75)		

INTERNATIONAL			CHANNEL	USA		
	Operating frequency (MHz)				*Operating frequency (MHz)*	
	Receive	*Transmit*		*Receive*	*Transmit*	
(duplex)	161.525	156.925	78	156.925	156.925	(simplex)
(duplex)	161.575	156.975	79	156.975	156.975	(simplex)
(duplex)	161.625	157.025	80	157.025	157.025	(simplex)
(duplex)	161.675	157.075	81	157.075	157.075	(simplex)
(duplex)	161.725	157.125	82	157.125	157.125	(simplex)
(duplex)	161.775	157.175	83	157.175	157.175	(simplex)
(duplex)	161.825	157.225	84	161.825	157.225	(duplex)
(duplex)	161.875	157.275	85	161.875	157.175	(duplex)
(duplex)	161.925	157.325	86	161.925	157.225	(duplex)
(duplex)	161.975	157.375	87	161.975	157.275	(duplex)
(duplex)	162.025	157.425	88	157.425	157.425	(simplex)
			WX1	162.550		
			WX2	162.400		
			WX3	162.475		
			WX4	163.275		
			WX5	161.650		
			WX6	161.775		

Appendix G

Glossary of British and American Terms

Although glossaries of useful words in foreign languages will be found in *The Macmillan's Nautical Almanac*, it is surprising how many words differ in meaning between the UK and the USA. Here is a list of some of the more frequently used terms, both nautical and general, and their cross-Atlantic translations compiled by Anne Hammick.

In a few cases one of the following terms may be common to both sides of the Atlantic, but the second used on only one side. Others may be regional. Some have nothing to do with boats or sailing, but are included as they may be of help with the catering or other shopping.

British	American
anchor cable (chain and/or rope)	anchor rode
aubergine	eggplant
autumn	fall
bill (restaurant)	check
biro	ballpoint
biscuit	cookie
boomed staysail	club staysail
boot top	boot stripe
bottle screw	turnbuckle
broad beans	lima beans
bungey cord	shock cord
cheque	check
chips	french fries
circular saw	skill saw
clinker (construction)	lapstrake (construction)
conical buoy	nun buoy
cornflour	corn starch
courgette	zucchini
cove line	railstripe
cramps	clamps
crisps	chips
crosstrees	spreaders
deckhead	overhead
dodgers	weather cloths
dowel	plug
draught	draft
echo sounder	fathometer/depth sounder
excess (insurance)	deductible (insurance)
eyelet	grommet
fairlead	chock
fortnight	two weeks
fretsaw	coping saw
frying pan	skillet
G-clamp or G-cramp	C-clamp
gas	LPG or propane
grill	broil
gumboots/wellingtons	sea boots

British	American
hatch boards	drop boards
jam	jelly or preserve
jelly	jello
jig saw	saber saw
jubilee clip	hose clip
kicking strap	boom vang
lee cloth	leeboard
lifejacket	PFD (personal flotation device)
lift (building)	elevator
margarine	oleo
methylated spirits	alcohol (denatured)
mince (beef etc)	ground beef etc
mole wrench	vice grip
nappies	diapers
off licence	liquor store
oilskins	foul weather gear
paracetamol	Tylenol
paraffin	kerosene
petrol	gasoline (gas)
polyester	Dacron
pontoons	floats
public telephone	pay phone
pumpkin (vegetable)	squash (vegetable)
rachet screwdriver	yankee screwdriver
range	distance
reverse charge call	collect call
rigging screw	turnbuckle
rowlock	oarlock
rubber	eraser
rubbing strake	rubrail
shifting spanner	crescent wrench
skin fitting	thru hull
slip	slipway
soya granules	TVP (texturised vegetable protein)
spanner	wrench
split pin/ring	cotter/pin/ring
spray hood	dodger
squash (orange etc)	cordial
staysail boom	staysail club
stopping	surfacing putty or trowel cement
Talurite	Nicopress
tap	faucet
term (school or college)	semester
Terylene	Dacron
torch	flashlight
transit	range
vang	preventer
Very pistol	flare gun
water biscuit	cracker or saltine
yacht	sailboat

American	British	American	British
alcohol (denatured)	methylated spirits	oar lock	rowlock
anchor rode	anchor cable (chain and/or chain)	oleo	margarine
		overhead	deckhead
ballpoint	biro	pay phone	public telephone
boom vang	kicking strap	PFD (personal flotation device)	lifejacket
boot stripe	boot top		
broil	grill	plug	dowel
C-clamp	G-cramp	preventer	vang
check (restaurant)	bill	railstripe	cove line
chips	crisps	range	transit
chock	fairlead	rubrail	rubbing strake
clamps	cramps	saber saw	jig saw
club staysail	boomed staysail	sailboat	yacht
collect call	reverse charge call	sea boots	gumboots/wellingtons
cookie	biscuit	semester	term (school or college)
coping saw	fretsaw	shock cord	bungey cord
cordial	squash (orange etc)	skill saw	circular saw
cornstarch	cornflour	skillet	frying pan
cotter/pin/ring	split pin/ring	slip	pontoon or finger berth
cracker or saltine	water biscuit	spreaders	crosstrees
crescent wrench	shifting spanner	squash (vegetable)	pumpkin (vegetable)
custard	baked custard	staysail club	staysail boom
Dacron	polyester	surfacing putty	stopping
Dacron	Terylene	check	bill
deductible (insurance)	excess (insurance)	thru hull	skin fitting
depth sounder	echo sounder	trowel cement	stopping
diapers	nappies	turnbuckle	bottle screw or rigging screw
dodger	spray hood		
draft	draught	TVP (texturised vegetable protein)	soya granules
drop boards	hatch boats		
eggplant	aubergine	Tylenol	parcetamol
elevator (building)	lift	vice grip	mole wrench
eraser	rubber	weather cloths	dodgers
fall	autumn	wrench	spanner
fathometer	echo sounder	yankee screwdriver	rachet screwdriver
faucet	tap	zucchini	courgette
flare gun	Very pistol		
flashlight	torch		
floats	pontoons		
foul weather gear	oilskins		
french fries	chips		
gasoline (gas)	petrol		
grommet	eyelet		
ground beef etc	mince (beef etc)		
hose clip	jubilee clip		
jello	jelly		
jelly or preserve	jam		
kerosene	paraffin		
lapstrake	clinker (construction)		
leeboard	lee cloth		
lima beans	broad beans		
liquor store	off licence		
LPG	gas		
Nicopress	Talurite		
nun buoy	conical buoy		

Appendix H   Metric Conversions

CHART DEPTHS

Metres	Feet	Fathoms
1	3.3	0.55
2	6.6	1.09
3	9.8	1.64
4	13.1	2.19
5	16.4	2.73
6	19.7	3.28
7	23.0	3.83
8	26.2	4.37
9	29.5	4.92
10	32.8	5.47

Feet	Fathoms	Metres
10	1.7	3.05
15	2.5	4.57
20	3.3	6.10
25	4.2	7.62
30	5.0	9.15
35	5.8	10.67
40	6.7	12.20
45	7.5	13.72
50	8.3	15.24
55	9.2	16.77
60	10.0	18.29
65	10.8	19.82
70	11.7	21.34
75	12.5	22.87
80	13.3	24.39
85	14.2	25.91
90	15.0	27.44
95	15.8	28.96
100	16.7	30.49

AREAS

Sq metres	Sq feet
1	10.8
2	21.5
3	32.3
4	43.0
5	53.8
6	64.6
7	75.3
8	86.1
9	96.8
10	107.6

Sq feet	Sq metres
10	0.93
15	1.39
20	1.86
25	2.32
30	2.79
35	3.25
40	3.72
45	4.18
50	4.65
55	5.11
60	5.58
65	6.04
70	6.51
75	6.97
80	7.43
85	7.90
90	8.36
95	8.83
100	9.29

MISCELLANEOUS

Metric	UK	US
1 litre	1.76 pints	2.2 US pints
10 litres	2.2 galls	2.64 galls
1 kilogram	2.2 lbs	2.2 lbs
1 kilometre	.62 mile	.62 mile
1 tonne	.984 tons	1.10 tons

The US cooking measurement of a 'cup' is equivalent to 8 US fl oz or 0.5 US pints.

UK/US	Metric
1 UK pint	.57 ltrs
1 US pint	.47 ltrs
1 UK gall	4.54 ltrs
1 US gall	3.79 ltrs
1 pound	.45 kgs
1 UK ton	1016 kgs
1 US ton	907 kgs
1 mile	1.61 kms
1 sea mile	1.85 kms

Rope Sizes

In Europe rope is measured in millimetres diameter and sold by the metre. In the USA it is measured in inches diameter and sold by the foot.

Index